LASELL COLLEGE

W9-AHA-402

Other Cultures, Elder Years

Second Edition

DATE DUE	

BRODART   Cat. No. 23-221

To our parents, grandparents, and those invincible aunts
who taught us volumes about aging.

305.26
H730
1995

Other Cultures, Elder Years

Second Edition

Ellen Rhoads Holmes
Lowell D. Holmes

LASELL COLLEGE
LIBRARY
AUBURNDALE, MASS.

SAGE Publications
International Educational and Professional Publisher
Thousand Oaks   London   New Delhi

Copyright © 1995 by Sage Publications, Inc.

All rights reserved. No part of this book may be reproduced or utilized in any form or by any means, electronic or mechanical, including photo-copying, recording, or by any information storage and retrieval system, without permission in writing from the publisher.

For information address:

SAGE Publications, Inc.
2455 Teller Road
Thousand Oaks, California 91320

SAGE Publications Ltd.
6 Bonhill Street
London EC2A 4PU
United Kingdom

SAGE Publications India Pvt. Ltd.
M-32 Market
Greater Kailash I
New Delhi 110 048 India

Printed in the United States of America

Library of Congress Cataloging-in-Publication Data

Holmes, Ellen Rhoads.
   Other cultures, elder years: An introduction to cultural
gerontology / Ellen Rhoads Holmes & Lowell D. Holmes. —2nd ed.
   p. cm.
   Lowell's names appeared first on previous edition.
   Includes bibliographical references (p.   ) and index.
   ISBN 0-8039-5133-7 (cloth: acid free paper). —
   ISBN 0-8039-5134-5 (pbk.: acid free paper)
   1. Aging—Cross-cultural studies.   2. Gerontology—Methodology.
   I. Holmes, Lowell Don, 1925- . II. Title.
   HQ1061.H574
   305.26—dc20   1995

This book is printed on acid-free paper.

   96 97 98 99 10 9 8 7 6 5 4 3 2

Sage Production Editor: Astrid Virding
Sage Typesetter: Andrea D. Swanson

Contents

Preface   ix

1. The Anthropological Perspective   1
    The Discipline of Anthropology   2
    Comparative Analysis   7
    Holistic Perspective   8
    Emic-Etic Perspectives   9
    Relativistic Perspective   10
    Case-Study Approach   12
    Process Analysis   13
    Summary   15

2. Longevity   17
    Life Span and Evolution   19
        Calculating Evolutionary Maximum Life-Span Potential   23
        Evolution and Senescence   24
    Demography and Aging   27
        Population Aging   30
    Shangri-las   34

	Abkhazia	35
	The Hunza	36
	Vilcabamba	37
	Paros, Greece	37
	Yagodina	39
	Validity of Shangri-la Claims	39
	Abkhazia	39
	Hunza	43
	Vilcabamba	44
	Cultural Factors in Longevity	45
	Summary	48
3.	**The Life Cycle**	**50**
	Age Stage Perceptions in Samoa and Colombia	57
	Aging as a Career	59
	Creativity and the Life Cycle	61
	Personality Changes in the Life Cycle	66
	Retirement	68
	Disengagement	73
	Roles of the Aged	77
	Political Leadership	82
	Differences in Roles of Aged Men and Women	83
	Death and Dying	90
	Summary	92
4.	**Status and Family**	**95**
	Modernization	98
	Prestige-Generating Components	99
	Personal Achievement	100
	Societal Types	101
	Property Control	102
	Status and the Decrepit Elderly	107
	Defining Status	109
	Family, Kinship, and the Aged	111
	Generational Reciprocity	116
	Childlessness and Its Consequences	120
	Summary	123
5.	**Community Studies**	**124**
	Retirement Communities as Age-Graded Phenomena	133

Non-Western Homes for the Aged 135
   Hong Kong 136
   Africa 137
   Japan 138
Social Networks 141
Summary 143

6. **Varieties of Aging Experience** 145
   Growing Old in a Hunting Society: Eskimos 146
      Cultural Change 155
   Life in a Simple Agricultural Society: Samoa 157
      Gerontocide 165
      Cultural Change 166
   Aging in an Industrial Economy: The United States 168
      The Cultural Setting 168
      How Old Is Old? 169
      The Aged Population 170
      Residence Patterns 170
      Early History 171
      Ceremonial Life 173
      Religion 173
      The Value Environment 174
   Summary 182

7. **Ethnic Aged in America** 183
   African American Aged 187
   American Indian Aged 196
      The Reservation 200
      The Navajo 201
      Urban Aged Native Americans 205
   Mexican American Aged 207
      The Changing Scene 212
   Asian American Aged 213
      Chinese Americans 214
      Japanese Americans 216
   Italian Americans 220
   Summary 223

8. **Applying Anthropology: Culture, Health, and Aging** 226
   Cultural Perspectives in Health Care 227

African American Concepts of Illness   232
Food Preferences   233
Dementia   234
Ethnic/Minority Support Groups   236
Black and Hispanic Caregivers   237
Long-Term Care Institutions   238
Ethnicity and Institutionalization   242
Nursing Homes in Other Cultures   245
Summary   248

9. **The Aged and Cultural Change**   251
Salient Aspects of Modernization   270
Criticisms of Aging and Modernization Theory   276
Case Study of Modernization: Japan   277
Summary   283

10. **The Future of Aging in America**   286
Summary   294

References   295

Index   316

About the Authors   323

▣ Preface

Early in my career I was fortunate enough to be hired as the first anthropologist in a combined sociology and anthropology department chaired by the late sociologist Donald O. Cowgill, a man who had a significant role in the development of social gerontology and who passed on his interest in aging research in this and other cultures to me. His research on aging in Thailand and East Africa inspired my own in Samoa, a locale that proved to be a most fertile field for investigation considering the culture's high regard for the elderly. In all of our areas of research, we were impressed by the fact that changing times were affecting attitudes toward the elderly, and our findings, plus deliberations with a score of colleagues, led us to formulate a theory of aging and modernization that we believed explained a good deal of change in attitudes and events in other cultures and have challenged a host of researchers to test and refine the theory.

One such researcher is the coauthor of this book, who put the theory to the test in the Samoan islands and with Samoan migrants in the United States. Her work involved investigating the impact of modernization on status of the aged in three communities with varying degrees of modernization influence, plus researching longitudinal changes in attitudes over time.

When I wrote the first edition of *Other Cultures, Elder Years*, published in 1983, *cultural gerontology* (a term some have credited me with using first) was still very much in its infancy. The area has expanded so much since that time that it is a daunting task to assimilate the rich variety of published sources now available. While I am retired from teaching, my work in research and writing continues for I, like Leo Simmons (1959), believe that aging is like riding a bicycle: "If you stop, you fall" (p. 6). Although I now tend to pursue selfish interests, my wife and coauthor, Ellen Rhoads Holmes, in her anthropology/gerontology teaching and research roles, must grapple constantly with this body of knowledge developed by anthropologists and other social scientists who see gerontology as a discipline that must take all people and all cultural traditions into consideration if we are to contribute to an understanding of the process of human aging. It was Ellen who had the primary responsibility for the organization and scope of this new edition of the book.

This edition represents a substantial revision of the original book. No single chapter remains unchanged. New sections have been added on the family, a comparative perspective on the implications of population aging, a case study of Japan in the chapter on cultural change; a separate chapter now deals with community as it relates to the aged. The chapter on applied anthropology is an addition to the volume. My own interests have always been more theoretical than applied, but Ellen is confronted daily with the challenge of educating students who will or already do work in long-term care facilities or in agencies that provide services to the aged. It is hoped that the inclusion of the material of an applied nature will facilitate students' understanding of the values of their own culture in regard to aging and care of the aged relative to the range of ethnic differences of the people they may serve.

This is a book written primarily for students in courses in gerontology and anthropology (or other social sciences) that focus on cultural aspects of aging. It attempts to survey the ideas that constitute what I have labeled cultural gerontology, an approach that involves an anthropological perspective and draws freely upon the findings of both anthropologists and social gerontologists who use cross-cultural data or who investigate cultural patterns of behavior of the aged or those who serve the aged within our own society.

Both Ellen and I are much indebted to our students who have taken our courses in the anthropology of aging over the years and forced us to stay current in the literature, kept us exploring new issues, and kept us on our toes by challenging our ideas and making us clarify concepts.

Ellen is grateful for sabbatical leave support from Wichita State University, which permitted further research in the San Francisco Bay Area on aged Samoan migrants and also gave us the opportunity of using the resources of Stanford University's excellent library in researching this volume.

We also would like to acknowledge some very special colleagues who made contributions to this project. We are indebted to Marjorie Schweitzer, whose untiring efforts resulted in the production of an invaluable bibliography of anthropological materials on aging; revision of *Other Cultures, Elder Years* would have been far more time consuming, if not impossible, without that bibliography. Thanks are due to David and Dorothy Counts for sharing their published and unpublished data, photographs, and anecdotes regarding their research on RV communities. We would like to acknowledge our debt to Neil Henderson of the University of South Florida for his suggestions on our treatment of applied aspects of cultural gerontology. He also provided us with the opportunity to work with him in the study of Hispanic and Anglo support groups for caregivers of Alzheimer victims. To Arthur H. Rohn, Lee Guemple, Nicolas Peterson, Jeff Beaubier, and the Mid-America All-Indian Center, we are extremely grateful for the photographs they provided for our use in this volume. Above all, we want to thank our editor, Mitch Allen, for his patience while waiting for us to finish this book as numerous problems involving our elderly parents caused a multiplicity of roadblocks to our progress.

To the many cultural gerontologists at work in the research vineyards whose findings have made this volume possible, we offer our humble thanks and applause and encouragement to keep up the good work.

Lowell D. Holmes

1

▣ The Anthropological Perspective

The authors of this volume are anthropologists—cultural anthropologists—who, because of their training and scientific interests, look at the contemporary world in all its cultural complexity and variety and attempt to understand and interpret human behavior. A book on gerontology written by anthropologists may seem unusual, because most gerontologists are sociologists, psychologists, or social workers. Anthropologists have long been interested in the aged, but unfortunately mostly as sources of information on a non-Western culture as it was when they were young or before contact with white people and Western civilization. When Franz Boas (the father of American anthropology) sent out his Columbia University graduate students (Margaret Mead, Alfred Kroeber, Ruth Benedict, Melville Herskovits, and others) with instructions to seek out the elders first as major sources of cultural information, it apparently never occurred to him or his students that they might also ask what life was like for the elderly. Many anthropologists are doing that today, and anthropology is bringing new information and a new way of looking at aging to the science of gerontology.

The Discipline of Anthropology

Anthropology is the study of human beings—total human beings. No other science or humanistic discipline examines the human animal as thoroughly. Anthropology addresses itself to the study of the physical makeup of humans, to their social and cultural behavior in the contemporary world as well as in historic and prehistoric days. It is the science concerned with the evolutionary development of humans as animals, with their patterns of group interaction, and with the nature of their cultural traditions in industrialized as well as tribal and peasant societies.

Anthropology maintains a broad, holistic approach to the study of humankind but, like other social scientists, anthropologists tend to specialize. The anthropological fraternity includes physical anthropologists, archaeologists, linguists, and social/cultural anthropologists. Physical anthropologists study people as members of the animal kingdom, recognizing that they are vertebrates, mammals, primates, and, finally, because of their superior brains and culture-building capacities, *hominids* or human beings. Physical anthropologists concern themselves with human evolution, demography, population genetics, and human variation (race), and they are valuable contributors to knowledge in such gerontological and geriatric areas as morbidity, mortality, health, longevity, and the genetic basis of aging. Given that there are both hereditary and environmental components to aging, these scholars can be expected to contribute heavily to gerontological science.

Archaeologists also contribute to our knowledge of aging, particularly in the area of longevity. While archaeologists are generally concerned with reconstructing the lifestyles of past cultures through excavation and analysis of artifacts such as weapons, tools, and ceremonial objects, those with interests in paleodemography calculate age at death from human skeletons, figure mortality rates, and construct survivorship curves and life tables. Excellent examples of such studies are those by Mann (1968) and McKinley (1971), who studied average age at death of South and East African populations of australopithecines (19.8 years), as well as by Acsadi and Nemeskeri (1970), who determined from skeletal material in Asia that *Homo erectus* had a maximum life span of 60-70 years and an average age at death of 37-48 years of those who had reached adulthood. Lovejoy and others (1977) analyzed 1,327 articulated skeletons of Native Americans in an ossuary (communal burial ground) at Libben site in northern Ohio. Evaluating age at death through skeletal maturation and dental condition over a period from A.D. 800 to 1100, the researchers determined that life expectancy for this hunting and fishing population was approximately 20 years and the maximum life span was approximately 55+.

Anthropological linguists also have a potential role in gerontology. These scholars specialize in language analysis, with interests ranging from the history of language development to the study of language structure and semantics and to the use of language as a reflection of class, ethnic, or sex differences within a society. The branch of linguistics known as *sociolinguistics* has demonstrated that our language reflects American racism and sexism, and it is now recognizing ageism in our patterns of communication.

According to Herbert Covey (1988), the terms used to refer to older people not only have changed over time but there has been a proliferation of negative terms since the late nineteenth century, reflecting change in the status of the aged. Some words that had a neutral or positive meaning are now viewed more negatively. For example, *old* has generally referred to a stage of life, but when used in expressions like *old maid* or *old geezer*, it becomes negative. Many older people now object to being called "old" at all (Covey, 1988). In a survey of adults that studied preferred labels for the aged, persons age 65 and over found *senior citizen* the most acceptable term (Barbato & Feezel, 1987). It is interesting to note that this positive label is not a recent development; *senior* denoted a person deserving of respect in the 1300s and *senior citizen* is also an early reference. *Senile*, which in the 1600s was a general reference to old age, has become much more negative, implying mental and physical impairment. Even some words typically used for grandparents have had negative connotations at times. For old women, *granny* has referred to a gossip and later implied stupidity. *Gramps* has frequently been used in a negative sense for old men since the 1800s. The use of *hag* for an old woman has a long history and has undergone a dramatic change in meaning. Its earliest meaning was "holy one," but since 1225 it has carried connotations of evil, ugliness, and even witchcraft. While there is an abundance of negative terms for old men, historical evidence of language usage suggests old women have experienced more negativism and do so beginning at earlier ages than men (Covey, 1988).

Social anthropologists (who specialize in studies of social structure and social interaction) and cultural anthropologists (who study cultural traditions and systems) consider the many societies of our planet to be multiple experiments in human adaptation and survival in a wide variety of physical environments. The customs evolved by the societies represent their *cultures,* or systems of traditional behavior. One of the traditions that all societies have evolved concerns how the process of growing old is to be handled by the society and by the aging person. The ways aging is approached are infinitely varied around the world.

Anthropologists not only specialize in specific subjects, but most of them also specialize in a particular part of the world. Although some choose to remain at home and study their own people, a considerable number take a special interest in the peoples of the Pacific, Africa, Asia, Europe, or the Middle East. Some may be American Indian specialists. Because anthropology is dedicated to studying all peoples in all times and to documenting their infinitely varied configurations of customs, anthropologists often feel they must live among foreign peoples—often for extended periods of time. They investigate the value systems, worldviews, and cultural norms of people in far-off lands because they wish to test hypotheses about the nature of human beings in a worldwide laboratory.

Ethnographers are cultural anthropologists who engage in field studies, and *ethnography* is the term used to describe the empirical, fact-finding activities carried out by anthropologists in the field. As Michael Agar (1980) succinctly describes it, ethnography "always involves long-term association with some group, to some extent in their own territory, with the purpose of learning from them their ways of doing things and viewing reality" (p. 6). *Participant observation,* a time-honored method by which ethnographic data are acquired by anthropologists, is explained by Hortense Powdermaker (1966) as follows:

> To understand a strange society, the anthropologist has traditionally immersed himself in it, learning, as far as possible, to think, see, feel, and sometimes act as a member of its culture and at the same time as a trained anthropologist from another culture. This is the heart of the participant observation method—involvement and detachment. (p. 9)

This approach basically amounts to sharing the way of life, participating as much as appropriate, and keeping one's eyes and ears open to patterns of behavior and value assumptions of the people under study.

A great deal may be learned about a cultural situation from observation alone, but when the researcher carefully augments it with interviewing, observation becomes even more valuable. Observations may prompt questions or topics for interview, and they can also be useful in verifying interview data. A particular social event, for example, can be described in great detail from observation alone, but the meanings, symbolism, and function of the event will be best understood through interviews with participants themselves. Participation in a people's way of life is also an excellent way to establish rapport and gain the trust of those being studied, but more than that, through participation the researcher begins to understand their day-to-day routine, their pleasures, and their problems, and the resultant description of the culture will be to a large extent from their point of view. Of course, the participant observer never really becomes a part of the group being studied, and he or she will be more respected for being a nonjudgmental, sympathetic representative of his or her own culture.

In conducting our own research on aging in Samoa, we spent many months living in the islands. During this time we went into homes to interview older people and younger family members living with them. This approach allowed us to observe not only the circumstances in which families lived but also the nature of interaction between young and old. We also became involved in a broad range of activities and institutions that are part of life in the islands. We visited the hospital and talked with some of the staff, spent time in classrooms of elementary and high schools and the community college, attended church in several villages, were able to observe weddings and celebrate holidays with Samoan friends. We shopped in the local stores and the farmers' market, ate in restaurants, stood in line at the bank and the post office, and traveled on the local busses and interisland boats and airlines. In short, we experienced firsthand many of the conditions and some of the frustrations that Samoans experience, and in doing so we gained a better understanding of the context in which Samoans live and grow old. And later on, when we extended our research to Samoan migrants living in California, this knowledge of their native culture was invaluable for assessing the challenges and adjustments they faced in a new environment. These experiences are the essence of the participant-observation method of gathering ethnographic data.

Ethnography, then, is literally the science of describing cultural phenomena. Accurate documentation of human ways of life is considered of vital importance in this social science, but it is also considered important to carry the fact-finding activity one step further to the level of *ethnology*, which is a theorizing activity where cultural descriptions (ethnographies) are compared and generalizations then made about human nature.

Fully understanding the nature and cause of the problems and adjustments in regard to aging in a given society (let us say our own) is important, but it is also important to gain the wider perspective that embraces all societies in all times and in all places. Worldwide comparisons allow us to bring our own culture into sharper focus, and they may suggest new solutions to common problems or new adjustments to meet unique needs.

Not only does the broad scope of anthropology establish it as a useful discipline in studying gerontological phenomena but its unique perspective is also valuable. That perspective may be described as being (a) comparative, (b) holistic, (c) concerned with *emic* and *etic* viewpoints, (d) relativistic, (e) case-study oriented, and (f) committed to process or dynamic analysis.

Before we can deal with the nature of these various approaches, we must realize that these are all ways of analyzing culture, and that culture is a major concept of reference in anthropological analysis. *Culture* is defined as the shared patterns of values and behavior that are characteristic of a society, because they are passed on from generation to generation through symbolic communication. Once transmitted through teaching and learning, culture shapes the lives of individuals and gives form and stability to societal behavior.

Although aging is a biological phenomenon, our attitudes toward the aged and our own aging, the treatment our aged receive, the evaluation of the importance of the aged, and the roles considered appropriate for the old are more a matter of cultural tradition than of physiology. As Gregory Bateson (1950) put it:

Man lives by propositions whose truth depends upon his believing them. If he believes that the old are no good, weak, stubborn, whatever terms of abuse he likes to attach to them, then to a great extent that will become true of the old in the population where that is believed, and the old themselves will believe it and will reinforce the general belief that it is so. (p. 52)

Culture lies at the heart of all anthropological thought and investigation, and the cultural perspective represents an important factor of insight for gerontology. With the exception of certain aspects of longevity covered in Chapter 2, this book will be focused on the sociocultural aspects of aging.

Comparative Analysis

Anthropology was once known as the science that studied "primitive" or "nonliterate" peoples. However, in these waning years of the twentieth century, cultural change in the form of industrialization, urbanization, mass communication, and Westernization has made it increasingly difficult to find such preindustrial peoples. But anthropology does not require the existence of these populations to be a relevant social science discipline. More and more anthropologists are turning to their own culture or to subcultures within it for their studies, and simple, isolated, preindustrial societies no longer dominate the interest and subject matter of anthropology. The science does continue to be comparative and cross cultural, however. Not only are *synchronic* studies (those comparing many cultures) important, but so are *diachronic* ones (where single societies are described at various time periods).

In *The Counterfeiters*, André Gide (1931) describes a particular species of fish that, because of its unique biological makeup, must swim at a particular depth in the ocean. It has never been able to descend to the bottom nor has it ever been able to rise to the surface. Such a fish, suggests Gide, has no insight into the nature of its watery environment because it has experienced neither sand nor air. Human beings who know only their own culture are in danger of this kind of provincialism. If one has never experienced another culture—through residence or reading—then there is a good chance that person does not fully understand the significance of what is happening in his or her own society.

Comparative analysis is frequently used in anthropology to determine whether a particular form of behavior—such as competitiveness, pugnacity, mother love, or acquisitiveness—is cultural behavior (and therefore learned) or whether it is a product of the human biological heritage (and therefore passed on genetically). In 1961 Cumming and Henry proposed that it was "natural" and beneficial for elders to disengage socially and economically. Because such disengagement was presented as "natural," anthropologists might expect to find the phenomenon in all cultures. They have not. In fact, they found that disengagement was quite common in Western industrial societies but relatively uncommon elsewhere.

Cross-cultural comparison has been tremendously helpful in investigating the concept of human longevity. Although the relative importance of nature and nurture are difficult to determine precisely, comparison of dietary differences, variations in work and play patterns, and differences in supportive social structures and respect patterns in various societies shed important light on some of the cultural influences on longevity.

In general, anthropology, because of its comparative emphasis, has much to offer in the study of aging. In addition to the question of disengagement and longevity, anthropology can enlighten us about many other issues as well: What defines a person as old? Is retirement a universal characteristic of old age? What roles are available to the elderly? How does family type affect the welfare of older persons? What can cross-cultural research teach us about the alternative approaches to long-term care within the family and in institutions? What are the determinants of status of the aged? Are the elderly the losers when cultural change occurs? Is it possible that elderly residents of a high-rise apartment building and those who travel about in recreational vehicles can be considered communities? Have people in certain areas of the world learned the secret to extreme longevity? These are just a few of the questions that comparative research on aging has examined and are among the topics that will be considered in subsequent chapters of this book.

Holistic Perspective

Anthropologists think of culture as a configuration of interrelated traits, complexes, and patterns, and they believe that one aspect of culture cannot be effectively studied without taking the totality into consideration. As Ruth Benedict (1934) so aptly phrased it: "All the miscellaneous behavior directed toward getting a living, mating, warring and worshipping the gods, is made over into consistent patterns in accordance with unconscious canons of choice that develop within the culture" (p. 48). Because life is really merely a series of events and people interacting, we must realize that to categorize human behavior as "economic," "political," or "religious" is to arbitrarily divide up human behavior for the convenience of study. Distortions occur when facts are taken out of context, and there has been a long history of faulty thinking that has resulted from this practice. Racial, economic, biological, and other forms of determinism are reductionist, oversimplified forms of analysis that have stressed one causal factor to the exclusion or underemphasis of others. Comparative and holistic analysis has proved to be a valuable weapon against this kind of reasoning.

Although anthropology recognizes a great advantage in specialization, it is more interested in the total configuration of culture—in its organic wholeness—than in documenting every minute detail of every facet of human life. If forced to do so, the anthropologist will sacrifice detail for a comprehension of form.

Not only have anthropologists stressed the interrelationship of all aspects of culture, they have also emphasized the biocultural totality of human experience. Human behavior is partly a response to physical or animal needs and partly a following of established traditions. Although humanity is one biologically, there are almost as many kinds of culture as there are societies. To consider one factor without the other is to distort human nature. People require a given amount of nutriment to survive, but whether they receive it in two meals a day or five or in the form of raw fish or sauerbraten is a cultural matter.

Emic-Etic Perspectives

Any cultural situation can be viewed from the *inside* and from the *outside*. Anthropologists believe that much can be gained by attempting to see the culture as its participants see it. This approach, sometimes called *ethnoscience*, attempts to discover "folk" or local categories of thought and reality. This insiders' window on the world is referred to as the *emic* perspective, and this term comes from the word *phonemic*, which refers to the combination of meaningful sounds unique to a particular language. Therefore *emic* is not a universal reference to language but a specific reference to a particular language. The *etic* approach (deriving from the word *phonetic*), on the other hand, is the scientific perspective that the well-trained anthropologist brings to the analysis. This constitutes his or her cross-cultural frame of reference and is an objective and controlled procedure for weighing and sifting facts and theoretical viewpoints. Its approach to human behavior is a general, outsiders' approach, just as *phonetics* is the term for the science of all human speech production.

The best way to distinguish between *emic* and *etic* perspectives is to imagine the difference in perceptions of a worshipper and an art historian who are both observing a great stained-glass cathedral window. The window no doubt represents something very different, very personal, and very meaningful for the worshipper, who would include the window in his total complex of worship. The window might move him spiritually as well as artistically. The art historian, on the other hand, might be moved by the window's beauty but not by its connections with worship. He would analyze it coldly and objectively in terms of other great cathedral windows and in terms of established scholarly criteria for judging such architectural or artistic features.

Relativistic Perspective

Because of anthropology's insistence on a cross-cultural perspective and because several generations of anthropologists have lived among their foreign subjects and have come to respect them and see the wisdom of their lifeways, anthropology has come to be dominated by a kind of philosophical stance known as *cultural relativism*. Cultural relativism is both a *methodological* tool that ensures objective data collection and a *philosophical* and *theoretical* principle that calls for open-mindedness in accepting cultural diversity. It emphasizes the idea that no single culture can claim to have a monopoly on the "right" or "natural" way of doing things. From this standpoint, anthropologists who study gerontology believe that the meaning of old age and the effectiveness of solutions to the problems of old age can only be understood and evaluated in terms of the cultural context in which the aged reside. Although the common biological heritage of human beings and the inevitability of senescence create elements of common experience, anthropologists are extremely cautious about declaring that the customs in one society are more accept-able or more honorable than those in other societies. Who is to say that locking the elderly up in nursing homes is more humane than allowing them to wander off on the ice flow and freeze to death as Eskimo elders are sometimes permitted to do? Cultural behavior that may imply low status for the aged in one society may mean something entirely different in another.

Cultural relativism also warns that cultural institutions within one society may not easily transfer to another. Proof of this was observed by the authors in American Samoa, where a nutrition program for the aged was attempted. To begin with, Samoa is not a society that has a history of volunteerism, a major factor in such programs elsewhere. In Samoa, *families* serve the elderly—not neighbors or strangers who volunteer. Thus, when the government's planning began, Samoans suggested that food or money be distributed among families who would then make sure that their elderly got proper nourishment. American government offi-cials (mostly funding agency personnel) objected to this on the grounds that other family members would perhaps get the food intended for the elderly. After long consideration, the government officials decided that the food should be cooked in the kitchens of the 26 consolidated elemen-tary schools where food was already being prepared by kitchen person-nel for government-subsidized hot meals for the schoolchildren. The elderly could simply go to the school for lunch. This solution created another problem because it did not take into consideration appropriate age status and role behavior, particularly in respect to titled chiefs, who maintained that it was beneath their dignity to go to school and line up like children just for a midday meal. Also, the usual time for Samoans to eat is not noon but at 10 a.m. and 7 p.m. A later attempt involved having restaurants provide meals for elders, again with little success.

In 1988, more than a decade after initial implementation of the nutrition program, older persons were being issued vouchers for $30 per month to use for food items at participating stores. These businesses were subject to penalties if they allowed purchase of nonfood items with a voucher. These approaches over the years have continued to highlight the conflict between foreign program guidelines and culturally accept-able behavior. In essence, an American program designed to assist elders who may benefit from meals and social interaction because many live alone does not translate easily into a culture "where the elderly live with and are adequately fed by their families" (Borthwick, 1977, p. 250). In Samoa, as in Micronesia where Borthwick did research, if an elder is in need of food, then the entire family is probably at risk.

Cultural relativism is a difficult concept to apply, because all peoples in all places tend to be *ethnocentric*, which means that they believe that their own values, customs, and attitudes are superior to those of people in other societies. Although respect for one's own cultural system and loyalty to one's own group is necessary and worthwhile, social scientists in particular must realize that there are many effective and efficient ways of doing things, and no one way of life is either "natural" or necessarily best. In fact, no technique of qualitatively evaluating cultures has ever been discovered.

Case-Study Approach

Anthropologists typically study small groups or communities through intensive long-term involvement as detailed earlier. In anthropological studies of aging and the aged, while the results of research in a retirement residence, a nursing home, a caregivers' support group, an ethnic neighborhood, or a small community are recognized as not necessarily representative of all such groups, each example would be a case study that can be compared with other similar studies to establish generalizations and theories about various phenomena. The title of the largest and most popular series of ethnographic monographs used in college courses, *Case Studies in Cultural Anthropology*,[1] is an indication of the fact that anthropologists consider their monographs cultural case studies.

Anthropology's use of the case-study method is similar in some respects to that found in the field of social work. Just as social workers go into homes to observe and document the lifestyle of individual families in their caseloads, so anthropologists go to communities or other cultures to investigate the circumstances of the peoples they wish to understand.

The holistic approach is characteristic of case studies, and in their book on case-study method, the Committee on the Family (1970) maintained that, in studying the family, four determinants of family functioning must be considered. They are (a) the cultural, (b) the interpersonal, (c) the psychological, and (d) the biological. This manual for social workers elaborates on the determinants:

> The cultural area includes the profile of value orientations associated with cultural affiliation of the family and the belief systems that pattern all role activities, including domestic roles, as well as the structure of the nuclear and extended family. The interpersonal area is composed of overt, day-to-day interactions between family members in maintenance of their role relations—their communications, alliances, and coalitions; expressions of feeling; ways of reaching decisions; methods of child rearing and control; handling of illness, finances, education, religion, recreation and losses through death or separation. The intrapsychic processes of individual members, including their unconscious cognitions, emotions, defenses, and object relations, comprise the psychological area. The biological area embraces the physical constitution of family members, including their age and sex, the state of their physical health, and the patterning of biological functions in nutrition, sleep, excretion, and motility. (Committee on the Family, 1970, pp. 258-259)

The above prescription for a case study for social workers could easily, with minor changes, serve as a guide for anthropologists studying cultures or cultural situations. Like social workers, anthropologists are not always sure what they will find, what aspects of the situation they will be required to document, or exactly what methods they will have to use in collecting their data. But they know without doubt that there will be some difficulties in establishing rapport, in comprehending the value systems of their subjects, and in understanding the complexities and subtleties of communication. Participant observation has proven effective in meeting these challenges.

Process Analysis

Anthropology's interest in change and process is perhaps older than any of its other interests. Beginning with speculations about the principle of cultural evolution before anthropology was even an established scholarly discipline, anthropologists have, for more than 200 years, attempted to understand the reasons for and ramifications of change under such headings as evolution, revolution, innovation, discovery, acculturation, diffusion, and modernization. Anthropologists interested in gerontology have been particularly concerned with modernization influences in developing countries and the effect that they have on status and roles of the elderly. The general assumption has been that the influence of Western industrial cultures will destroy the traditional values and agencies of support and recognition for the aged and that the status and authority of the aged will be reduced, despite a general increase in the number of elderly. Because change is an ongoing process in all societies, we will note the impact of cultural change on the elderly throughout this book and also in the chapter devoted to the issue.

We begin our exploration of aging in other cultures by drawing upon knowledge from physical anthropology to investigate human longevity, an evolutionary perspective on the hominid life span and senescence, the demographic transition occurring throughout the world, and, finally, the validity of claims of unusually long average life spans in enclaves long heralded as Shangri-las. We then discuss the work of anthropologists and other social scientists in regard to the status and role of the elderly, a topic that has dominated the interest of gerontologists since Leo Simmons wrote his classic volume, *The Role of the Aged in Primitive Society*, in 1945. This will be followed by cross-cultural considerations of the nature of the life cycle (including such topics as retirement and death), the structure and function of family, and the concept of community and how the nature of community affects senior citizens.

Because we believe that it is of vital importance to study human phenomena in cultural context, Chapter 6 will focus on what it means to grow old in a hunting society, that of the Eskimos, in a simple agricultural society, that of the Samoans, and, finally, in a modern industrial society—the United States. A chapter on ethnic and minority aging concentrates on subcultures in the United States, explaining how cultural tradition shapes the needs and roles of seniors. The chapter on applying anthropology also deals with cultural differences as they affect health and long-term care of the aged in America. Our final concern is with change, especially modernization and accompanying demographic change, and its effect on the status and well-being of the elderly. With a theoretical foundation established in regard to the many facets and factors of change and its ramifications, we will close with a prophetic chapter, "The Future of Aging in America," and a hope that our book will help our readers move into the next century with confidence, comprehension, and anticipation for their own golden years.

SUMMARY

From this brief treatment of the nature of anthropology, its interests, and its potential for gerontological research, we can see that anthropology's concern for cultural, biological, and historical dimensions of humankind makes it unique among the sciences that deal with aging. Even though anthropology has only recently developed its interest in aging and the aged, its somewhat different approach can profitably supplement the work of sociologists, psychologists, social workers, and biologists. Because it concerns itself with all peoples everywhere in the world today and at all times in history and prehistory, anthropology is specially equipped to deal with universal problems of aging and, through its comparative data, is able to shed valuable light on the relative adequacy or shortcomings of solutions to gerontological problems in America. Anthropologists consider the many societies of the world as so many experiments in human adjustment and survival in a variety of physical, ideological, and sociological environments. It is appropriate that they include in their study each society's adjustment to the process of growing old and societal accommodation to this phenomenon. A famous American anthropologist, Clyde Kluckhohn (1949), once suggested that "anthropology provides a mirror for man wherein he may see himself in all his infinite variety" (p. 11). This is anthropology's most important contribution to gerontology.

Growing out of anthropology's insistence on cross-cultural comparison is a philosophical attitude toward other cultures that greatly affects both its methodological approach and its theoretical conceptualizations. That philosophical position is known as *cultural relativism*, and it basically represents an open-mindedness in accepting cultural diversity around the world. Cultural relativism demands that no one culture be held up as offering the "right," "moral," "natural," or "superior" solutions to growing old or dealing with old people. Furthermore, moral or scientific judgments based on experience with but a single culture are suspected of being unfair and invalid. Anthropological gerontologists believe that problems or understandings relating to old age must be analyzed only in terms of the cultural context in which they occur. The relativist approach also warns that cultural institutions cannot easily be transplanted from one culture to another. One society's solutions to their aging problems could prove disastrous to another society with different basic values and institutions.

NOTE

1. This series was edited by George and Louise Spindler and published by Holt, Rinehart & Winston, 1960-1961; it is currently published by Harcourt Brace Company.

2

▣ Longevity

All societies value life and seek to prolong it even in old age. Although the statement is often made that "life is cheap" in non-Western societies, this is an ethnocentric assumption with very little evidence to back it up. The truth is that most societies see life as extremely precious, and the bulk of cultural practices are dedicated to survival and maintenance of human life. This is not to say that life will be protected at all costs. When environmental conditions are extreme (as in the Arctic), when life no longer seems worth the effort, or when people are suffering poor health, death is often chosen over life. Simmons (1945) found that abandonment of decrepit or ill elderly was practiced in 38 of the 71 tribal societies in his study *The Role of the Aged in Primitive Society*, but close scrutiny of the literature reveals that people are abandoned only as a last resort and often at the request of the elderly themselves, who are too sick or too tired to go on.

It is notable that all societies have a prescription for long life, and in many societies respect and prestige continue to increase with age. In such a situation only the foolish would not want to sustain life as long as possible and thereby bask in the admiration of their community. Few cultures have failed to look on long life as a positive goal, provided it could be lived in relative comfort. Weyl (1977) writes: "Man's quest for longevity outdates both Genesis and Greek mythology. It has roots as universal as man's consciousness of the inevitability of his own death" (p. 163).

In this chapter we consider human longevity from an anthropological perspective. This involves differentiating the concepts of *life expectancy* and *life span*, and taking an evolutionary view of the life span, including the question of why humans live so much longer than other animal species. The demographic evidence for increasing life expectancy and population aging on a worldwide basis is examined, along with current and anticipated implications of these developments. We conclude with discussion of the several cultural groups who claim achievement of extraordinary longevity. Such an issue provides an excellent example of the value of cross-cultural research for distinguishing biological and cultural components of aging.

All organisms, from plants to human beings, have fixed, finite life spans. A mayfly can survive but a day, a dog 20 years, an elephant 85 years, a Galapagos turtle 150 years, and a human being 110 to 120 years. These figures should not be confused with the average length of life of each of these organisms, however. Most representatives of the above-mentioned species die much earlier, as the term *maximum life-span potential* (MLP) refers to the outside limit of survival. In other words, a person 120 years old is rarely found. In fact, it has been calculated that the chance of a human attaining that ripe old age is 1 in 2 billion. This means that there should be about two such remarkable individuals in the world today and about six in human history. One who has nearly achieved that extraordinary accomplishment was the subject of a Knight-Ridder news service dispatch ("French Woman," 1993): "At 118 years and 9 months, a French woman living in Provence, is thought to be the world's oldest living human being" (p. 5a). French scientists are convinced of the legitimacy of Jeanne Calment's age due to the existence of "unusually reliable birth, marriage and other civil records" (p. 5a). It is reported that she "has been remarkably healthy. She barely saw a doctor until she fell off her bike and broke her arm at the age of 100. She avoided one unhealthy habit for decades, taking up smoking only at age 110, after she entered a nursing home" (p. 5a). While she does have serious vision and hearing problems, she is described as having "a lively, not-in-the-least demented mind" (p. 5a; reprinted by permission: Knight-Ridder Tribune News Service). Calment turned 120 in February 1995.

The proper term for the number of years actually lived is *perform-ance,* and the term *life expectancy* is a projection applied to populations. Life expectancy is computed from life tables that predict the average number of years remaining for a hypothetical group of individuals based on the current set of age-specific rates of dying. Table 2.1 is an abridged life table for the United States for 1989. The table shows that, based on current mortality rates, a newborn could expect to live an average of 75.3 years. The age-specific death rate for that child in its first year of life is 1%. That is to say, approximately 1,000 of every 100,000 newborns will not survive until their first birthday. Of the ones who survive, the average person can expect to live to be 75 (National Center for Health Statistics, 1992).

The life expectancy figure tells people how long (on the average) they can expect to live when they are born; the figure changes as they get older. For example, although the average American man can expect at birth to live to about age 73 and a woman to age 79, once that age is attained a man can expect another 9.4 years of life and a woman, 11.9. Table 2.2 shows changing life expectancy at various ages from birth to age 85 (U.S. Bureau of the Census, 1992d).

Life Span and Evolution

While life expectancy has increased in modern times with better medicine, better diet, and fewer environmental hazards, the maximum life-span potential (MLP) that was achieved thousands of years ago by the human species appears to be relatively static. There has, however, been a dramatic rise in MLP throughout the 26-million year history (or prehistory) of hominid evolution (see Table 2.3). Hominids, defined as "humanlike" primates, have experienced a steady increase in their MLP from 17.8 years for *Aegyptopithecus* to nearly 100 for modern humans *(Homo sapiens sapiens)* (Cutler, 1975) as a result of biological modification, dietary changes, and lifestyle alternations, the most important of which was the acquisition of culture. With the acquisition of culture, "the learned, shared behavior that people acquire as members of a society" (Holmes & Schneider, 1987, p. 164), perhaps as early as australopithecines

Table 2.1 Life Table of the United States: 1989

Age Interval	Proportion Dying	Of 100,000 Born Alive		Stationary Population		Average Remaining Lifetime
Period of Life Between Two Exact Ages Stated in Years, Race, and Sex (1) x to $x+n$	Proportion of Persons Alive at Beginning of Age Interval Dying During Interval (2) $n^q{}_x$	Number Living at Beginning of Age Interval (3) l_x	Number Dying During Age Interval (4) $n^d{}_x$	In the Age Interval (5) $n^L{}_x$	In This and All Subsequent Age Intervals (6) T_x	Average Number of Years of Life Remaining at Beginning of Age Interval (7) e_x
All races						
0-1	.0099	100,000	986	99,154	7,525,922	75.3
1-5	.0019	99,014	192	395,606	7,426,768	75.0
5-10	.0012	98,822	117	493,791	7,031,162	71.1
10-15	.0013	98,705	132	493,269	6,537,371	66.2
15-20	.0043	98,573	428	491,894	6,044,102	61.3
20-25	.0056	98,145	548	489,382	5,552,208	56.6
25-30	.0062	97,597	604	486,474	5,062,826	51.9
30-35	.0076	96,993	734	483,173	4,576,352	47.2
35-40	.0097	96,259	932	479,097	4,093,179	42.5
40-45	.0127	95,327	1,213	473,819	3,614,082	37.9
45-50	.0186	94,114	1,753	466,508	3,140,263	33.4
50-55	.0292	92,361	2,694	455,493	2,673,755	28.9
55-60	.0463	89,667	4,154	438,547	2,218,262	24.7
60-65	.0707	85,513	6,044	413,274	1,779,715	20.8
65-70	.1026	79,469	8,156	377,836	1,366,441	17.2
70-75	.1522	71,313	10,851	330,381	988,605	13.9
75-80	.2235	60,462	13,511	269,356	658,224	10.9
80-85	.3348	46,951	15,720	195,668	388,868	8.3
85 and over	1.0000	31,231	31,231	193,200	193,200	6.2

SOURCE: National Center for Health Statistics (1992).

Table 2.2. Life Expectancy at Various Ages in 1989: United States

Age	Total	Male	Female
Birth	75.3	72.7	79.2
15	61.3	58.6	65.1
25	51.9	49.4	55.3
35	42.5	40.1	45.7
45	33.4	31.1	36.1
55	24.7	22.5	27.1
65	17.2	15.2	19.0
75	10.9	9.4	11.9
85	6.2	5.3	6.5

SOURCE: Compiled by the authors from U.S. Bureau of the Census (1992d) data.

Table 2.3. Estimated Maximum Potential Life Spans for Early Hominids

Hominid Predicted	Antiquity (years)	Body Weight (kg)	Cranial Capacity (cm^3)	Predicted Sexual Maturity (age)	MLP Observed[*] (years)	MLP (years)
Ramapithecus punjabicus	14 million	32	300	8-9	?	42
Australopithecus africanus	3-4 million	32	450	10-11	35-40	51
Homo habilis	1.5 million	43	660	12-13	?	61
Homo erectus (Java)	700,000	53	860	13-14	40-60	69
Homo erectus (Pekin)	250,000	53	1,040	15-16	40-60	78
Homo sapiens (Mt. Carmel)	100,000	57.6P	1,310	17-18	40-60	89
Neanderthal	45,000	58.1P	1,460	18-19	40-60	93
Homo sapiens sapiens (Cro-Magnon)	15,000	58.4P	1,460	18-19	?	94
Homo sapiens sapiens	present	63.5	1,410	18-19	95	91

SOURCE: Adapted from R. G. Cutler (1975); used by permission.

NOTE: ? = not sufficient data available; p = predicted.

*Figures in this column were derived from fossil evidence and survival time in contemporary preindustrial societies with similar cultural development.

(1.4 to 5 million years ago) hominids became domesticated animals—self-domesticated to be sure, but still they were the recipients of the special security provided by an artificial (human-made) environment. In regard to the domestication of the human animal, Melville Herskovits (1949) has suggested: "As one of the domesticated animals, man lives a life that is quite different from that he would have to live under natural conditions. . . . If there is any one word which summarizes the criteria of domestication and the conditions under which domesticated animals live, it is protection" (pp. 629, 146).

While the artificial environment no doubt contributed to greater life expectancy because of reduced hazards, the coming of culture could also be responsible for increasing the life span of hominids. The important consideration is that with the introduction of culture we enter the sphere of learning and teaching. Cutler (1978) reasons that

> the MLP of a mammal may be related to the ability to learn from experience, as compared to instinct abilities. To take full advantage of the ability to learn from, and to teach what is learned, more time is necessary than in animals solely dependent upon instinctive behavior. (p. 332)

The larger and more complex brains capable of learning also take longer to grow and mature. According to Washburn (1981), the larger human brain was also reorganized especially in areas relating to linguistic capabilities and hand usage, the latter of which would have been associated with tool making and use. Both speech and the ability to manipulate the environment are hallmarks of culture.

The learning process associated with generation-to-generation transmission of culture is called *enculturation*. As George Kneller (1965) has observed: "The greater the knowledge and the more complex the skill required for cultural life, the longer education takes" (p. 79).

Margaret Mead (1967) also believes that postponement of sexual maturity (which is closely tied to life span) was an evolutionary development associated with human acquisition of culture. She writes:

> We also know that the postponement of the reproductive period in man has tremendous value for the development of human culture. . . . It is possible that what actually occurred was a shrinkage of the

reproductive period at both ends. That is, puberty was postponed later and later and the menopause appeared—itself an exceedingly important biological change. Human groups with such genetic characteristics would have a superior chance of survival. (p. 33)

Mead goes on to suggest that the factor contributing to female longevity was the reduction of the dangers and stresses of childbearing because of a shorter period of fertility, but that the factors contributing to male longevity were not biological but social and cultural. Better cooperation in hunting, a new division of labor, better hunting tools that reduced fatal accidents, and ways of negotiating disagreements between groups (thereby reducing open conflict) permitted more men to live into middle and old age.

Calculating Evolutionary Maximum Life-Span Potential

At this point the reader might question how scientists know what the MLP was for hominids who lived millions of years ago. In some cases, analysis of skeletal material has allowed researchers to "observe" what the average age of death might have been and then calculate the life-span figure from that. For example, analysis of skeletal material (mostly teeth and jaw fragments) of 114 specimens of australopithecines by Mann (1968) revealed (based on tooth development and wear) that the average age of death for *Australopithecus africanus* was 22.9 years. When a survivorship curve was constructed, that is, a table showing percentage of population alive at various ages, it was found that no one would have survived past the 35- to 40-year bracket. Where a large amount of fossil material is not available for analysis, maximum life spans are calculated on the basis of body weight/brain size ratio, age of sexual maturation, maximum calorie consumption, and specific metabolic rate. The most important of these for our purposes is the body weight/brain size ratio.

According to Cutler (1975), the maximum life span of an animal can be estimated within 25% using the ratio of brain weight and body weight; Table 2.3 shows the agreements between calculations and observations of mortality. Assuming that the natural world operated in much the same way a million years ago that it does today, we can make educated guesses as to the life span of early hominids, given that we do have fairly accurate knowledge of body and brain size for most of these early forms.

Another indicator of life-span potential is age of sexual maturation (Table 2.3). It has been found that there is a ratio of about 5 to 1 between life-span potential and the time required to reach full reproductive capacity. In humans the sexual maturation age is between 18 and 20 years and the human MLP is a little more than 100 years—roughly five times the sexual maturation period (Cutler, 1975). Washburn (1981) cautions that sexual maturation age is a variable phenomenon, at least partly influenced by diet. He questions the validity of Cutler's use of 17-19 years for sexual maturation of humans and suggests that "maturation at 14-15 years was usual for human beings" (Washburn, 1981, p. 19). This lower age range would greatly reduce MLP ($15 \times 5 = 75$).

Other indices of MLP are metabolic rate and caloric intake, and these tend to relate to overall size of the animal. Smaller animals (and early hominids were small) have a higher rate of metabolism so as to maintain their 37°C body temperature. Metabolism used to generate heat is harmful to an animal, and the higher rates are associated with shorter life spans. This rule, which was put forward by Max Rubner in the early 1900s, is not perfect, however. Some of the living fossil-like animals have unusually low metabolic capacities and so do human beings, a few other primates, and rodents.

It should be noted that some of the figures in the table for MLP of prehistoric human beings have been calculated from observations of contemporary preindustrial societies with cultures and environments similar to those of early hominids. For example, many Australian aboriginal populations in Victoria were found to subsist at a cultural level not greatly different than a number of Paleolithic populations. They are hunting and gathering peoples with stone tools. A demographic study of these peoples during the years 1876 and 1912 revealed that 2% of the full-blood population survived into the 86- to 90-year bracket. Infant mortality claimed approximately 25% of the population, but after the first two years of infancy chances for survival increased greatly. This type of evidence is considered of great value by paleodemographers seeking some perspective on performance and life-span potential of prehistoric populations.

Evolution and Senescence

According to Beall and Weitz (1989):

One meaning of biological aging is "the cumulative result of multiple basic processes which occur primarily after maturity, which are characteristic of individuals in a population, and which as a whole decrease the functional capacities of the organism and render death increasingly probable." (p. 189)

Senescence is the term used to describe this process of aging. Much research effort has been directed toward trying to determine why we age, and a variety of theories have been proposed, but evolutionary biologist Michael Rose (1991) states that "all evolutionary theorists who have published on the causes of aging have agreed that the ultimate cause is the declining force of natural selection with age" (p. 16). Two genetic mechanisms are offered in explanation of aging: (a) antagonistic pleiotropy, in which genes having advantageous effects early in life are disadvantageous at some later time, and (b) age-specific genetic effects, in which "alleles having deleterious effects at later ages are essentially neutral, because of a lack of effects at earlier ages and weak selection at later ages due to the declining force of selection with age" (p. 62).

Hayflick (1988) suggests that, rather than being concerned with why we age, a more appropriate question is this: " 'Why do we live as long as we do?' " (p. 87). Humans are unique in the animal world for living so long past the reproductive stage, and from an evolutionary perspective it is reasonable to ask why. Because evolutionary success is based on reproductive success, what is the value of survival of individuals long past the reproductive stage?

There has been some speculation as to whether there was some evolutionary advantage to having aged adults in a population that contributed to extension of MLP. Some arguments in favor of this view have focused on the menopause. Mayer's (1982) research on four New England families, using genealogical records for a 200-year period, led him to conclude that women who died after menopause had more inclusive fitness than those who died before menopause. As explained by Moore (1987): "Inclusive fitness not only involves an individual's fitness but also any contribution the individual's behavior makes to the reproductive success of his or her close relatives" (p. 70). For the New England study, the postreproductive grandmothers' caregiving assistance improved the fitness of their grandchildren. Mayer also suggests that in nomadic early hominid groups, where very young children had to be carried during their early years, there is evidence that selection favored reduction of intervals between births, leading to increased population. With this change in birth spacing, mothers would need assistance with transporting additional dependent infants. Older women who were no longer reproductive could assist with care and carrying of the young. Mayer (1982) offers the theory that this behavior "became physiologically, hence genetically, manifested in the menopause as required by selection for reduced birth intervals among mobile hominids" (p. 490).

Washburn's (1981) position on evolution of the human life span is that old age is only a "byproduct of selection for evolutionary success at much younger ages" (p. 11). He describes a life span in three phases: preparation (about 18 years), adaptation (ages 18-45), and decline (ages 45-75). The evidence indicates humans were not adapted for life beyond 45 years or so. Even at the present time various physiological functions start declining at about age 30. He concludes:

The attainment of maximum life-span potential is partially the result of the new environment of modern technology and medicine, and it is partially luck. If none of the aging systems reaches a fatal level then great age may be achieved. But for most, great age will be associated with handicaps, impairments severe enough to have caused death in our ancestors. (p. 27)

Hayflick (1988) takes a similar view in denying natural selection for long life. Instead, he emphasizes that "the forces of natural selection have provided sexually mature animals with an extraordinary reserve capacity in virtually all organs" (p. 82). This ensures functional efficiency through the reproductive years and, as a bonus, allows some individuals longer life as they use these declining reserves. This loss of functional capacity has been outlined by Leaf (1973b), who tells us that by the age of 75 the basic metabolism rate has diminished 16%, cardiac output has been reduced by 30%, the maximum breathing capacity has dropped 57%, and the filtration efficiency of the kidneys has diminished by 31% from the level of the 30-year-old. Brain weight diminishes 8% and nerve-conduction velocity is lowered approximately 10%.

Fries and Crapo (1981) also present vignettes describing the increasingly common scenario of the 80+-year-old persons who have functioned quite well until some seemingly simple health incident initiates a sequence of events that, over a short time, result in death. As Hayflick (1988) says:

> With few exceptions, no one over the age of 65 ever dies directly from what is written on the death certificate. People die from the *normal* decrements of old age that *increased their vulnerability* to what was written on the certificate. (p. 78)

Demography and Aging

Although extended old age as we know it is a relatively new phenomenon in human history, the evidence is clear that life expectancy has increased significantly. Gains are greatest in more developed countries, but increased life expectancy is occurring worldwide. United Nations (1990) data indicate that during the period 1985-1990 life expectancy for the world as a whole was 64 years; in more developed regions it was 74 years, and in the least developed countries, 49 years. Table 2.4 illustrates some of the variability in life expectancy in different countries. Generally speaking, highest life expectancies are found in the most developed countries and lowest life expectancies are found in Africa, as shown by the figures for Chad and Nigeria. Analyzing data from 50 countries in the developing regions of Asia, Africa, Latin America, and the Caribbean, Kinsella and Taeuber (1992) state that those areas with currently low life expectancy—Asia and Africa—are predicted to improve most by the year 2025.

With very few exceptions, a well-established pattern of greater longevity for women than men is found throughout the world. Deviations from this pattern tend to be associated with cultures where women are in a disadvantaged status relative to men (Kinsella & Taeuber, 1992). Within a particular country, life expectancy may also vary according to occupation, socioeconomic status, or race. Recent studies in the United States, for example, indicate that income and educational levels are important factors in explaining differential mortality rates and life expectancy. Higher income and more education are predictive of less risk of death (Pappas, Queen, Hadden, & Fisher, 1993), and of both greater overall life expectancy and greater active life expectancy (Guralnik, Land, Blazer, Fillenbaum, & Branch, 1993), the latter being the "number

Table 2.4. Life Expectancy in Selected Countries, 1985-1990

Japan	78
Canada	77
Sweden	77
Australia	76
France	76
United States	76
Israel	75
United Kingdom	75
Samoa	71
China	69
Mexico	69
Brazil	65
Fiji	64
Mongolia	61
Peru	61
Vietnam	61
South Africa	60
India	58
Bolivia	53
Zaire	52
Yemen	50
Nigeria	45
Somalia	45
Sierra Leone	41

SOURCE: Compiled by the authors from United Nations World Population Chart (1990).

of remaining years of life expected to be free from disability at specific ages" (Guralnik et al., 1993, p. 110). Kinsella and Taeuber (1992) refer to this as "healthy life expectancy" and suggest that in time it may equal life expectancy in importance.

Differences in life expectancy in various parts of the world or in various segments of our population can be accounted for in large part by differences in environmental hazards such as disease, diet deficiencies, radiation, chemical pollution, accidents, rigors of the physical environment (climate), and mental and physical stress.

Much of the increase in longevity can be attributed to improvements in medical care and nutritional status, along with better sanitation. The result has been the "virtually complete elimination of major infectious diseases" (Fries & Crapo, 1981, p. 63), and an older population that is now characterized by the prevalence of more chronic disease. This is not to say that infectious disease is no longer a problem; in fact it is still a major cause of death in aged Africans (Kinsella, 1988). The change in the primary causes of death over time has been called the "epidemiologic transition," a term credited to Abdel Omran (Kinsella & Taeuber, 1992; Olshansky, Carnes, & Cassel, 1993).

Whether life expectancy can be extended further without individuals simply living more years with physiological decrements remains a matter of debate (Cutler, 1981). One view is that if a major risk factor associated with the leading causes of death could be reduced or eliminated, the resulting decline in mortality might be equivalent to eradicating one of the major diseases (Olshansky, 1993). The evolutionary model, however, asserts that disease in old age results primarily from genetically based processes, that is, postreproductive "declines in cellular maintenance and repair mechanisms" (p. 87). For this reason Olshansky (1993) believes that life expectancy is unlikely to increase indefinitely. In his view, conquering one cause of death in old age (like cancer) "will reveal new or infrequently observed diseases that will be ever more difficult to conquer. I contend that because humans are not designed for immortality, life without disease or some life-threatening disorder is not possible" (Olshansky, 1993, p. 88). His recommendation is that, rather than attacking death, the goal of medicine should be to work toward slowing both the aging process and the onset of the common disabling conditions of the aged.

Fries and Crapo (1981) emphasize that we now have knowledge that individuals can use to make choices—for example, exercising, eating a balanced diet, avoiding smoking, seeking preventive health and dental care—that may modify (in the sense of delaying) the onset of disease. It is their view that by doing so people could live relatively healthy lives to about age 85, after which decline might be quite rapid. Illness and disability would be "compressed" into a shorter period of time. While the value of healthy lifestyle choices is generally accepted, and widely publicized in popular and scientific sources, the position of Fries and Crapo (1981) on the "compression of morbidity" (p. 92) very late in life remains controversial. A contrasting position is that these lifestyle changes "do not change the onset or progression of most debilitating diseases" (Olshansky et al., 1993, p. 51), and may lead to an expansion of morbidity.

Population Aging

Populations, like people, can age. An aging population is one in which older people constitute an increasing proportion of the population, as has been occurring in the United States. "This process . . . is primarily determined by fertility (birth) rates and secondarily by mortality (death) rates. Populations with high fertility tend to have low proportions of older persons and vice versa" (Kinsella & Taeuber, 1992, p. 13).

The typical young population is characterized by high birthrates, high death rates, and a relatively low median age. The *median age* indicates the point at which half the population is below that age and half are at and above that age. A young population can be shown graphically to have a pyramid-shaped age structure (Kinsella, 1988). As population aging occurs, a more rectangular structure becomes apparent. As described by Cowgill (1986), an aging population, usually as a result of modernization influences like access to better health care, experiences reduction of infant mortality, which leads ultimately to improved life expectancy overall. With greater survival in the early years of life, fertility rates decline thereby contributing to the shift in proportion of young to old. An aged or old population is one in which this demographic transition is well established, with low birth- and death rates.

A higher median age is also characteristic of aging and old populations. In Kinsella and Taeuber's (1992) study of 50 countries, median age ranged from 15 to 39 years, and future projections indicate that we can expect median ages to continue increasing. Some countries with low median ages in 1990—for example, Kenya (15.3), Malawi (16), Liberia (18.1), and Pakistan (18.1)—are expected to show increases of only two to three years by 2025. In many developing countries, projected increases of 8 to 10 years in the same period are more typical. In developed regions like North America and Europe, and the countries of New Zealand and Japan, where median age already exceeds 30 years, and in most instances is 35 or more years, all but the United States are expected to be above 40 years in median age by 2025, with projected highs of 48.4 in Italy and 47.9 in Japan. In the United States median age is predicted to increase by less than six years over the 1990 level of 32.8 years to 38.5 (Kinsella & Taeuber, 1992).

On a regional basis, those geographic areas with the lowest percentage of their population aged 65 and over include most of Africa, Latin

America, Asia, and Oceania. Within these regions there are some more developed countries with 9% or more in this age group—Uruguay, Argentina, Japan, Hong Kong, Cyprus, Australia, New Zealand, and several Caribbean islands, for example (United Nations, 1990). It is in these countries, along with Europe, Canada, and the United States, that significant population aging has occurred. Sweden has the distinction of being the world's "oldest" country with 18% of its population aged 65 or more years, an increase of 4.3% just since 1970. Most other European nations have slightly lower percentages of old persons, ranging around 13% to 15%. In the next three decades, Poland, with only 10.1% in 1990, is expected to double its proportion of aged, reaching 20.3% by 2025. The rest of Europe will continue to age, with most countries having 20% or more aged 65 and over, and Luxembourg will become the oldest European country with 25.5% in this category. At that time, Japan may well be the oldest country in the world with a projected older population of 26.7% (Kinsella & Taeuber, 1992).

It is predicted, however, that it will be in developing countries where dramatic increases will occur in the next few decades, especially in absolute numbers of older persons. According to Kinsella and Taeuber (1992): "Sixty-two percent of the world's monthly net gain of elderly— half a million people—occurs in developing countries" (p. 9). To give some specific examples of expected future increases, the size of the elderly population will increase by 220% in China, 271% in Zimbabwe, 321% in Malaysia, and 414% in Indonesia. Many of the developing countries in Kinsella and Taeuber's (1992) study will double the percentage of elderly in their populations. On the other hand, Malawi, Kenya, Zimbabwe, and Bangladesh, with very low percentages in 1990, are expected to increase but will still have relatively low proportions of aged persons. This reflects what is observed in the early stages of population aging, when fertility rates are still high but mortality rates are declining.

In the United States it is often noted that those referred to as the "oldest-old," usually those persons aged 80 or older, are a rapidly increasing part of the older population. In the 1990 census 2.8% of the elderly population was in this age group. Although the oldest-old are a relatively small group, between 1980 and 1990 the number of Americans aged 85 or older increased by 38% (U.S. Bureau of the Census & National Institute on Aging, 1991). Kinsella and Taeuber (1992) indicate that "the oldest-old constituted 16 percent of the world's elderly in 1992" (p. 15).

While developing countries are also experiencing an increase in numbers of oldest-old, developed countries tend to have larger percentages. "Nearly 40 percent of the world's oldest-old in 1990 lived in . . . [t]he People's Republic of China, the United States, and the former Soviet Union" (p. 16). Even when they represent a small proportion of a population, it is the increase in sheer numbers of oldest-old that has important implications for the future.

The implication of the demographic changes outlined here is that aging is, or will become, an important issue throughout the world. It has been said that aging was not considered a social problem in the United States until the twentieth century, when sizable numbers of people began surviving into old age (Fischer, 1978). In the United States we now have a wide array of programs and services for the aging—pension plans, health insurance, specialized housing, nursing homes, adult day care, home health care, nutrition programs, and senior centers, for example. Even so, there are older persons with unmet or inadequately met needs. The continued growth of the older population, especially the oldest-old, suggests that this situation will perhaps be magnified in the future. The demand for more health care and nursing facilities, additional housing, and all manner of support services will be even greater than at present. Such issues are already a source of concern for families and government alike and have begun to create intergenerational tensions. *Caregiving* and *burden* are frequently linked terms in the United States. Questions arise about the solvency of the Social Security system, and the incompatibility of the trend toward early retirement with the societal age structure in the future. The cost of health care, especially for the 12.6% of our population who are 65 or older, increasingly raises the issue of the possibility of rationing of health resources for the aged and other ethical dilemmas unheard of in the past.

Currently, these concerns may be most prevalent in the developed countries that have already aged significantly. But as population aging progresses in developing countries, they too will be confronted with similar problems, for, regardless of cultural variation in views and customs regarding aging, biological aging is a common denominator we share as humans. Lower fertility rates, which eventually accompany population aging, imply that fewer children will be available for care of elderly parents. Because elders tend to live with children in developing countries (Kinsella & Taeuber, 1992), decreasing family size represents a potential threat. Martin (1988) indicates that in Asia about 75% of elders share a household with children, but this is changing. Fewer elders are living with children and more older couples and older women are living alone. This trend is especially apparent in Japan, but there is evidence in other Asian countries of an increase in older women alone or institutionalized. Martin suggests these residential changes "indicate a significant change in attitudes and actions" (p. S104). This situation also implies weakened support for the value of filial piety.

According to Kinsella and Taeuber (1992), "the highest rates of institutional use are found in many of the world's 'oldest' countries" (p. 55), and in the United States institutionalization is often associated with lack of an available caregiver. In the developing world, homes for the aged are a relatively new phenomenon, but with smaller families and the projected increases in the oldest-old population, it seems likely many more such facilities will be needed. These "frail" elders are also most likely to require a variety of health and social support services.

The Parent Support Ratio (PSR) relates to this oldest-old population and is derived from "the number of persons 80 years and over per 100 persons aged 50 to 64" (Kinsella & Taeuber, 1992, p. 61). The PSR is expected to rise in most of Kinsella and Taeuber's 50 study countries but the rates of change will be variable. Japan stands out with a predicted increase in PSR from 13 to 45 by the year 2025. The PSR is important because of the nature of needs of this oldest-old age group and because the potential caregivers are relatively old themselves, and thereby more likely to have needs and responsibilities of their own that conflict with those of their aged parents. And because it is a well-established fact that most of the family care of the aged is provided by women, changing roles of women in industrializing countries may further complicate family support of elders.

If traditional mechanisms of support for the aged are eroded in the future, which seems a real possibility in countries facing tremendous increases in numbers of elders, there may be great pressure on governments to provide solutions to address the economic and social needs. Martin (1988) says, however, "it is clear that elderly people are viewed as a low priority in most Asian countries, especially those that are less developed" (p. S105). This may also be the case in other developing areas of the world as well. Olshansky et al. (1993) describe the challenge facing an aging world:

The demographic evolution of the age structure will have an impact on many aspects of human society, including the job market, housing and transportation, energy costs, patterns of retirement, and nursing home and hospice care, to mention only a few. . . . Social structures have simply not evolved with the same rapidity as age structures. . . . All older people, both the healthy and the sick, will need the chance to contribute meaningfully to society. Achieving that end will require an economy that provides ample, flexible opportunities for experienced and skilled older persons, as well as modifications in the physical infrastructures of society. Changes in attitudes about aging will be essential. (p. 52)

Dealing with this issue is far from simple in the developed countries of the world. It may be even more difficult in the developing countries, many of which lack strong economies and have too few people engaged in "full-time wage-related employment to support programs that are based on principles of social insurance—that is, payroll contributions, as in most industrial nations" (Tracy, 1991, p. 3).

Shangri-las

For many years the world has been intrigued by reports of little pockets of people who, apparently for genetic, environmental, or cultural reasons, have managed to achieve surprisingly high longevity. In the novel *Lost Horizon* (Hilton, 1933), Shangri-la was a place where people were immortal, and this term is often used now to describe the populations and locales for which claims of extreme longevity are made. Lewis Aiken wrote in 1978 that

examples of very long lifespans are found in sizable numbers among the Hunza people in the Karakoram Range of the Himilayas, the Abkhasians of the Republic of Georgia in the USSR, and the Andean "Viejos" of the village of Vilcabamba in Ecuador. Nearly 50 out of every 100,000 people in the Caucasus region of the Soviet Union, compared to only 3 out of 100,000 (in the United States), live to be 100. (p. 8)

These societies not only claimed high percentages of centenarians, but two areas reported people living well beyond what we have established as the maximum life-span potential for human beings—120 years. For example, Sula Benet's (1974) informant among the Abkhasians, Madame Khfaf Lasuria, was reported to be 140 years old, and in Vilcabamba, Ecuador, several investigators set the age of Miguel Carpio at 129. Claims for the Hunza of Pakistan have been a bit more conservative, with the oldest in this region reported to be only 110.

Since Aiken's book was published, several more Shangri-las have come to light, principally the island of Paros in Greece and Yagodina in southern Bulgaria. Both have reported unbelievable percentages of centenarians in their populations; Paros, for example, claims an index of 185 per 100,000 population, while in the United States the current figure is 10 per 100,000.

To explore the factors of heredity and environment (geographic and cultural) in long life and to assess the reliability and validity of claims of extreme longevity, let us look at each of the five societies cited above where claims of unusual longevity have been recorded.

Abkhazia

The Abkhasians live in the northern part of the Republic of Georgia in a mountainous region bordered by the Black Sea on the west and the Caspian Sea on the east. Abkhazia was previously part of the former Soviet Union, and in early 1994 negotiations over the political status of this area were still under way. It is not an isolated area, and the population of the region is so ethnically mixed that Berdyshev (1968) postulated that the high proportion of long-lived people in this area can be explained by hybridization (heterosis). The people of Abkhazia eat little meat, eggs, or sweet foods but acquire great amounts of natural vitamins from fresh vegetables. Protein is derived from beans, nuts, and yogurt, and they get large amounts of vitamin C from wild apples and pears. Food is chewed slowly and well, and a calm atmosphere prevails while eating (Benet, 1976, p. 93). The consumption of wine, however, is very high in the area (higher than in France), and Leaf found an Abkhasian claiming to be over 130 years old who said he had smoked a pack of cigarettes daily for the last 62 years. Another, believed by Benet to be 140 years old, reportedly had a glass of vodka before breakfast every day.

The Georgian population is very active. Everyone works hard, even the aged. Sichinava (1965) reports that almost three fourths of the men and women over 80 still do varied light tasks, and about 10% still work in the gardens and orchards. People of all ages walk and climb a great deal, often on very rocky paths.

Benet (1976) writes:

> In the Caucasus, the old people remain involved in their family, their lineage, and their community. They are involved emotionally and physically. Their work provides them with physical exercise but also with the knowledge of their own meaningful contribution to the community. (p. 164)

The Hunza

At the northern apex of West Pakistan, between Afghanistan and China, the Hunza Valley lies within the Karakoram mountain range. This area, which is actually located in an extension of the Himalayas, has an altitude of between 5,000 and 7,000 feet. The climate is temperate with warm summers (often reaching 90°F) but winter brings snow and cold temperatures. The land is arid, and although the Hunza Valley looks like a great formal garden, this is made possible only by use of water from glaciers and springs high in the hills above in an ingenious irrigation system. The inhabitants of the valley, called Hunzakuts, subsist on grains, vegetables, and fruits (principally apricots). The people suffer neither obesity nor malnutrition. There is no alcoholism, and elderly people do not smoke.

Where the people inhabiting this valley came from originally is unknown, but their language, Burashaski, indicates that they have been isolated in these mountains since about 1500 B.C. It is not a written language and therefore there are no birth records. The only event that can be used to establish any kind of time frame is the invasion by the British in 1892. Although no census has ever been taken, Hunza is believed to have a relatively high percentage of healthy and vigorous elderly people, some of them over 100. It is difficult to understand just why Hunza gained its reputation as a "Himalayan Shangri-la" (Taylor & Nobbs, 1962) although the area has long been considered a healthful environment and it has long been rumored that the people had an extraordinary capacity for rapid healing of wounds or infections (a phenomenon attributed to their diet).

The social and political system is described by Leaf (1975) as follows:

> The old people are esteemed for the wisdom that is thought to derive from long experience and their word in the family group is generally the law. . . . Most continue their work until the age of 100. There is no fixed or forced retirement age, and the elderly are not dismissed when they reach a certain age as occurs in our industrialized societies. (pp. 153-154)

Vilcabamba

The village of Vilcabamba (meaning Sacred Valley) is 4,500 feet above sea level in the Andes mountains of Ecuador. Paul Martin (1976) describes the Vilcabamba region as an ecological paradise with pure air and water and a moderate climate. The inhabitants of this small rural agricultural community are of mixed ancestry—Spanish and Indian—but with a tendency toward European features. This farm community subsists mainly on corn, bananas, potatoes, wheat, barley, beans, peanuts, grapes, but very little meat.

In 1969 a Peruvian doctor, Miguel Salvador, brought a medical team to Vilcabamba to investigate health and longevity claims. Salvador concluded that he had found a natural island of immunity to the physical and psychological problems that shorten life elsewhere and he claimed to have found nine persons over the age of 100 in a population of 819 (Leaf, 1975). This would represent an index of approximately 1,100 centenarians per 100,000 population. If the United States had such an index, we would have 2 million centenarians instead of our 36,000.

Salvador theorized that the constant physical exertion required to live in this mountainous terrain kept the people's bones mineralized, dense, and strong and their hearts robust. Although hygienic and public health conditions are poor, the diet was seen as conducive to good health and long life.

Paros, Greece

Paros is a community on the island of Paros in the Grecian archipelago. The area has a moderate Mediterranean climate and is free of

This 105-year-old Paros Island farmer and his wife, 87, relax between chores in the courtyard of their farm. He still directs work on his land. (Photo courtesy of Jeff Beaubier; used by permission.)

infectious disease. Major causes of death are heart disease, cancer, and stroke. The community has "extremely low or nonexistent rates of alcoholism, drug abuse, homicide, truancy, illiteracy, civil suits, felonies and misdemeanors, insanity, illegitimacy, venereal disease, bankruptcy, accidents, divorce or suicide" (Beaubier, 1976, pp. 131-132). Inhabitants fish, farm, and provide services to tourists. A few are merchant seamen. Paros is described as "a society that requires physical work, and rewards and prizes mental activity. There is good nutrition, lack of pollution, excellent medical care, folk medicine and preventative health, good family life, lack of crime and social strife" (Beaubier, 1980, p. 41). The standard of living is relatively high and great respect is shown to elders. The diet of the people is much like that found in other areas claiming high longevity—large quantities of fresh fruits and vegetables and very little meat. Protein comes from fish and eggs, and yogurt and cheese are plentiful in all homes.

When Paros was studied by Jeff Beaubier in 1970-1972, he claimed to have established documentary proof that, out of the population of 2,703, 5 were 100 years old or older. That represents an index of 185 centenarians per 100,000, or 18.5 times greater than what is found in the United States. Beaubier also maintains that the age claims of centenarians as well as the rest of the community were corroborated by birth registrations and baptism records, all complete with family members' and officials' signatures. Other substantiating evidence included records of taxation, property ownership, and military service.

Yagodina

Yet another Shangri-la has been located in Yagodina, Bulgaria, by Los Angeles Times staff writer Mathis Chazanov (1987). He reports that this village in the Rhodope Mountains near the northern border of Greece has an extraordinarily high percentage of people 100 years of age and older, most of whom are "physically fit and mentally alert" (p. 1). The region has been researched for more than 20 years in an effort to isolate the reason for such long and healthy life. Popular wisdom claims that it is the yogurt that people eat three times a day, but Dr. Argir Hadjihristev, a local scientist, maintains there is no single factor. Instead, he believes their long life stems from family histories of longevity, stable marriages, and the fact that the people "spent most of their lives hard at work outdoors; drank herbal tea and boiled oats instead of coffee; ate nothing but fresh food; slept moderately; and benefited from the sunny, pollution-free and oxygen-rich atmosphere of the Rhodope Mountains" (Chazanov, 1987, p. 1). He describes the lives of the Yagodina oldsters as characterized by moderation and the environment by an absence of stress.

Validity of Shangri-la Claims

Abkhazia

Over the last few years there has been a cloud of doubt over the validity of claims of extreme longevity in Abkhazia, Hunza, and Vilcabamba. Gerontologists maintain that the 110- to 120-year human life-span maximum is valid for everyone, even the citizens of these purportedly unique enclaves. Some scientists, like Medvedev (1974), have claimed that these so-called centenarians of Abkhazia, have falsified their age to avoid the military service.

Medvedev's doubts are prompted by a great deal more than his assumption that ages were altered for draft evasion, however. He maintains that state documents about age distribution are not valid, because all information was obtained verbally and without corroborating documents. He asserts that the 1970 census in the Caucasus showed a decrease in centenarians from 8,890 in 1960 to 4,925, although there is no reason to believe that any natural or man-made cause should bring this about. The answer is that the methods of collecting accurate information improved.

The purported concentration of centenarians is highest in Moslem areas and here there is no practice of birth registration at all. Even in Christian areas it is difficult to find birth registrations, because about 90% of churches (and their birth records) were destroyed between 1922 and 1940.

Of the 500 people in the Caucasus claiming to be between 120 and 170, not a single one has been able to produce documents proving his age. Even if some of these people were correct in assessing the number of years they have survived, there is also the complicating fact that many in this group are Moslem and the Moslem year is only 10 months long.

Bennett and Garson (1986) cite the work of the Soviet scientist Krupnik in regard to inaccuracy of reported ages in Abkhazia. Prior to the Russian revolution, there was no system of recording precise dates of birth or age; "broad age categories" (p. 359) were used instead. When a system intended to produce more exact data was implemented following the revolution, some questionable methods were employed. One such method involved adding years as a sort of reward to a person. This was done apparently in recognition of life experiences or to elevate their position.

Some researchers claim that the people are able to establish their correct age by associations with historical events. But many of these events concern only the village—such as the year of a famine or a plague—and cannot always be accurately placed in time. Also troubling is the fact that often more people are reported in the very old categories than in the younger ones. For example, in the Altay area of the Caucasus, the 1959 census showed 15 people between the ages of 111 and 113, but 19 individuals between 114 and 116. In one area, statistics showed 72 persons between the ages of 100 and 104, 44 persons between 105 and 109 (a mortality rate of 39%), but then only a 12% mortality drop to 39 people in the 110-114 age bracket. Theoretically, this pattern of attrition is not possible, and such statistics can be of little use in scientific research.

Although the average life span in the Caucasus is about the same as that for the rest of the former Soviet Union, the reported number who reach 80 is 40% higher, the number who reach 100 is 410% higher, and the number who reach 110 is 2,000% higher than the average for the whole country.

Palmore (1984) cites a Soviet study that appears to provide more believable data concerning Abkhasian longevity. Using what is known as the "anamnestic method" (determining one's age through family records of marriages and births correlated with dated national and local events), a carefully controlled study of 115 people reputed to be over 90 years of age in four Abkhasian villages revealed that only 38% could actually be verified as being over 90. None was found to be over 110. Palmore (1984) maintains that in 1970 Soviet scientists determined that the percentage of Abkhasians counted as over 90 was 0.9, but

> if the percentage over 90 is corrected by multiplying it by .38 (the proportion verified), the result is that only 0.3% of Abkhasians were actually over 90. . . . This percentage was slightly higher than that for the U.S.S.R. as a whole but no higher than that for the United States. (p. 95)

What would seem to be operative in Abkhazia as well as in all of the areas discussed in this chapter, with the possible exception of Paros, Greece (with its abundance of documents establishing age), is age exaggeration, a factor that has been carefully researched by Rosenwaike and Preston (1984), Rosenwaike and Logue (1985), Bennett and Garson (1986), and others. Rosenwaike and Preston (1984), investigating age overstatement in Puerto Rico, discovered a tendency among the elderly there for what they call "age heaping," which is "the tendency of respondents to report ages with terminal digits of zero and five more frequently than other ages" (p. 506). This phenomenon was found to be more pronounced among females than males, and such misreporting tended to be associated with illiteracy and with those in poorer living conditions. The highest rate of illiteracy was found among the oldest individuals.

Even in the United States this phenomenon prevails. The 1980 census recorded that 1.2% of whites claimed to be centenarians while 4.1% of the nonwhite population made that claim. Considering that life expectancy among whites is greater than among nonwhites, this figure must be inaccurate.

Age overstatement can have a significant effect on population statistics. As Rosenwaike and Preston (1984) point out:

Life tables for populations such as U.S. whites indicate that at older ages there generally is an increase of 9 or 10 percent in the death rate with an increase in age of one year. Thus, if the average age recorded on census and death records for a particular age group is one year older than the true age, the result would be an error of about 10 percent for that group. An average overstatement of two years could produce an error of about 20 percent. (p. 522)

After conducting a study of Soviet mortality and census data from 1959 and 1970, Bennett and Garson (1983), using cross-checks for consistency between census age distributions, age-specific growth rates, and life tables, found old age mortality greatly underreported and the percentage of centenarians in the U.S.S.R. exaggerated. True mortality levels were understated in all republics with official Soviet life tables (eight), and the 1959 number of centenarians was overstated by 28.9% and that for 1970, by 7.5%.

Berdyshev (1968) believes that social and political factors can partially explain the claims of high longevity in the Caucasus. He points out that in this area villagers seek out the elderly for advice and help in solving of difficult problems, and the older the adviser, the greater the respect and honor extended to him or her. This has a tendency to encourage age exaggeration.

Another encouragement is the great deal of attention that the international media have given in recent years to the phenomenal longevity of these people. This has resulted in considerable competition between villages to be able to claim the oldest individual or the greatest number of centenarians. A generation ago villages were claiming 115-year-old residents, but it is not unusual today to find claims of 160- or 170-year-old people.

Moreover, the region encompassed by the former Soviet Union as a whole has enjoyed the publicity and feels that a long life is a unique

Soviet accomplishment. Many of the old people working on collective farms have been given special recognition by the state and applauded as national heroes. The fact that Stalin was from the Caucasus area is also significant. He encouraged the reports of longevity from his area of birth and did everything he could to establish the validity of such claims. We might suspect that few social scientists during Stalinist years would have had the courage to challenge the claims so much relished by their leader.

Even if the claims of long life could be safely rejected, today it would not be a good business, given that the reputation of longevity has brought droves of foreign and domestic visitors to the region, and the residents are the recipients not only of material advantages but also of a great deal of flattering attention.

Finally it must be recognized that Abkhazia has essentially been assumed to be a closed population, that is, there has been no migration. No doubt documentation of rural to urban migration patterns of young people would have some impact on recorded percentages of elderly in these rural areas.

Hunza

Statements concerning Hunza longevity are extremely subjective. No census has ever been taken in the Hunza Valley, there is no written language and therefore no records, the only event that can be used to document people's ages is the 1892 British invasion, and there is a political advantage in being elderly. The Hunza appear to have the characteristics of a gerontocracy, where elderly wield considerable power as members of the Mir's court.

As Leaf's conclusions appear to be more impressionistic than scientific, no controlled study of the validity of claims for high percentages of very elderly or cases of extreme age among Hunzakuts exists that would compare with those made in Abkhazia, and we are left with statements such as the following:

> I was not able to confirm exact ages in Hunza. Yet I had the definite impression of an unusual number of very vigorous old folk clambering over the steep slopes that make up this mountainous land. It was the fitness of many of the elderly rather than their extreme ages that impressed me. (Leaf, 1973a, p. 96)

In nearly every recorded case of a society reporting extraordinarily long life or high percentages of centenarians, one of the primary explanations is invariably that the people live in a mountainous region and the exertion required in negotiating the rugged terrain produces physically fit people even up into advanced age. However, Beall, Goldstein, and Feldman (1985) in their research in the mountains and flat terrains in Nepal state that

> there was no evidence that the sample residing in rugged terrain was more physically fit than the sample residing in flat terrain. . . . The findings of this study indicate that the rural, agricultural, unmechanized lifestyle of these traditional Nepalese residents does not result in an especially high level of physical fitness. The data offer no support for the common notion that residence in rugged terrain per se is associated with greater physical fitness during old age. (pp. 533-534)

Vilcabamba

After Leaf's (1975) visit to the Ecuadorian village of Vilcabamba, he suggested that "because of the apparent family ties linking the elderly . . . I felt with a strong suspicion that genetic factors were of prime importance" (p. 58). In fact he felt genetic reasons could account for an index of 366 times more centenarians in Vilcabamba than in the United States, but a subsequent study by Mazess and Forman (1979) revealed another explanation—*that they systematically exaggerate their age.* These researchers claim to have found not a single centenarian in the lot. The oldest person in the village was, according to them, 96. Explaining that "age exaggeration appears to be a common finding in the extreme elderly throughout the world . . . associated with illiteracy and absence of actual documentation" (p. 94), they set about investigating claims of extreme longevity in this Ecuadorian village.

Mazess and Forman (1979) found some baptismal records, but many had been destroyed in a church fire. Those that did exist were difficult to read because of faded writing and the poor condition of the pages. Positive identification of individuals soon loomed as the major problem. They discovered

> there were frequent duplications of given names and surnames. Misidentification and sloppiness of identification have characterized

previous descriptions of this population. In Vilcabamba there are relatively few familial names in use, and several of these, such as Toledo and Carpio, are extremely common. (p. 95)

They also found that the same given names have been used again and again over many generations. When it was possible to compare birth records of individuals with their reported ages, it was found that there was a consistent and predictable pattern of age exaggeration. Mazess and Forman (1979) state:

Systematic age exaggeration was found beginning at about 70 years; at a stated age of 100 the estimated actual age would be only 84 years. . . . We were able to demonstrate that nearly all cases of reported centenarians in Vilcabamba were in their 80s and 90s. (p. 98)

Mazess and Mathisen (1982) found that "life expectancy (corrected for exaggeration) at all ages in Vilcabamba (and Loja) is in fact less than in the U.S." (p. 522).

Other factors that would appear to falsify Vilcabamba longevity claims are cited by Mazess and Mathisen (1982). The factors are (a) that the authors suspect that deaths in early infancy and childhood were underreported, thereby affecting life expectancy figures, and (b) that

the elevated proportion of persons over 60 in the town population was largely due to the influx of older persons from surrounding rural zones and the out-migration of younger persons to a nearby urban center. The percentage of elderly in the entire "longevity" area is no different than in the rest of the province of Loja, or in rural Ecuador in general. (p. 518)

Cultural Factors in Longevity

Although claims of extremely high longevity (above the human maximum life-span potential) appear to be highly questionable, there are, without doubt, conditions that can prolong life and increase the percentage of elderly that survive to the century mark. Every society has its prescription for long life. The ideas of individuals in a society may vary somewhat on this issue, but there will be consistency within the society based on the group's concept of health, illness, and important values.

Ideas of desirable physical and psychological environments also vary from culture to culture. Members of different societies may respond negatively or positively to the same stimuli. For example, in America stress is often cited as a factor detrimental to longevity, and noise pollution has often been cited as a major contributor to stress.

In Hong Kong, however, where there is tremendous crowding (20,000 persons per acre), noise does not contribute to stress. E. N. Anderson (1972) writes:

> Noise, demonstrably a stressful problem in many crowded cities and households around the world, is not a problem here. . . . Noise in a household is the sign of life and action, and the household moves in a shimmering ambience of sound from waking to sleep. . . . I have never heard anyone complain about noise in a Chinese household. Noise is desirable or at worst ignored. (pp. 145-146)

In spite of cultural differences in what are perceived as harmful or helpful factors in longevity, the similarity of the responses to what contributes to long life is remarkable. Generally, societies value work as a way of maintaining health and vigor, although few have as strong a work ethic as Americans. Moderation in eating, drinking, and smoking is often cited, as is the value of a proper diet. In a large number of societies, even preindustrial, people believe that one will live longer if one has had long-lived parents. The pleasures of sex and pleasant companions are often seen as advantageous, and in many societies large, supportive, and respectful families are believed to contribute to longevity of elders. In most of the world, the general formula for a long life is to be happy, to be adequately (but not overly) fed, to be respected, to be moderate in one's vices, and to be active.

The following are a few formulas from elders around the world explaining why they have lived so long:

Ali Murad (Hunza, age 91) attributes long life to "normal work, no smoking, no suffering, adequate rest, and a moderate amount of wine; and one should eat a lot of green vegetables" (Leaf, 1975, p. 39).

Four aged Abkhasians (ages 95-106) when asked the secret of their long life stated: "The clean Abkhasian air," "good food and pure mountain water," "constant exercise and exertion of farm life keeps you fit and helps strengthen the heart," and "heredity. Long living individuals tend to marry other long lived, and longevity is concentrated in certain lineages (Rodi) in the community" (Crawford & Oberdieck, 1978, p. 37).

Charlie Smith (former African slave claiming to be 130) recommends that the way to achieve very old age is to "eat raw sausages and crackers and drink 7-Up. I never drank green (raw) milk—only chocolate" (Weyl, 1977, p. 167).

Sei (Samoan chief in his eighties) explains his longevity by the fact that "I work hard every day" (Holmes, 1972, p. 75).

Aline Pierce, who died in San Francisco in 1993 at age 109, "the oldest living survivor of the '06 quake till her death . . . attributed her long life to a nightly straight-up martini and her beloved Jaguar, 'the only car worth driving' " (by Herb Caen, 1993, p. B1; © *San Francisco Chronicle.* Reprinted by permission).

Bessie and Sadie Delany (ages 102 and 104) say they're "still here" because "we never had husbands to worry us to death!" These never-married sisters also give a "serious reason they've lived so long . . . they need each other" (Hearth, 1993, p. 144).

Belarmino Carpio (Vilcabamba, age 85) attributes longevity to "god and climate," and "we almost never eat meat" (Leaf, 1975, p. 52).

"Satchel" Paige (former major league pitcher, age unknown but well over 65) maintains his formula for "stayin' young" is as follows:

1. Avoid fried meats which angry up the blood.
2. If your stomach disputes you, lie down and pacify it with cool thoughts.
3. Keep the juices flowing by jangling around gently as you move.
4. Go very light on the vices, such as carrying on in society. The social ramble ain't restful.
5. Avoid running at all times.
6. Don't look back. Something might be gaining on you. (Broeg, 1989, p. 48)

Democritus (Greek philosopher, age 100) volunteered the secret of his longevity: "Application of oil without, and honey within" (Bailey, 1857, p. 16).

Ancient Hebrews believed that one must "honor thy father and thy mother, that thy days may be long in the land" (Exodus 20:12).

Hopi Indians maintained that "whoever is not mean will live long" (Stephen, 1936, p. 11).

The Palaung of Burma attribute long life to virtuous behavior. (Apparently, there are no "dirty old men" among these people.)

SUMMARY

All organisms have fixed, finite life spans, and the maximum potential for humans appears to be approximately 110 to 120 years. Most individuals will die much earlier, and life expectancy (a projected average calculated at birth) varies from country to country and for different races, classes, and occupations. It also differs for males and females. While life expectancy has increased in modern times with better medicine, better diet, and fewer environmental hazards, the maximum lifespan potential for humans has not changed to any great degree since the time of Neanderthals, 45,000 years ago. Length of life span is a property of the species, but in understanding the matter of human longevity it is necessary to understand the evolutionary history of our ancestral primates. From the first apelike progenitor through modern *Homo sapiens*, there has been a steady and progressive increase in life span with a noticeable gain with the shift from instinctive to learned behavior and the advent of culture.

Consideration of life span logically leads to the question of what aging is and why it takes place. Aging, known as senescence, is a natural loss of organic functions that begins in humans at about age 30, which is after the peak of the reproduction cycle. Human beings are one of the few species that experience senescence. Most animals die shortly after they have reproduced and guaranteed the continuation of the species. In the case of human beings, culture has provided a margin of safety, allowing longer life and therefore senescence. Although the security provided by culture is important, we must remember that the greater part of human longevity is determined by genetic endowment and is a product of the species' evolutionary history.

From a demographic perspective, it is clear that population aging is, or soon will be, occurring throughout the world. This process, which is associated with declining birth- and death rates, results in an increasing proportion of older persons in a population. The most highly industrialized countries are well into this demographic transition while developing countries exhibit varying degrees of the trend toward population aging. It is in these latter countries where the most significant change in life expectancy and percentages of older persons in the population is expected in coming decades, a situation likely to present serious challenges to families and governments alike as they attempt to meet the needs of larger numbers of elderly persons.

As the volume of knowledge concerning longevity grows, we are struck more and more by the necessity for holistic analyses of the interaction between genetic and environmental components. Even though humankind is one species biologically, the fact that life-expectancy rates vary as much as 40 years among various cultures means that studies of the quality of genetic endowment must always be linked with data concerning climate, diet, technology, disease, emotional stress, war, and genocide. Believing that environmental factors are of great importance in determining average length of life, scientists have sought to find cultures where the lifestyle appears to promote long life. Such societies as Abkhazia in the Republic of Georgia, Vilcabamba in Ecuador, Hunza in the Himalayas, Yagodina in southern Bulgaria, and the island of Paros in Greece have been purported to be pockets of extreme longevity and have often been labeled Shangri-las. However, in nearly all of these areas serious questions exist about the validity of the data. Often there are no documents officially recording dates of birth and in some cases patterns of institutional exaggeration of age have been discovered. In societies where great respect is given to the very old, it pays to add a few years. Many of the claims of extreme longevity have come from tourists and travelers rather than scientists, and in some cases local and national political and economic interests may have led to the exaggerated claims of long life.

3

□ The Life Cycle

Margaret Clark (1967) once pointed out that "anthropologists have long claimed the study of cultural patterning of the human life cycle, with its various phases, transitions, and rites of passage, as one of their special concerns" (p. 55). Crane and Angrosino (1992) maintain that "every complete ethnography should give the reader an understanding of the life cycle of the people in question—what it is like to be born, to live each phase of life, and to die in that particular society" (p. 75). Unfortunately, however, the focus in anthropology has been on the earlier years in the life cycle—infancy, childhood, adolescence, and early adult years. Only since Simmons (1945a) have the final years of life received any great amount of attention.

In this chapter we focus on a number of interesting questions and issues that anthropological gerontologists explore in studying the life cycle: When does old age begin? How is one supposed to behave when identified as old? Do all cultures use the same criteria in determining the onset of old age? Is there potential for creativity in late life? Is retirement a universal phenomenon? What do cross-cultural data reveal about disengagement theory? What role options are available to the elderly in various societies? Completing our overview of the life cycle, we consider how age relates to views of death and ceremonial response to this event.

Of course, all societies in the world recognize a number of phases of the life cycle. Even Shakespeare, in his late sixteenth-century play *As You Like It*, referred to divisions of the life cycle:

> All the world's a stage,
> And all the men and women merely players;
> They have their exits and their entrances;
> And one man in his time plays many parts,
> His acts being seven ages. At first the infant,
> Mewling and puking in the nurse's arms;
> Then the whining school-boy, with his satchel
> And shining morning face, creeping like snail
> Unwillingly to school. And then the lover,
> Sighing like furnace, with a woeful ballad
> Made to his mistress' eyebrow. Then a soldier,
> Full of strange oaths and bearded like the pard,
> Jealous in honour, sudden and quick in quarrel,
> Seeking the bubble reputation
> Even in the cannon's mouth. And then the justice,
> In fair round belly with good capon lin'd,
> With eyes severe and beard of formal cut,
> Full of wise saws and modern instances;
> And so he plays his part. The sixth age shifts
> Into the lean and slipper'd pantaloon,
> With spectacles on nose and pouch on side,
> His youthful hose, well sav'd, a world too wide
> For his shrunk shank; and his big manly voice,
> Turning again toward childish treble, pipes
> And whistles in his sound. Last scene of all,
> That ends this strange eventful history,
> Is second childishness and mere oblivion,
> Sans teeth, sans eyes, sans taste, sans every thing. (Act 2, Scene 7)

This is but one of many systems of dividing up life. There may be great variation from one society to another in the number of categories recognized, and the age range of each grouping may be quite vague.

There are, however, societies where "precisely defined, self-conscious, corporate age groups" (van den Berghe, 1983, p. 73) are an integral part of the social structure. Africa is notable for this tendency to form *age grades* and *age sets*. To distinguish between these two terms, van den Berghe (1983) explains:

> When the emphasis is on the position of that age category in relation to similar others, for example, "The sophomore class at Harvard" is in our terms an *age grade*. We shall reserve the term *age set* for the specific group of individuals who move as a group through an age grade system. For example, "the Harvard class of 1970" is an age set until its last member dies. (p. 73)

In American society we generally do not place much emphasis on such precisely delineated age groupings, but the Nandi of East Africa provide a good example of a system where age is an important basis for organization. According to Huntingford (1960), the social system of the Nandi has four age grades for males (small boys, initiates, warriors, and elders) and two for females (girls and married women). Although there are only four major age grades for males, there are actually some seven named age sets in all—four of them made up of elders. Each set is composed of all those who underwent their initiation into manhood together. A circumcision ritual marking the advent of manhood takes place about every 15 years, accommodating boys varying in age from 10 to 20 years. Before this ritual, the boys must spend two years in military instruction, because after the initiation they are officially warriors. After several years as warriors, when they concentrate on making war and making love, they graduate to the status of elder and as such are expected to settle down, marry, and raise a family. Eventually, if a man lives long enough, he, along with his surviving age-mates, serve their society as statesmen and tribal advisers (Hollis, 1909). Age-graded societies are often labeled gerontocracies, but it is also possible to have a gerontocracy (society governed by the elderly) without an age-grade system.

Regardless of how the life cycle is divided, all societies recognize old age as a definite status. Most societies also believe that certain kinds of behavior are appropriate to the different life stages, and most societies have well-agreed-on markers by which to recognize the beginning of old age. In the United States and in much of the Western world, one becomes

Table 3.1 Nandi Age Grades

Grade	Expected Behavior
Males	
1. boys	Cattle herding; servants to warriors
2. warriors	Warfare and courtship
3. elders	Marry, raise a family, and then serve as statesmen and tribal advisers
Females	
1. girls	Household chores
2. married women	Childbearing and rearing; homemaking

old at age 65, regardless of one's biological condition. That is when most individuals are given their gold watch for long and faithful service to their employers and told to go home, retire, and start collecting their pensions and Social Security. This system of determining the onset of old age is based on an arbitrary sum of years (65) and bears no relationship to the nature of the individual's personality, vitality, biological condition, and mental acuity. Such a system is *chronological.*

The alternative method of reckoning age, and the one used by most non-Western cultures, is a *functional* system. That is, a person is considered old when he or she is no longer able to be a fully productive, participating member of society. A person who has reached this stage does not necessarily command less respect, but special considerations are forthcoming from fellow societal members. People who are considered old are given the right to work at their own speed, to engage in special kinds of duties, or perhaps to do nothing at all, having already put in a lifetime of productive labor.

Various circumstances seem to determine how and when old age is recognized. Cowgill and Holmes (1972) postulated that "the concept of old age itself appears to be relative to the degree of modernization" (p. 7). That is to say, as societies become more modern, the age at which one becomes old goes up. Moreover, in some areas where the elderly were eligible for government assistance or Social Security, evidence indicated functional definitions for old age had been completely replaced by a chronological one.

Christine Fry (1980) conducted a study of age markers and appropriate age behavior in the United States and she sought answers to questions such as these: What makes us old, culturally? How is age differentiated and structured into a cultural system? What are the expectations and standards of acceptable behavior for different age groups? Fry used an ethnoscience (involving establishment of emic categories) approach to age cognition. Believing that aging is more than a series of birthday celebrations, she developed a methodology for understanding aging in terms of such dimensions as engagement-responsibility, reproductive cycle, and encumberment. Fry (1980) discovered that the following was characteristic of the American life cycle:

> As the life time becomes longer, the statuses are marked by increasing responsibilities and engagement in the social system. This progression is then "intersected" by further responsibilities with the possible arrival of children and then their maturation. Finally, the horseshoe is complete as the sequence of statuses is marked by an increasing withdrawal primarily from occupational engagement. (p. 53)

In general, Fry found the typical American life history to run something like this: Before the age of 25, role changes are frequent and marital status is likely to change from single to married. Between 25 and 35, Americans establish their major work commitments and are involved with preschool and beginning school children. Ages 35 to 50 are marked by highly productive job activity; family households contain high school children but during this period the "empty nest" becomes a reality. Beyond 50, reference to children disappears and widowhood and retirement become typical. Approaching aging as something multidimensional rather than unidimensional (in terms of years) permits the investigator to discover "how age is interlaced with basic issues that must be resolved by all cultures" (Fry, 1980, p. 44). Fry believes her cross-cultural approach could be fruitful in understanding "the underlying cultural organization, the commonalities and variations, of an issue which is universal for all humankind—aging" (p. 61).

Growing out of Fry's analysis of age-appropriate life-cycle behavior in the United States has come a much more ambitious research project that goes by the acronym A.G.E. (Age, Generation and Experience). This project, carried out between 1982 and 1988, involved a team of seven anthropologists working in seven community sites around the world, using a methodology that included participant observation, that is, living in the community and observing the lifestyle; 200 interviews in each site with people of various ages; life history analysis; and a card sorting task that they referred to as the "Age Game." This device consisted of asking "informants to sort written and sketched descriptions of imaginary people into piles representing stages of life" (Keith, Fry, & Ikels, 1990, p. 246).

They then asked the people to explain why they made the choices they did, what might be the main concerns of the people in these age categories, and what were the things that might make these people perceive that they were doing well or doing poorly. The investigators were also interested in how many piles (representing stages of the life course) the people created, what the age ranges were in each, and what events they depicted as thresholds between each of the stages.

The various communities in which the research took place represented a diverse selection of cultural and socioeconomic environments. They included the following:

1. Swarthmore, Pennsylvania, a small (4,650) suburban college town near Philadelphia with somewhat mobile, well-educated, and economically comfortable residents: More than 25% were over 65.
2. Momence, Illinois, a small (4,000) blue-collar community 50 miles south of Chicago with mostly a high school educated, middle-income population: Its relatively stable population was politically conservative, valuing personal independence, stable family relations, and participation in community activities.
3. Blessington, Ireland, a farming and light manufacturing town of 1,322 residents 18 miles south of Dublin: People over 65 constituted 40% of the population and most of these elders had government pensions and health benefits.
4. Clifden, Ireland, a community in the west of Ireland with 805 residents and another 851 in the hinterlands: While only 16% were over 65, there was considerable emigration of young people. Those who remained behind farmed, fished, or worked as shopkeepers.
5. Hong Kong, an industrial and commercial metropolis of 5.3 million (57% of whom were locally born Chinese and 40% of whom were born in China): Four neighborhoods with varying socioeconomic characteristics were studied. Confucian ideals of family are still honored but not always implemented (see Chapter 4). Elderly people make up only 10% of the population.

6. Herero: This research population consisting of 5,000 Bantu-speaking pastoralists in Botswana, Africa, is a culturally conservative group with strong familial and religious values. They are polygynous, have unilineal descent patterns, and show great respect and concern for the elderly, who make up 17% of the population.

7. !Kung: This research population of about 1,000 Bushmen lives in the northwest Kalahari desert in Botswana. Once nomadic hunters and gatherers, these people now raise livestock, tend gardens, and live a sedentary existence. Here the monogamous nuclear family prevails, and marriages are stable. Old age is determined more by physical condition and functionality than actual years.

A.G.E. was "intended to reveal how the life course is perceived and what old age means in a range of societies that vary systematically in scale, complexity, subsistence patterns, residential mobility, and population structure" (Ikels et al., 1992, p. 80). Researchers were interested in whether the elders in each community viewed old age as an improvement over earlier periods of life or whether it was viewed more negatively. But whatever their feelings, the investigators wanted to know why they felt that way. Because the seven research sites represented very different cultural environments, particular aspects of growing old were viewed positively in some contexts and negatively in others, and quite different strategies were perceived as most effective in achieving a satisfying old age in the various groups.

In comparing the two American sites with Hong Kong, Keith et al. (1990) found that differences in perceptions of doing well or doing poorly in old age appear to be most clearly evidenced in regard to such factors as good health and functionality, finances, independence/dependence, and relationship to children and family. In Momence the ability to work is important even in advanced years so there is a major concern with health. Health is also important in Swarthmore, but not for employment reasons. These relatively affluent subjects see it as a major factor ensuring independence, a most cherished value. In Hong Kong, on the other hand, where there are traditional expectations that the elderly will be cared for by their children, health is seen as less of a consideration for well-being. Furthermore, while Hong Kong subjects identify dependence (on family) as a reason for well-being, those from Swarthmore identify independence as a necessary condition for successful aging.

While Momence and Swarthmore subjects saw adult children and family as having little effect on the quality of life in old age, those in Hong Kong (where traditional Confucian values such as filial piety obtain) regarded adult children as very important in determining whether the elderly will do well or poorly. The extent to which children are willing or able to meet their filial responsibilities is a paramount consideration.

It is also interesting to note the impact of finances on the residents of the three research sites. As might be expected, the well-to-do Swarthmore people were not greatly concerned with this issue whereas those from Momence and Hong Kong saw finances as a key determinant of the quality of life in old age.

The category "Personal Characteristics" included "personal qualities" and "active." Personal qualities that affect interactions with others, such as being "easygoing," ranked high among elders in Hong Kong as contributing to successful old age. Americans, on the other hand, placed less emphasis on the category, but those who did stressed being active and personal qualities like "optimistic," reflecting their outlook on the world in general (Keith et al., 1990, p. 256). Overall, the findings of Project A.G.E. indicate that the vision of a "successful" old age differs for residents of these communities, and that in each there are pathways, shaped by the social system and by many intervening factors, such as values, peer groups, or residential stability, that lead some individuals to great satisfaction with their later years (Keith et al., 1990, p. 259).

Age Stage Perceptions in Samoa and Colombia

A study that in some ways resembled Fry's early work in regard to documentation of life-cycle stages and use of "age game" methodology was that of Bradd Shore, who asked informants in Western Samoa in 1975 to associate age-appropriate behavior or to make associations with recognized age categories. That is, informants were asked to match such reference terms as *free life, protected, sits, evil behavior, respected, peaceful, stupid, dignity, does chores* with the age divisions *pepe* (0-3 years), *tama'ititi* (4-12), *tagata talavou* (13-20), *tagata matua* (30-60), and *lo'omatua* and *toea'ina* (over 60) (see Table 3.2).

Dianne Kagan (1980) carried her interest in indigenous age designations to the peasant village of Bojaca, Colombia, where she found the

Table 3.2. Survey on Aging in Samoa: Cultural Associations With Stages of Maturation

	Age (years)*				
	0-3	4-12	13-30	31-60	Over 60
Free life	142	120	18	20	63
Protected	171	88	50	23	49
Controlled	4	21	66	162	74
No judgment	86	144	45	9	2
Evil behavior	0	110	121	16	4
Smart	6	52	114	91	29
Sits	71	126	6	23	173
Serves	36	29	163	105	6
Does chores	—	124	183	54	6
Roams about	12	152	58	10	11
Respected	2	4	17	139	142
Works	—	16	183	88	7
Stupid	69	48	7	6	46
Stays at home	61	5	1	22	200
Runs the family	—	2	3	154	132
Lives happily	95	145	54	19	30
Peaceful	142	72	6	16	77
Hard life	4	7	72	98	32
Dignity	—	1	16	137	127
Strong	53	65	146	63	6
Difficulties	46	82	56	36	44

SOURCE: Data from Bradd Shore.

*Informants were asked to place an X in the column under the age category that each description in the left column best suggests and to use only one X for each descriptive phrase.

life cycle divided into "babies," "children," "young people," "adults," and "old people." Although informants had no trouble conceptualizing the stages, they also warned that chronological boundaries could not or should not be assigned to these age grades. One informant pointed out, for example, that many Bojaca females of 15 are married, have children, and function as responsible adults. Although a precise number of years could not be assigned to old age, the greater share of local inhabitants believed that the elderly should be given greater deference and respect than those in other age categories and that old age is a period marked by greater dependency. They did not see old age as a period of idleness but as one where active contributions could be made to community life in such areas as religion, food preparation, manual skills, folk medicine, horticulture and nature lore, personal counseling, and advice on questions of justice.

> The Bojaca model was found to be one where during the life cycle the aging adult experiences increasing degrees of biological change and psychological change as he or she passes from middle years into old age. The aging individual must also come to terms with the changes in the manner in which he or she is perceived by others. . . . The older person is often expected to drop former roles and activities and assume new ones more appropriate to the new category. (Kagan, 1980, p. 77)

Although those in Bojaca occasionally disagree over age-appropriate behavior, both young and old share values that preclude any identity crisis that might be experienced by anyone just entering the category of *vejez* (old age).

Aging as a Career

One of the more unique approaches to the life cycle is that of Myerhoff and Simic (1978) in their book *Life's Career—Aging*. Here aging is presented as *career* or a life's work. The authors explain their perspective as one that

> stresses old age as a period of activity, participation, self-movement, and purposefulness. It holds that aging cannot be understood in isolation but rather must be conceived as the product of a building process involving the entire life span. Old age is not a passive state but one evoking dynamic responses. To live each day with dignity, alertness, control over one's faculties, and mobility necessitates the output of tremendous energy, and in the most general sense of the word, it is a kind of *work*. (Simic & Myerhoff, 1978, p. 240)

The volume brings together the research conclusions of five anthropologists, each of whom considers old age and aging in relation to a particular cultural tradition, including the Chagga of Tanzania (by Sally Moore), the slum residents of Mexico City (by Carlos Velez), the Mexican Americans in East Los Angeles (by José Cuellar), the Yugoslavs in central Europe and the Yugoslav-Americans in northern California (by Andrei Simic), and the Jewish Americans from east Europe living in Venice, California (by Barbara Myerhoff).

The study has three major focuses: continuity, sexual dichotomy, and aging as a career. *Continuity* emphasizes process and relates to exploring the way events and ideas of one period are tied to those of the next. It concerns stability of ideas, values, and symbols and the permanency of interpersonal relations through time. Although all human beings value continuity, the authors propose that for those approaching the end of their lives interconnectedness becomes a dominant theme and "that there is a tremendous impetus toward the maintenance of continuity, and where it is lacking, toward its reestablishment" (Simic & Myerhoff, 1978, p. 236).

Sexual dichotomy relates to the way society defines appropriate areas of influence, responsibility, and behavior for men and women. These change during the life cycle, and it is important to understand how men and women pass from one status to another and how power peaks and wanes at various periods in life.

Finally, viewing aging as a *career* provides an alternative to the usual conception that growing old is simply a series of losses to be endured. On the contrary, it introduces the idea that although

> losses do occur with the passing of years, gains are clearly accrued as well. However, these gains are not distributed equally to all, and the analogy to a career in its everyday sense of the meaning also suggests the idea of differential success. . . . In every society the rewards possible in old age depend to a great extent on the individual ability, resourcefulness, good judgment, and luck at every point during the life cycle. (Simic & Myerhoff, 1978, pp. 240-241)

An excellent example of how individual ability, good judgment, and resourcefulness can determine the quality of old age is found in the chapter by Andrei Simic (1978) titled "Winners and Losers" in *Life's Career—Aging.* Here he compares the life histories of two Yugoslav seniors, Mitar and Djole.

Mitar lives with his son's family. He has never had any serious conflict with his children or grandchildren or with his parents or siblings as he was growing up. Simic states that

> until recently the entire responsibility for the management of the family's limited resources had fallen upon him. . . . Though their household had been . . . somewhat poorer than average, Mitar had earned the respect of his fellow villagers and had been chosen to serve as a member of the governing council of the village church. (p. 91)

What had created Mitar's satisfaction with old age was his careful nurturing of reciprocal relations with his descendants and his collateral kin through his life plus his skillful use of Serbian culture. His treatment of his kin over the years was not unlike a bank account upon which he could draw in his old age. He was a happy man surrounded by loving family and with no fear of being left alone and without resources.

Djole had also spent a lifetime influencing the conditions that have contributed to his unfortunate old age as a charity case in a county-supported old age home. His father and elder brothers were ill-tempered, abusive drunkards, and Djole has followed in that pattern. He has no land and no children to care for him. He separated from his wife, saw his children move to the city, and feels that no one has any respect for him. He has long ago alienated his kinsmen, and his only pleasure in life is drinking up his monthly allowance of 200 dinars (U.S. $1.30) at a local bar on the day he receives it.

Creativity and the Life Cycle

For many years Americans have labored under the misapprehension that middle age marks the end of any capacity for creativity or intellectual growth. Renaldo Maduro (1974) points out that

> although there has been general interest in both aging and creativity, a more focused consideration of artistic creativity in relation to different phases of the life cycle has been neglected. Anthropological studies of culture and aging have not stressed the expressive symbolic dimensions of human existence. (p. 303)

Harvey Lehman (1953), a psychologist, is one of the few behavioral scientists who has been concerned with the idea of creativity and the life cycle. While Lehman has stated that "with some dramatic exceptions, our greatest creative thinkers have been long-lived" (p. 333), he also maintains that superior creativity generally rises rapidly to a high point in the thirties and then slowly declines. Wechsler (1958) also supports this position, but Irving Lorge (1963) believes that longitudinal studies might produce counterevidence. Kogan (1973) suggests that decrements may not be associated with age but could be causal, for example, a decline in physical or mental abilities or in competitiveness, motivation, or curiosity. John Dacey (1989), who sees ages 60-65 as one of the peak periods of creativity in the life cycle of Americans, also cites impediments to creativity in old age. He points out that this is the period when retirement takes place and

> most adults are faced with a major adjustment of self-concept. . . . Although some [fare] badly as a result of this change, and begin withdrawing from society, others use it as a chance to pursue creative goals that had previously been impossible for them. (p. 243)

One of the main problems with this kind of investigation is a lack of consensus on the meaning of creativity. Artistic creativity, scientific creativity, and creativity as a generalized personality trait are often confused. In addition to this, much of Lehman's (1953, 1962, 1966) research actually deals with productivity rather than creativity. Tallies were made of the number of symphonies, paintings, books, poems, and scientific discoveries produced by artists, scholars, and scientists of various periods in their lives. Given that production was greater in the early adult years of most of his sample, he assumed that those were their most creative years. Romaniuk and Romaniuk (1981) have suggested that the problem with these tallies of productivity is that they measure quantity and not necessarily quality.

Anthropological data indicate that the capacity to grow intellectually and creatively has no bounds, but we also know that both the ability to learn and the ability to create can be greatly influenced by cultural ideas about these abilities. Margaret Mead (1967) points out that the capacity to adopt or relinquish roles at different ages is something that is learned within a culture. For example, the Balinese have no concept that age has anything to do with the ability to learn and be creative. If a person who has never carved or painted wants to begin at age 60, no eyebrows are raised whatsoever. A man of 60 may start to play a musical instrument for the first time, or a woman of that age may decide to become a dancer. On the other hand, a child of 6 may learn to play one of the more important instruments in the village orchestra or even begin to lead it without anyone objecting or finding it inappropriate.

This disregard for age-grading activities must be considered in cultural context to be understood. Because the Balinese believe in reincarnation, what is begun in one lifetime may be carried on in the next. Perhaps our own popular beliefs about learning and creativity grow out of the Christian tradition in which a person has only one life to live on earth.

Pertinent to our consideration of creativity in senior years are two anthropological studies: a study of aged jazz musicians in New York and Los Angeles and a study of Brahmin folk painters in West India. In 1978 and 1979 Lowell D. Holmes and John W. Thomson (1986) studied 15 elderly jazz musicians to explore such subjects as capacity for creativity as judged by their colleagues, their assessment of their own capacity to play and create, the effects of age on performance, and their acceptance by younger musicians and jazz aficionados. Believing that jazz improvisation is the essence of creativity in jazz performance, the researchers were oriented by the following concept of Charles Nanry (1979):

> Improvisation in music means pretty much the same thing it means in other areas of life. It is a synonym for spontaneous creativity, for solving a problem that has not been solved before when working with existing materials. In jazz playing, improvisation usually refers to melodic invention that is created out of conventional melody. (p. 17)

Most students of the creative process agree that birth of the new comes from the old, that no new work, however original, is without roots in the past, in the tradition of the art itself. Being creative in jazz does not necessarily mean being avant garde; creativity is possible within any style. Nor does the fact that a number of elderly musicians maintained that they are making no effort to keep up with modern trends mean that they are no longer playing inventively.

Top flight New York jazz star of the 1930s, Shirley Green, still playing creatively. (Photo by Lowell D. Holmes.)

When creativity was defined in these terms, neither the researchers nor the musicians themselves felt that creativity must cease or begin a downhill slide in advanced age. Playing jazz was seen as putting together musical ideas in a new and inventive way, and the larger the stock of these ideas and figures and the more experience one has in putting them together, the more creative the jazz player. All artists interviewed had been around so long and had heard and played with so many fine musicians that they were able to recall an idea from here, borrow a musical phrase from there, and in putting them all together could achieve a result that no younger player without equivalent background and experience could accomplish. A particularly interesting example of creative capacity in old age was Doc Cheatham, who did not start playing improvised jazz until he joined the Benny Goodman quintet in 1971 at the age of 66. Up until that time he was strictly a lead trumpet player in large dance bands. Today, at age 90, Cheatham is still working in nightclubs and appears in at least a half-dozen jazz festivals every year. John Guarneiri, a former pianist with Benny Goodman and Artie Shaw, was in his middle sixties but was constantly experimenting. Several years ago he began playing many of his numbers in $\frac{5}{4}$ time instead of $\frac{4}{4}$ because of the different effect it produced. He predicted to the researchers, "I think I'm going to do some very interesting things in the future" (Holmes & Thomson, 1986, p. 17). Milt Hinton, in his eighties, is still one of the most sought-after jazz bassists in the country for jazz festivals and record dates. He explains his much heralded capacity for outstandingly creative playing as follows: "I think I'm doing more interesting things now because of the variety in my background—I'm drawing on a lifetime of playing—and also because I'm listening to what young people are doing" (p. 17).

In 1974 Renaldo Maduro conducted a study of creativity in quite a different setting—West India. Maduro studied 110 male Brahmin folk painters in Rajasthan to determine whether artistic creativity declines with age. He concluded that in India creativity appears to peak in early middle age and then remains constant into old age. In measuring creativity, Maduro asked the painters to rank each other along a creativity continuum, and they were also given the Barron-Welsh Revised Art Test for scaling creativity. What is most interesting about this study is the relationship between the various stages of the Hindu life cycle and creative activity. For example, the onset of old age is identified as the "forest hermit" stage. This is a time when a man has

met his family obligations and performed his duties to caste and his society. He can turn inward and contemplate the inner light. At this time a man's powers of imagination increase fourfold because he has learned to reach into himself for light, bliss and balance. (Maduro, 1974, p. 308)

The artists maintain that with increasing years they become "more open" to the nuances of intuition, to "conceiving," and to "the unfolding of the self" (p. 308). They are no longer interested in acquiring power or wealth, and they are free to grow in new psychological and symbolic directions.

Personality Changes in the Life Cycle

In an article in the *Gerontologist* in 1967, Margaret Clark cited gerontology as "a new area for studies of culture and personality," and she lamented the fact that in spite of a great body of such psychological research by eminent anthropologists little or no attention had been given to the later stages of the life cycle. "Culture and personality" as an anthropological specialization developed originally from a fusion of cultural anthropology and psychoanalytic theory during the 1920s. Its primary function has been to study how personality development is influenced by participation in a given cultural system. Because it focuses on culture (a group phenomenon), this research area differs from psychology in that it concentrates less on individual personality than on the extent to which personality types, or at least traits, are shared within societies. Workers in this field have also concentrated on documenting early childhood experience to understand the impact of cultural norms and practices on adult personality. Some of the basic theoretical positions of this school of inquiry are presented by Clark (1967):

> The assumption persists that human beings are basically unchanging, at least in their deeper and "more important" aspects. This orientation has led students of culture and personality to confine their work to four major areas: (1) the enculturation of children and adolescents, and the role of childrearing practices in the determination of adult personality; (2) status personality characteristics, as influenced by sex role and class or caste differences—these, too, thought to be group differences for which the individual is shaped quite early in life; (3) modal personality and national character, usually derived from studies of young and middle-aged adults (those whose personalities are now assumed by the observer to be "fixed" or "set" into a particular shared pattern through common early life experiences); and (4) individual deviance and its cultural interpretation. (p. 57)

Culture and personality scholars still tend to think of personality as a static commodity, and a significant number of scholars stress continuity of personality types. Clark (1967) and a few others believe, however, that personality is "an on-going process of interaction between the sociocultural world and the internal life of the individual—a process that continues throughout the life cycle" (p. 63). Scholars who believe that personality reflects life experience ask, and rightly so: How could forced retirement in America, age discrimination, the necessity for a total reorganization of ideas of goal achievement, leisure activities, changes in residence, and ideas of personal worth not affect personality characteristics of those past 65 years of age?

Even though culture and personality studies of the aged are few and far between, there has been some movement in this direction. The study of ongoing personality by David Gutmann (1976) is worthy of mention. Although not an anthropologist, Gutmann's approach is cross cultural, and data were acquired through investigation in the field. Gutmann's study used Thematic Apperception Test (TAT) protocols in the study of perceptions of self and the world at different ages in four cultures—Western Navajo, Mayan, midwestern American, and Israeli Druze. Believing that "important psychological orientation, based around passivity and aggressiveness, dependence and autonomy would discriminate age groups within culturally homogeneous societies" (p. 88), Gutmann proceeded to investigate ego states of men between the ages of 40 and 70. In a Kansas City sample of 140 men, he found that, between 40 and 54 years, men exhibit an ego state that he labeled *active mastery*. This involved a deliberate pursuit of achievement and independence and was marked by an attempt to control external conditions. Men aged 55 to 64 exhibited traits that were labeled *passive mastery*. This involved more internal than external control and a greater tendency to accommodate than was true of younger men. Those men who were 65 or over exhibited an ego state termed *magical mastery*. This life-cycle characteristic was described as featuring self-deception and denial of unpleasant realities.

Gutmann (1976) believes that he found many similarities in his Navajo, Mayan, midwestern, and Druze populations. Finding that all four societies exhibit "an age shift away from Active Mastery and towards the Passive and/or Magical orientations" (p. 89), Gutmann believes that ego states are distributed more reliably according to age than according to culture. In other words, he believes that he has found a universal feature of personality change that is immune to cultural influences. His more recent work has presented a more detailed analysis of this predictable personality development, including the tendency for women to exhibit a reverse trend from passivity in younger years to more aggressive tendencies in late life (Gutmann, 1987).

Retirement

Retirement as we know it in the United States tends to be nonexistent in preindustrial and even in many non-Western industrial societies. Formal retirement, which ends career activities, is associated primarily with bureaucracies that have complex military, civil service, educational, commercial, and industrial enterprises. To understand retirement, we need to understand the significance of work in the society in question—how it provides roles and status in the society and what kinds of rewards in money, goods, or prestige it yields.

Margaret Clark (1972) suggests that two aspects of retirement deserve study: the cultural and the psychological. From the cultural standpoint, it is important to investigate retirement in terms of its history, form, function, and meaning in a given society. The psychological approach, on the other hand, concerns itself with recording the personal meaning of the institution for the individual. Some cultural systems permit second careers for retired persons and although this occurs only occasionally in America (e.g., Colonel Sanders or Ronald Reagan), it is fairly common in preindustrial societies. These societies often have a well-defined category of activities known as "old people's work." These activities may represent modifications of roles occupied by younger people or in some cases entirely different roles that are appropriate to the declining energies of the elderly, but they are seen as no less important than roles occupied by younger people. Examples of second careers are those of elder statesman and political adviser, folk medicine specialist, storyteller, choreographer, or ceremonial director. Although all societies observe sex divisions of labor, age divisions of labor are of consequence primarily in preindustrial societies.

In the United States, the categories of "children's work" and "old people's work" are not significant because neither category is expected to be involved much in the way of productive labor. About the only kind of work the elderly are consistently permitted to do is baby-sitting and domestic work (these tend to be children's jobs also), but even these prestigeless tasks are not reserved for them. Even if Americans were to find the concept of a second career appealing, the scarcity of such employment opportunities for those over 65 would quickly discourage any such notion.

In tribal and peasant societies, the retirement experiences are much the same for men and women, and the situation resembles to a certain extent what has been the situation in the past for women in our own society. In other words, in the United States and in the West generally, men traditionally retire but women do not. This is changing as more and more women join the commercial labor force, but for homemakers the domestic work of their later years differs little from what they have done for most of their lives. There may not be children to raise any more, but the cooking, cleaning, mending, laundering, and marketing go on. Men in retirement, however, are completely cut off from the work activities that gave their lives meaning and status. Unless a second career is started, their lives are often nonproductive and without purpose. In one investigation of death anxiety (Schulz, 1980), work role continuity was found to make women in our society much more accepting of the inevitability of death than men. There is a positive correlation between role satisfaction and lack of anxiety about one's own death, and middle-class men face a real crisis. During their working years, role satisfactions enabled them to repress and deny the possibility of death, but when role satisfaction no longer exists, the anxiety over death surfaces.

In preindustrial societies, there is a continuity of useful roles for men also, and they do not expect to cease functioning in productive activities until they are unable to make contributions to either family or community. Most societies of this type believe that the elderly should have the option of enjoying complete leisure if they so desire, but few elders make this choice. Most continue to find satisfaction and personal rewards in productive labor of some type.

Any study of retirement in America must consider American concepts of work, leisure, and work-derived status. For many years, the American work ethic has dominated perceptions of personal worth and status, but evidence now indicates that American values in this sphere are changing. Although America continues to condemn idleness, the work ethic is being replaced by an activity ethic. Activity may be recreational but it must be purposeful. One aspect of our puritan heritage is that recreation and sports are acceptable if the physical activity contributes to physical health and makes more efficient work habits possible. The energy expended on modern-day vacations is often greater than that exerted on the job, and people in the United States often return from vacations a day or two early to rest up before going back to work.

Jerry Jacobs (1974b) describes, in his monograph on Fun City, what developers have instituted as attractions for potential residents of the age-homogeneous community. He writes:

> The *Fun City News*, a weekly community newspaper lists the week's events by date and time of day. A typical week's calendar lists about 150 separate social events, most of which are conducted within the activity center. Approximately 65 of these are morning activities, 60 afternoon, and about 25 evening. Fun City boasts a total of 92 different clubs and organizations. (pp. 6-7)

The planned activities include Camera Club, Garden Club, band practice, Bridge Club, American Legion, lawn bowling, golf, chess, checkers, Square Dance Club, Glee Club, Bicycle Club, typing classes, dinner club meetings, Scrabble Club, TOPS (Take Off Pounds Sensibly), ballroom dancing, language classes, Pinochle Club, Canasta Club, art classes, Lapidary Club, jewelry making, sewing, ceramics, woodworking, and photo lab. Jacobs points out, however, that those who want to work at a part-time job often have to travel outside the community.

Regional as well as urban-rural differences in values affect attitudes toward work, leisure, and retirement in the United States. An example of this can be found in the phenomenon peculiar to Appalachia (and perhaps some other rural areas) that is known as "retiring to the porch." This behavior is associated primarily with men and involves a set of social arrangements in which a person has, over a long period of time, won the respect of the community and therefore its support in his retirement. Lozier and Althouse (1975), who have studied this phenomenon, maintain that porch sitting is a way of receiving social attention and care but only if the recipients have established "social credit" by their own lifetime contributions to neighbors and the community in general. It is a form of idleness permitted people who have "paid their dues" and now have a right to dividends (in the form of communication and privilege).

Clark (1972) also suggests that it is not possible to understand the full impact of retirement in a society without making some reference to age segregation. America is one of the most segregated societies in the world in regard to class, race, religion, and age, and our industrial system also tends to segregate us in terms of our role behavior. Only on farms do Americans work close to their homes, and children in urban areas often have no idea of the work their father does because they have never seen him on the job. This kind of segregation means that work colleagues are a separate group of people from neighborhood, church, or social club acquaintances. When the American worker retires, he or she loses not only a job that has provided meaning and status but also a group of fellow workers with whom he or she has shared a lifetime of work cooperation. Because men and women in preindustrial societies do not have occupational segregation, and because they do not retire, they obviously do not experience this kind of social separation. Loneliness, so much a fear in industrialized societies, is not a serious consideration in less complex ones.

According to Barbara G. Anderson (1972), retirement in America does more than separate people from jobs and colleagues, it is actually a period of *deculturation*. The learning of a culture (by a child or an adult immigrant) is referred to in anthropology as enculturation. This learning usually takes place informally in the family and community and formally in school. It is a process vital to the continuity of society, given that human behavior is not inherited genetically but must be taught and learned. A number of anthropologists—Margaret Mead, Ruth Benedict, Ralph Linton, John Whiting—have carefully researched this period of cultural transmission, but Anderson is the first to document the process of unlearning culture, which she believes is forced on the elderly in our society. She writes:

> If it is during childhood that the individual comes to learn the given ways of a society so that he can function within it, then in the United States at least, it is through old age that he is made to unlearn these ways so that eventually he can and does cease to function culturally in it. There is no doubt in my mind that, through a system of conscious and unconscious conditionings, the older American is gradually groomed by his society for total cultural withdrawal. (Anderson, 1972, p. 210)

America today is faced with a dilemma. It now has greater numbers of old people than the society can comfortably support. Since 1900 life expectancy has increased by 28 years (U.S. Senate Special Committee on Aging & American Association of Retired Persons, 1991). More than 32 million people in the United States are 65 or older (U.S. Bureau of the Census, 1992b), but in spite of this no appropriate or meaningful lifestyle for the elderly has evolved. Anderson (1972) maintains that old age in our society is merely a "degenerate extension of middle-years, already negatively valued in a youth-invested, action-oriented culture" (p. 210). When the aged were few in number and the rate of cultural change was moderate, American society seemed to be able to cope with people growing old, but today there is mostly confusion. Mead (1967) observes that

> we are retiring many men at the height of their creativity. This is one of the slow death-dealing mechanisms of present-day society. . . . Early retirement was primarily based on an attempt to make room for other people in a society built on the kind of productivity that ties together a job and the right to eat. We don't need this any more. We can build a society in which social contribution is not related to keeping someone else out of a job. (p. 36)

A few exceptional elderly—artists, judges, professors, statesmen, business tycoons—have been integrated into the system, but the majority of aged have been forced into a condition of statuslessness and culturelessness. Their lives, states Anderson (1972),

> are lived outside and apart from the viable body of tradition that constitutes the daily patterns of younger Americans. More accurately, perhaps they are a lost generation in the sense that they are carriers of a defunct or dying culture. In the thirty or forty years since the world revolved around them . . . [w]ays of making a living, the pace and orientation of life—all have changed. (p. 211)

The deculturation process that has been forced upon our elderly is somewhat like the enculturation process in reverse. Society insidiously communicates that in old age acquisitiveness, mobility, creativity, and innovation are improper and that the aged should be content with only modest social involvement. Society demands that the elderly not only relinquish their earlier status and roles but that they also begin to value themselves as the society values them. Just as children begin to value themselves by observing society's approval of their behavior, so the elderly learn to devalue themselves as they sense society's disinterest or disapproval of their behavior.

Disengagement

Even social science appears to have contributed to the effort of American society to devalue the aged by its formulation of what is commonly known as the disengagement theory (Cumming & Henry, 1961).

Actually, disengagement is a controversial issue in social gerontology. According to Cumming and Henry, withdrawal from societal involvement is a normal and beneficial aspect of aging. "Aging is an inevitable act of mutual withdrawal or disengagement, resulting in decreased interaction between the aging person and others in the social systems he belongs to" (p. 14). The authors believe that disengagement applies not only to industrialized societies but to traditional or "primitive" ones as well.

Although Cumming and Henry insist that disengagement is a universal phenomenon, evidence from numerous anthropological studies conducted in a variety of cultures shows that had the basic theoretical orientation of social gerontology been established by anthropologists (with their cross-cultural perspective and relativistic approach), there would be no such thing as a "disengagement theory." Disengagement would merely be recognized as a phenomenon that may or may not be present in the society, depending on the unique social and economic cultural patterns.

In fact, disengagement is rare in tribal or peasant societies. Most elderly in these groups continue to play important roles in family enterprises, and in many cases their value to the greater society increases with age. They tend to be called upon more than ever for decision making and for advice in those areas where their experience and knowledge of traditional matters are valued. Disengagement in preindustrial society is not a matter of societal pressure but depends entirely on the strength and mental clarity of the individual.

A study by Andrei Simic (1977) that contrasts intergenerational relationships in the United States with those in Yugoslavia reveals that disengagement and deculturation are peculiar to American culture and should not be considered universal phenomena. He does, however, maintain that disengagement and deculturation are culture-specific models that have value in that they provide a contrasting framework for analyzing aging in other societies.

Simic believes that disengagement and deculturation are not simply products of seniority but that they reflect the American values of individualism, independence, and the right to unrestricted freedom in decision making. What we must understand about America, states Simic (1977), is that "individuals do not suddenly find themselves isolated in their declining years, but are socialized for this role almost from the time of conception in the context of the family and community" (p. 55).

Simic (1990) also maintains that American children are socialized toward a goal of independence and Yugoslav children are taught the importance of reciprocal roles that they will play throughout their lifetime with family members and other relatives. Isolation (often verbalized as privacy) is a part of an American's life from the very beginning. Even babies in cribs have their own rooms, each child must have a separate bedroom, and children are not expected to relate as much to family as to peers outside the home. Yugoslavian children, by contrast, live in a social environment where "privacy is notably lacking, that is, the recognition of a need to be periodically alone and to control private space and possessions" (Simic, 1990, p. 101). Yugoslav children are expected "to identify more strongly with members of their own families than with their age mates" (p. 102).

There are marked contrasts in the world of work as well. Americans labor as a moral obligation to achieve personal, spiritual, and emotional fulfillment, but Yugoslavs work to maintain and enhance familial and other important social relationships.

At every point in the American life cycle, evidence points to a lack of family solidarity, cooperation, or reciprocity. With this kind of ethos, societal members can expect little support in old age either from families or from an independence-oriented society. Although disengagement and deculturation are compatible with "individualism and generational replication," Simic (1977) points out that it does not seem to be compatible with the Yugoslavian stress on "kinship corporacy and generational symbiosis" (p. 63).

Old age in India involves a withdrawal from certain productive roles and household obligations but a movement toward greater spirituality and religious involvement. (Photo by Lowell D. Holmes.)

David Gutmann (1976), whose research has primarily centered on personality change in old age among the Maya, Navajo, midwestern Americans, and Druze of Israel, has also turned his attention to disengagement as a purportedly inevitable, universal phenomenon. In his article "Alternatives to Disengagement: The Old Men of the Highland Druze," Gutmann describes an apparent cross-cultural tendency for men over 65 to move from an orientation marked by active production-centered, competitive motives and attitudes to a passive orientation labeled *magical mastery.*

Even though Cumming and Henry hypothesize that old people move toward a more passive orientation, Gutmann's (1976) study indicates "that disengagement need not be compulsory, and it particularly demonstrates that passivity is not inextricably tied to disengagement" (p. 106). Gutmann found that the movement toward passivity and magical mastery among aging Druze men is actually a shift from allegiance to productive and secular-productive life to one concerning traditional Moslem religion and the moral life. Pointing out that elderly men have a tendency to move into an active religious role, Gutmann states: "While the religious role fits the special needs of older men, their tendencies toward mildness and accommodation are particularly fitted to the requirements of the religious role" (p. 104). In other words, the Druze elder does not disengage but merely shifts his interests and activities from a life of economic striving to one of religious service. He is no less involved, but now in old age he carries forward the moral rather than the material work of this society. It is not a disengagement but a social rebirth.

Sylvia Vatuk (1980) has worked among the people of India, where social and psychological disengagement are a part of the traditional culture, but even there she does not find the social disengagement described by Cumming and Henry. There is in India a pattern of withdrawal in old age known as "dwelling as a forest hermit" (p. 135). Old age is regarded as a period of rightful dependency with the security of the aged dependent on the support of the extended family, particularly the adult sons. But in regard to disengagement, there is a great discrepancy between the ideal and the real. As elderly parents increase in age, many of their roles are turned over to the young, but the aged do not usually drop out and they do not really become hermits. Activity levels actually are increased but, as among the Druze, they are in different areas than those engaged in when younger. The situation is much like the second-career situation described earlier. Retirement from household affairs and rejection of attachments to other human beings is sanctioned by age-old sacred Hindu texts and cultural traditions but, in reality, aging brings disengagement from certain roles and relationships. Moreover, aging means forming new relationships and assuming new roles that are more in line with "the activity theory," a concept that holds that successful aging requires maintaining reasonable activity levels and role substitutions in retirement.

A test of disengagement theory in Fun City (Jacobs, 1974b) reveals that only about half the residents fit the Cumming-Henry model and then perhaps imperfectly. Jacobs found that about 10% of Fun City's population was clearly engaged and participating in the community's 92 planned recreational activities. These people had been actively engaged preretirement and they continued this lifestyle in retirement. A second group—disengaged in both pre- and postretirement periods— also represented an exception to the disengagement rule. They were never active in clubs or recreational activities, and retirement has brought no change in their lives. These individuals constituted upward of 15% of the total. A third group—representing about 25% of the population— were happily engaged in pre- and early postretirement periods but were now disengaged, not by choice but because their health had failed. This group and the two just described represented a total of approximately half of the residents of Fun City and therefore a strong challenge to the Cumming-Henry theory.

Approximately 50% of Fun City's residents do fit the disengagement model. These people have voluntarily disengaged at retirement. They clearly intended to withdraw from society, watch television, do a little reading, play a little cards, and walk the dog. Their lifestyle was, according to Jacobs, regarded as "vegetating" by the more active members of the community and by outsiders, and they were looked upon with pity. Of this group—the truly disengaged—Jacobs (1974a) writes: "There is no proof for or against the contention that their disengagement is beneficial, either for them or society" (p. 486). Generally Jacobs felt, however, that living in Fun City, with all its isolation and segregation, could not be beneficial socially or psychologically.

Roles of the Aged

While disengagement may not be characteristic of preindustrial, developing countries, the roles that are filled by the elderly often differ from those held at other periods in the life cycle. There is a general tendency in old age to shift toward sedentary, more advisory and supervisory activities, and to those directed toward group maintenance more than economic production. In societies rich in ceremonialism and religious ritual, there is a tendency for the elderly to assume positions of responsibility and authority in the religious establishment not open to younger people. Because of their recollections of and involvement with the traditional, unchanging ritual phenomena of a society, the elderly man or woman is the appropriate person to be its caretaker. Old people are not only able to teach the details of the ceremonials but they represent in their remarkable long life a kind of liaison figure between the things of earth and the realm of the supernatural. Ritual is the celebration of the traditional and the orthodox, and what is traditional is best known by those who have lived the longest. de Beauvoir (1972a) expands on this point:

> As the custodian of the traditions, the intercessor, and the protector against supernatural powers, the aged man ensures the cohesion of the community throughout time and in the present. . . .
>
> Generally speaking, the services, taken as a whole, that the old are enabled to render because of their knowledge of the traditions, mean that they have not only respect but also material prosperity. They are rewarded with presents. The gifts that they receive from those whom they initiate into their secrets are of particular importance—they are the surest source of private wealth, a source that exists only in societies that are sufficiently well-to-do to have an advanced culture. (p. 83)

Many of the ceremonial and ritual roles performed by the elderly are described by Simmons (1945a):

> They have served as guardians of temples, shrines, and sacred paraphernalia, as officers of the priesthood, and as leaders of the performance of rites associated with prayers, sacrifices, feast days, annual cycles, historic celebrations, and the initiation of important and hazardous enterprises. They also have been prominent in ceremonies associated with critical periods in the life cycle—such as birth, puberty, marriage, and death. (p. 164)

Ceremony and religious ritual have long been recognized as cultural foci of the Northwest Coast Indian tribes. Religion was extremely formalized and the complex ceremonies of religious societies made a great impression on the minds and emotions of their members. Membership

This maker of ceremonial paraphernalia is a resident of a senior citizen complex on a Kickapoo reservation. (Photo courtesy of "Photographic Narrative, Indians of Kansas Exhibition," Mid-American All-Indian Center Museum; Photographer, Ken Engquist; used by permission.)

in these societies conferred great status, and the ceremonies they conducted were seen as vital to the well-being of the society. One tribe in this area, the Coast Salish of western Washington and British Columbia has been described by Pamela Amoss as a society in which the aged, because of their knowledge of ritual and ceremonial detail, have continued to command considerable respect in spite of the influence of modernization. Amoss (1981) contends that

> old men and women maintain prestige and high social rank through their control of scarce information about the old ritual practices and through the spiritual power people believe they possess. Far from losing ground as Coast Salish society has changed, they have actually improved their position in the last twenty years. (pp. 227-228)

On the other hand, a society without a ceremonial tradition may provide little opportunity for prestige or participation for the elderly. In the western subarctic region of North America, ceremonial and religious ritual have never been a particularly important part of Indian life. Spencer and Jennings report, for example, that there was an absence of feasting and communalism in religion and that individualism and personal power were important elements in the belief system. They point out that although there was a modified guardian-spirit quest it could hardly be considered a ritual or dramatic happening, and while shamanism was present

> it lacked the drama of either Eskimo shamanism or certainly that of the Northwest Coast. While there is some suggestion that shamans might sing at various occasions, such as before hunting, and sometimes in association with girls' rites, the practices associated with the complex appear essentially rudimentary and imperfectly developed and integrated. (Spencer & Jennings, 1977, p. 112)

Among the Chipewyan Indians of this subarctic region, elderly men who are no longer able to hunt command no respect, and they are not able to gain it by telling myths or legends, as there is little interest in such things. This is not a society that engages in ritual behavior, and therefore the elderly are left almost no opportunities for societal participation.

The elderly may also function as repositories of traditional lore and history. The memories of the aged often are depended upon to provide traditional solutions to survival problems, to instruct young people in the valuable subsistence or occupational skills, to maintain the mores, and to perpetuate the sacred tenets of the culture. Although the capacity to remember is perhaps a bit less important in societies with books and libraries, there is still a great demand even in modern societies for the personal reminiscences (oral history) that can only be supplied by old people. Given the recent interest on the part of American minorities in discovering their cultural roots, the information grandparents and great-grandparents can provide on now-extinct cultural ideas and ways of behaving has become eagerly sought after by the young. Gerry Williams (1980) notes that among Oklahoma Indians

> the trend toward "Indianism" or a revitalization of the Indian cultural traditions may in part account for conflicting attitudes

between generations. That is, we would expect an idealization of the aged for they are, chronologically at least, closer to an older form of social behavior which is now being stressed by the younger Indian. This stress upon the older Indians' knowledge of traditional behavior often times is an expectation which the aged Indian cannot fulfill. Individuals in their 60's and 70's today, except in a few instances, cannot begin to recall earlier forms of ceremonial behavior, past life-styles, and the movements and exploits of a hunting and gathering subsistence. (p. 109)

Similar demands have been made on the elderly in the People's Republic of China. In old China respect for the aged was maintained through the principles of filial piety enunciated by the Confucian tradition, but these concepts were to a large extent rejected under the Marx-Mao ideology that was established when the Chinese communists came to power in 1949. At that time Mao believed that the skills of the elderly would be beneficial to his Revolution. He called for including the elderly in a coalition of people of all ages, and he challenged them to continue the Revolution and to build a socialistic society. Ganschow (1978) reported that the basis for respect in China in 1978 had changed from the Confucian-based ideology to one based on respect for the makers of the Revolution. And the aged were valued because they had within their memories the facts about the Revolution that young Chinese wanted to know. They could relate personal experiences involving the suffering, the struggle, and the hardships of the Revolution and the happiness associated with establishing the new order. The elderly were therefore valued for their memories not of traditional China but of the birth and growth struggles of the new China.

de Beauvoir (1972a) comments that, for the Miao who live in the high forest and bush country of China and Thailand,

it is the old who hand on the traditions, and the respect in which they are held is chiefly based upon the ability to do so; their memory of the ancient myths can provide them with a very high standing. They are the community's guides and counsellors. (p. 71)

Among the Mende of West Africa, the recollections of the elders are even more important, for it is the aged who possess the traditions upon which Mende political organization is based. Mende society is constituted of two quite distinct classes. An upper class is made up of descendants of the hunters and warriors who first settled the territory, and this group consists of the chiefs and their families. The lower class, on the other hand, is made up of newcomers to Mende country and the descendants of slaves. The land is owned by the upper class and worked by lower class tenants. The comprehension and perpetuation of the system depends in large part on the memories of the elderly.

> It is memory alone that makes it possible to state whether a person belongs to one class or the other. A man who aims at becoming a chief must know the country's history, the genealogies of the Mende, the lives of their first founders and of their descendants; and this knowledge is necessarily passed on to them by their ancestors. It is they, the old people, who possess the traditions, and the Mende's political organization is therefore based upon them. (de Beauvoir, 1972a, p. 72)

The fact that the elderly represent the repositories of traditional knowledge in preindustrial societies has been widely recognized, and Maxwell and Silverman (1970) found that control and transmission of useful traditional knowledge by the elderly is a major factor associated with their good treatment and high status. Margaret Mead believes that even the survival of early hunting and gathering societies in early prehistoric times depended upon the knowledge possessed by the elderly. She conjectures:

> We have to assume a period in man's very early history when, in all probability people could not describe the places where food could be found; they had to lead others there. Nor were there any ways of communicating information on distance or direction. But some old or older people (old probably meant 40-50 under these conditions) knew where food had been found 10 years ago, when there was a scarcity of food, and they could lead others there. This made such people extremely valuable. (Mead, 1967, p. 33)

Political Leadership

Some old men (and, in rare cases, old women) continue to act as political and judicial leaders in modern as well as preindustrial societies.

Jack Goody (1976) has observed that "politics is an area, even in industrial societies, where old age is rarely an impediment to office. In the
Western world, political leaders are often active after others have retired,
and the same is true in non-industrial societies" (p. 127). Shortly after
Ronald Reagan was sworn into office as the fortieth president of the
United States, he celebrated his seventieth birthday, an age by which the
average American has been retired for several years. By law, mandatory
retirement based on age occurs in relatively few occupations, but incen-
tives or pressures to encourage early retirement are not unknown for
employees in their fifties.

In 1991, 100 members of the U.S. Congress—28 senators and 72
representatives—were age 65 or older, and 49 of these 100 were 70 or
over, with the oldest being 90 years old. At the same time the Supreme
Court of the United States, which is a lifetime appointment, included
among its members four justices aged 68, 73, 75, and 84 (Barone &
Ujifusa, 1991).

Turning to nonindustrial societies, Simmons (1960) informs us that

> the office of chieftainship and/or membership in official council,
> regulative organizations, clubs and secret societies have afforded
> old people, especially men, positions of usefulness and prestige in
> which established prerogatives, ripe experience, and special knowl-
> edge often could more than compensate for physical handicaps or
> waning vitality. (p. 78)

The ongoing value of elders politically is confirmed by the existence
in many parts of the world of gerontocracies, which, of course, are
political systems where the political power rests in a council of old men
who, by virtue of their purported wisdom, serve as community decision
makers, counselors, and arbiters of disputes. Such societies, which often
operate on an age-grade principle, are found in Africa, Australia, and
Melanesia.

Differences in Roles of Aged Men and Women

Old age does not have the same meaning or involve the same
circumstances for men as for women. Simone de Beauvoir (1972a) points
out, for example, that there is a great difference in the sexual potential of

the two sexes. While men are capable of siring offspring when they are well into their seventies or eighties, after menopause a woman is no longer considered sexual. In some respects, her status may be likened to that of a prepubescent girl in that in many societies she is free to ignore a number of repressive taboos and regulations. In Samoa, for example, the strong "brother-sister avoidance" patterns that begin at puberty no longer are in force with elderly women. They may sit and talk informally, make suggestive remarks, or even gossip about sexual matters with male siblings or cousins without shame or guilt.

Lee (1992) reports that !Kung women "undergo a blossoming" (p. 43) beginning in middle age. He attributes this change to a decline in work required of older women, the political authority based on the size of their kin networks who owe them respect, and "the changing evaluation of women's sexuality" (p. 44). The latter issue is the source of serious conflict in this otherwise peaceful society during young adult years, but gives way to more acceptance of open expression of sexuality by older women.

Hamer (1972) writes concerning the Sidamo woman in Ethiopia that with senescence

> there is a noticeable change in her manner or approach to others. The essence of this change is relaxation and warmth in social interaction with old and young of both sexes. She is no longer subject to all the tension surrounding the importance of her fecundity and labor in enhancing the prestige of her husband. Symbolic of this change is the fact that she no longer keeps her eyes focused on the ground when approaching other men, and may speak casually with them without first obtaining permission from her husband. An old woman may even be invited to eat and converse with the old men. (p. 23)

There are also striking differences in the extent to which men and women are able to acquire and control property, and this particularly affects the welfare of the elderly. Simmons (1945b) found that, although women have property rights in fewer preindustrial societies than do men, aged women seem to have had some advantage in this respect among collectors, hunters, and fishers. Among farmers and herders, however, men have had a great advantage over women, and their control of property seems to increase with cultural and technological complexity in general. Where elderly women control property, the situation tends to be greatly influenced by the prevailing form of social organization—for example, by matrilocal residence or by matrilineal descent, inheritance, and succession (see Chapter 4).

Role reversal may also occur in old age. While young and middle-aged men and women are, in most cultures, locked into certain kinds of roles and certain kinds of behavior that are thought of as "masculine" or "feminine," old age brings a blurring of these identifications. David Gutmann's (1987) research leads him to conclude that gender roles of adults are significantly influenced by what he calls "the parental imperative." He believes that humans possess a combination of male and female traits, but that parental roles in young adult years—passive, nurturing activities by women and aggressive, protective behavior by men—require sublimation of the opposite characteristics in both sexes for the well-being of the family. Once the children reach adulthood and the parental role is no longer dominant, older adults can safely allow these dormant tendencies of the opposite sex to emerge. In Gutmann's (1987) words:

> Just as men in late middle life reclaim title to their denied "femininity," middle-aged women repossess the aggressive "masculinity" that they once lived out vicariously through their husbands. The consequence of this internal revolution, this shift in the politics of the self, is that the sharp sex distinctions of earlier, parental adulthood break down, and each sex becomes to some degree what the other used to be. (p. 203)

Quain (1948) reports that Fijian men invest increased amounts of time and affection in their wives and in household chores as they reach old age. They, in effect, become more "domesticated" as they age, and they find no stigma in spending a great deal of time gardening—normally a pastime of women. This kind of movement toward interests and activities that are not typically masculine is also found among old Hopi Indian men. Simmons (1945a) reports that when they were

> unable to go to the fields any longer they sat in the house or kiva and spun, knitted, carded wool, or made sandals. . . . Corn shelling

Although a "big man" politically in his village, this aged New Irelander encounters no stigma in his baby-sitting role. (Photo courtesy of Nicolas Peterson; used by permission.)

was woman's work but men would do it, especially in their dotage. . . . They darned old clothes, cared for children, and guarded the house; and when there was nothing else to do, they would sit and watch the fruit drying in the sun. (p. 86)

Simic and Myerhoff (1978) point out, on the other hand, that in Yugoslavia and in parts of Mexico, women, required to be submissive in early adulthood, "become more assertive and independent with advancing years, and in old age participate to a far greater degree than men in both familial and nonkinship social areas" (p. 238).

On the island of Vanatinai, Papua New Guinea, the roles of men and women are less differentiated throughout the life course. This is an egalitarian society where both sexes pursue similar activities and achieve equal recognition for their knowledge and expertise. An exception to this pattern is that sorcery is a "virtual monopoly" of men, but even in this case some women have become skilled (Lepowsky, 1985).

Among the Chipewyan Indians of the Canadian Northwest Territories, performance and physical capacity are respected and are the basis for authority and prestige. Throughout much of their adult lives, men dominate their wives on this basis, but as a woman's children become adults there is a reversal in role dominance within the family. A father can continue to exercise his authority over his sons and command their respect as long as he remains competent and active, but as a man's strength begins to fail he begins to lose his ability to maintain this influence, and his position relative to his wife's suffers. In some cases, the wife actually dominates her husband. Sharp (1981) writes:

> In a real sense, the position of a man within his domestic unit is one of progressive diminution of influence throughout his life while a woman's position in her domestic unit is one of increasing influence until their respective statuses are virtually reversed. (p. 102)

Although this emphasis on competence among the Chipewyan has become less important recently because government agencies now compensate for the inability of the elderly to provide for themselves, competence is still admired and the lack of it is a matter of great anxiety. Women can remain competent in this society longer than men, for men have but one important skill—hunting—and women have three—childbearing, handicrafts, and food processing. Although a woman's role as childbearer ceases at menopause, her role as child-rearer does not. Grandparents have the right in this society to adopt a child from each of their children's marriages, and through such adoption elderly women not only find satisfaction in an ongoing role of "mother" but also are assured of the presence of young people to aid with such tasks as fetching water and firewood.

Chipewyan women are also valued for their handicrafts—sewing and beadwork—and the preparation of hides. Most elderly women are capable of performing most of these activities, but even very decrepit ones can teach their skills to younger women and supervise their work.

Finally, Chipewyan women continue to command respect well into old age through their skills as food processors. In addition to cooking, they cut dry meat and debone fish for drying. Much of this work is strenuous and takes place outside the comfort of the house, but most of this work is done by several women working together, and the very elderly ones invariably are able to get considerable help from the younger ones or are permitted merely to supervise the work.

In most societies women seem to have a distinct advantage over men in adjusting to their senior years. Even in societies where there is no formal retirement, women seem better able to continue in a familiar, valued role—that of homemaker and nurturer. While a man may no longer be able to go to the fields to farm or to the bush to hunt, the elderly woman is usually able to carry on business as usual or at least some degree of it. The nurturing role also gives the elderly woman a special place in the hearts of her children that a husband can seldom compete with. Simic and Myerhoff (1978) also found that elderly women may adjust to cultural change better than elderly men. They can migrate with their children to the city and perform a useful role—caring for and socializing children, preparing meals, and keeping the house in order—while the young people are off doing wage labor. Old men, however, have greater difficulty finding ways of contributing to family welfare.

An excellent example of the respect accorded to the mother because of her nurturing role is found among the Chinese of Taiwan. Here respect and responsibility for parents' welfare has been based on the time-honored concept of filial piety, but this standard, although it ensures security, does not necessarily guarantee love. In fact, in Chinese society filial piety is a culturally imposed imperative, and it often involves deep resentment toward parents because obedience is demanded and is primarily based on a combination of fear and duty. This greatly influences how elderly men and women are treated. Harrell (1981) reveals:

> Growing old is quite different for Taiwanese men and women.
>   Paradoxically enough, women, who are unquestionably treated as inferiors and even oppressed from childhood through middle age, are usually happier and less lonely in their final years than their once powerful husbands and brothers. (p. 199)

Elderly Chinese women are recipients of considerable respect and affection and tend to be happier and have more authority than their once powerful husbands. (Photo by Lowell D. Holmes.)

When no longer able to do physical work, the elderly father will turn over control of the family farm to his sons, but due to the harshness of the filial piety system, they will probably neither listen to his advice nor consider his wishes. In fact, they will probably ignore him. Their mother, on the other hand, will be the recipient of considerable affection, and sons will often seek her out and sit and talk for hours. At her advanced age, she no longer can boss her sons' wives about, but she often is able to retain support and affection from them.

In some societies, however, men and women have been equally able to maintain a position of respect and areas for meaningful participation. One such society is that of the Kirghiz of Afghanistan. In Kirghiz society, there are important roles for both elderly men and women, and therefore the experiences of the two sexes do not differ greatly in prestige, although they do in kind. The Kirghiz believe that as one declines in strength one increases in wisdom, and consequently respect and authority should increase. Old age is viewed as a triumph for both men and women. Old men are considered to have extensive knowledge of oral history, local ecology, veterinary medicine, and curing rituals for humans. Old women are equally valuable because of their special knowledge of arts and crafts, of problems associated with both human and animal birth, and of curing diseases not associated with supernatural spirits. It is not remarkable therefore that, among the Kirghiz, old age is never referred to as the "declining years" nor does old age bring disengagement even among those handicapped by blindness or other forms of physical deterioration (Shahrani, 1981).

Death and Dying

Old age is seen as a period of preparation for death in many societies, and senior years are therefore a time for planning, reflecting, and summing up. Although death may occur at any stage in the life cycle, and often does during infancy in preindustrial societies, there is a natural tendency to associate old age with death and dying. If old age is the final act of the human drama, then surely death is the final curtain. Leo Simmons (1945a) established the precedent of linking old age and death in his study of roles of elders in preindustrial societies, and most social scientists agree that it is a valid association, because the aged, more than any other age group, have to come to terms directly and realistically with this inevitability. But anthropologists know that the way the elderly handle the prospect of death varies from culture to culture, depending on the society's worldview, religious orientation, conception of the hereafter, and extent to which the society accepts or denies the reality of death.

Anthropologist/psychologist Ernest Becker, in his book *The Denial of Death* (1973), maintains that the human fear of death is the source of much individual and institutional behavior—heroism, neurosis, and religion. Geoffrey Gorer (1967) goes so far as to describe the Western attitude toward death as similar to its attitude toward pornography, explaining that we find death disgusting and immoral and yet we have a morbid fascination with it that results in grotesque fantasies and perversions. On the other hand, some social gerontologists (Jeffers & Verwoerdt, 1977; Kastenbaum & Aisenberg, 1972) present evidence that aged Americans handle the idea of death well. Although they are not overly apprehensive, they are more prepared for the event than younger people. Two thirds of the elderly in America have wills, for example, compared with the national average of one fourth.

While anthropology's interest in death and dying has been as slow in developing as its interest in gerontology, the discipline is now making worthwhile contributions to both areas with studies of funeral and bereavement practices of American ethnic groups and non-Western cultures, the role of the aged as intermediaries between the living and the dead, and attitudes and institutions of our own and other cultures associated with preparation for death. An outstanding contribution to our understanding of the cultural aspects of aging and death is a volume edited by Dorothy Counts and David Counts (1985a), *Aging and Its Transformations: Moving Toward Death in Pacific Societies*.

When we look beyond our own culture to beliefs and practices relating to death, we find some stark contrasts with our own experiences. In many societies death is rarely seen as a natural occurrence, especially where beliefs in sorcery are prevalent. People with this view attempt to determine who or what is responsible for a death. Among the Managalase of Papua New Guinea, death may be attributed to suicide, sorcery, murder, or malevolent spirits, and depending on one's stage in life, one's parents or other kin or even the village may be seen as being at fault for not providing adequate protection (McKellin, 1985).

There is a widespread belief in Pacific cultures that the soul or spirit can and does travel while a person sleeps, especially during dreams. In Tahiti, for example, it is thought that death occurs when the soul leaves the body, and if a sleeping person is awakened abruptly the soul may not have returned, thus leading to death (Levy, 1973). Older people, who may sleep more than others, are perhaps more at risk of this occurrence.

In contrast to Western societies where death is an event of finality, the Kaliai of New Britain, Papua New Guinea, see death as a reversible process. Dorothy Counts and David Counts (1985b) report that the word for death, *mate*, has a range of meanings: "to be ruined, fatally injured or terminally ill (*ngamatene*, 'I'm dying'); to be unconscious or partially dead (*isolo matenga*, 'he's half dead'); to be 'really dead' (*imate gasili*) or 'completely dead' (*imate kuvu*)" (p. 151). The Kaliai believe it is possible to recover from any of these states. Tahitians also refer to people who are unconscious as being "dead," a potentially reversible condition, but one who is "very dead" has no chance of recovery (Levy, 1973).

In some parts of the world—in a number of Melanesian societies, for example—death is still far more likely to occur long before what most would consider to be old age. Dying in the prime of life may be the rule and may be considered "loss of life" as opposed to the "passing away" of a very old person. Both occasion mourning, but death of a vigorous younger adult causes more disruption in the social order (McKellin, 1985).

Age may play a significant role in determining the nature and extent of ceremonial activity associated with death. In general, in non-Western societies the death of a very young person is marked by relatively simple and brief mortuary rituals. For an older adult, who has an extensive network of kin and friends, funerary rites may be quite elaborate and extend over a long period of time. Such is the case for the Sidamo of Ethiopia, who delay burial of an old man for several days, during which time honey and spices are used to preserve the body. Burial takes place in an underground tomb around which an elaborate bamboo fence is built. After several months, which allow time for the required preparations, a mourning ceremony is held, complete with receiving lines, presentation of mourners by age, singing, mock battles, and sacrifice of a calf. Because it is a patrilineal society (see Chapter 4), burial and attendant ceremonies are less elaborate for older women (Hamer, 1972). In contrast, among the Managalase of Papua New Guinea, ceremonial activities surrounding death and burial of an old person tend to be very limited because the people normally responsible for preparation of the body for burial (siblings, for example) are likely to be dead. For this same reason the associated rituals involve only close family members (McKellin, 1985). Similarly, Counts and Counts (1985b) report that in Kaliai when death is attributed to "old age" mourning involves only "the quiet grief of his immediate family" (p. 152).

SUMMARY

All societies have a system and a rationale for dividing up the life cycle of their members. Whether it is the seven ages cited by William Shakespeare or the formal four age grades for males and two for females of the Nandi of East Africa, each recognizes appropriate behavior and responsibilities for the several phases of aging, and members of each are accorded a particular status. In the West, life stages tend to be determined *chronologically*, while in the non-Western world, age stages are *functionally* determined, that is, one is old when unable to carry on a normal work pattern expected of adults.

One group of gerontological researchers conceive of the passage through the life cycle as a kind of *career*, where individuals negotiate and actively shape their own destinies through individual ability and ingenuity and are not merely content to passively take life as it comes.

A common misapprehension is that during the period of advanced age there is a decline in intellectual and creative activity, but studies of elderly jazz musicians and Brahmin folk painters in West India indicate that the capacity to grow intellectually and creatively has no age bounds, but the ability to create may be greatly hampered by cultural ideas concerning appropriate age behavior. Other research has investigated the capacity of personality to change with age. Some see personality as relatively stable while others maintain it is shaped by ongoing circumstances such as role and status changes. Gutmann's cross-cultural studies dealing with active, passive, and magical mastery ego states occurring at different ages stress that personality change is immune to cultural circumstances.

A significant event in the life cycle of Western men and women of advanced aged is *retirement*, which marks the end of career responsibilities and ideally inaugurates a period of financial security and leisure during their remaining years. Retirement as we know it does not exist in preindustrial societies, but old age—however it is defined—often forces alterations in role behavior. In most of these societies, the role changes are much the same for both men and women. Neither is required to abandon productive roles altogether, although their activities may be quite different than those of their earlier years. Occasionally there is actual role reversal with males feeling no sense of shame at engaging in activities that are normally recognized as those of women. In most cases the new roles of both sexes are useful ones but probably involve less expenditure of energy, less stress, and less emphasis on quantity and quality of production. In the United States, on the other hand, there is a tendency to force men into idleness in their senior years but to allow women, at least those who are homemakers, to continue working at familiar domestic tasks as long as they are able.

Not only does retirement in America rob the individual of a most important source of status and identity—the work role—but according to Anderson (1972), retirement is a period of life in America when people are systematically forced to undergo *deculturation*. That is, they are required to relinquish cherished values and goals and accept a secondary social and economic role. And gerontologists Cumming and Henry (1961) suggest that there is a universal and natural tendency, which they label *disengagement*, for aged individuals to withdraw socially, economically, and politically. They see such behavior as "mutually advantageous" both for the elderly and for the society. However, most anthropologists hold that cross-cultural data do not support the claim that disengagement is universal, natural, or beneficial to either old people or societies.

Significant research is also being carried out concerning the termination of the life cycle. Cultural gerontologists are exploring the attitudes, anxieties, and perceptions concerning death and dying of elderly in a variety of cultures. Although death is by no means an event that takes place only in old age, it is the elderly who most directly and realistically must come to terms with this inevitability.

4

▣ Status and Family

Anthropological interest in gerontology did not really begin until Leo Simmons (actually a Yale University sociologist) published *The Role of the Aged in Primitive Society* in 1945. An earlier encyclopedic volume by J. Koty, *Die Behandlung der Alten und Kranken bei den Naturvolkern*, had been published in Stuttgart in 1933, but it had little or no impact on American research interests. Simmons's (1945a) book purported to be a "report on the status and treatment of the aged within a world-wide selection of primitive societies," and it addressed itself to such questions as these: What in old age are the possible adjustments to different environments, both physical and social? What uniformities or general trends may be observed in such a broad cross-cultural analysis? Simmons's study was unique in its day, because it used elaborate and complicated statistical measurements; one reviewer described it as the "first systematic comparative analysis of the role of the aged in primitive society" (Kimball, 1946, p. 287).

It was Simmons's work that established the concept of status as an important focus in the study of the aged, and we begin this chapter with discussion of that work. Many other social scientists since that time have been interested in learning what factors contribute to or detract from the status of old people in different cultures. We will also see that, although the family takes a variety of forms throughout the world, it is essentially a primary source of support and care for the aged regardless of culture. Consideration of the nature of generational reciprocity and the implications of being childless conclude this chapter.

Simmons selected 71 widely distributed preindustrial societies and carefully analyzed the monographs in which they were described with an eye to differences in environment, level of technological development, and degree of cultural complexity. He correlated 109 cultural traits pertaining to (a) habitat and economy, (b) religious beliefs and practices, and (c) social and political organization with 112 traits dealing particularly with status and treatment of the elderly. Among the latter were traits pertaining to property rights, food sharing practices, community and family support, ceremonial roles, and political authority. Although some reviewers objected to some of Simmons's statistical procedures, they generally applauded his attempt to establish universals and variables of aging. Solon Kimball (1946) conceded that the book did have value as a "reference work," but he criticized Simmons's methodology on the grounds that "there is the ever-present danger that the use of isolated cultural facts, called 'traits,' outside their context may produce distortion of meaning" (p. 287). Even though this pioneer work may have contained methodological problems, Simmons must be applauded for creating a great deal of interest in aging and for laying some important groundwork for future investigation. He established, for example, that old people the world over seek (a) to preserve life as long as possible, (b) to be released from wearisome exertion and to be protected from physical hazards, (c) to maintain active participation in group affairs, (d) to safeguard prerogatives—possessions, rights, prestige, and authority—and (e) to meet death honorably and comfortably.

Simmons further established that the status of the aged had a tendency to stem from the force of tradition and from the special skills and knowledge that they possessed. To a large extent, their security, he thought, was derived from their control of property, and in many cases food for the elderly was assured through communal sharing, through kinship obligations, or through food taboos from which the elderly were exempt. The general welfare of the aged was at least in part seen as resulting from the routine economic and personal services they perform for their family or community, and from their ability to wield civil and political power either because of individual ability or because of a combination of social and cultural factors. Simmons found that old people usually have high prestige in preindustrial societies, the only exceptions being in very rigorous climates that require great energy and stamina to survive.

Although Simmons was technically a sociologist, his methods of cross-cultural analysis in this study were certainly more anthropological than sociological. The same can be said for his earlier life history study of a Hopi Indian, *Sun Chief* (1942). Also of an anthropological nature was the work of Western Reserve University sociologist Irving Rosow, who in 1965 used much of Simmons's data in assessing the cross-cultural factors that seem to contribute positively to the treatment of the elderly. Rosow's analysis revealed that the position or status of the aged is higher (a) if they own or control property that younger people depend on; (b) if their experience gives them a vital command or monopoly of strategic knowledge of the culture, including the full range of occupational skills and techniques as well as healing, religion, ritual, warfare, lore, and the arts; (c) if they are links to the past and to the gods in tradition-oriented societies; (d) if the extended family is central to the social structure; (e) if the population clusters in relatively small, stable communities where the governing values are sacred rather than secular, where roles are formally age graded, and where contacts are face-to-face; (f) if the productivity of the economy is low and approaches the edge of starvation—the greater the poverty, the relatively better off old people are by the standards of their group—and (g) if there is high mutual dependence within the group—the greater the interdependence among members, the greater the reciprocal aid in meeting survival problems.

Following both Simmons's and Rosow's suggestion that the aged are generally revered in preindustrial society because of the traditional knowledge they command, Robert Maxwell and Phillip Silverman (1970) hypothesized that societies value their aged in varying degrees, depending upon the amount of useful information they control. In their study, which they described as using the "general rubric of system theory," they analyzed data from 26 widely distributed societies, directing their attention to such aspects as (a) information control among the aged, (b) treatment of the aged, (c) rate of institutional change, and (d) ecological factors affecting the aged. Analysis of the key variable—information control—was directed at such aspects of social participation as roles in feasts and games, consulting, decision making, entertaining, arbitrating, and teaching.

As anticipated, Maxwell and Silverman found a strong correlation between control of useful information and good treatment and high status of the aged. They stated, however, that rapid institutional change (as found in industrialized societies) generates a high rate of information obsolescence and therefore leads to an eventual deterioration of prestige for the elderly.

Modernization

Another study that assessed the impact of change and technological development on the status and roles of the elderly was Donald O. Cowgill and Lowell D. Holmes's *Aging and Modernization* (1972). Modernization in this study was equated with industrialization, urbanization, and Westernization and was analyzed as a major factor affecting the fortunes and activities of elderly men and women in 14 societies ranging from what traditionally have been called "primitive" to those of western Europe and the United States.

Although cross-cultural in its emphasis, the study differed from those of Simmons or Maxwell and Silverman in that aging was considered entirely in terms of complete cultural contexts. The contributors to this study—eight anthropologists, seven sociologists, two psychologists, and a social worker—had all conducted extended, in-depth studies in the societies on which they reported. Cowgill and Holmes had provided each with a list of topics to discuss to ensure uniformity and continuity in the several studies, but the contributors were totally ignorant of the general theoretical propositions that their data would be used to test. The theoretical orientation for the study consisted of a number of hypotheses on the way the aged would be affected along a societal continuum from primitive to modern. A general hypothesis was that there is an inverse relationship between status of the aged and the degree of modernization, but the study also set forth 30 propositions, 8 labeled as "universals" and 22 identified as "variations" (to be considered in terms of unique social and cultural contexts). The uniqueness of the contexts was in this case related to the society's place on the primitive-modern continuum.

Although the data generally supported the hypotheses, a few exceptions—Russia, Israel, and Ireland—provided an interesting and unexpected
challenge to the hypothesis. In general, the researchers concluded:

> The theory with which we began this study has survived the test
> for the most part. In some cases we did not get adequate or relevant
> evidence. A few of our propositions were found wanting and must
> now be deleted or modified. These were more than balanced by
> serendipitous findings which we have not anticipated and were not
> looking for. Thus our theory has been extended and strengthened
> and is now ready for further testing. (Cowgill & Holmes, 1972,
> p. 321)

Further developments regarding this theory will be discussed in the
final chapter.

Prestige-Generating Components

Status considerations were also paramount in the study of Middle-
American aged carried out by Irwin Press and Mike McKool (1972). Here
the investigators isolated four prestige-generating components in a select group of Meso-American and perhaps all societies. These components are *advisory, contributory, controlling,* and *residual.* The advisory
component involves the extent to which the advice and opinions of the
aged members of the society are heeded; the contributory component
concerns the degree to which the aged are allowed to participate in and
contribute to ritual and economic activities. The control component
concerns the degree to which the aged have authority over the behavior
of other persons, institutions, or ritual processes, and the residual component pertains to the degree to which the elderly continue to retain
prestige from roles performed earlier in life.

Press and McKool concluded that at least in Meso-America the aged
are disadvantaged in societies featuring economic heterogeneity, diversity, and discontinuity in father-son economic interests and occupations.
Status of the aged was also found to be low where achieved rather than
ascribed roles, nuclear families, and independence from larger kin structures are emphasized, and also where there is an early turnover of family
resources. Status also declines for older persons in societies marked by

ritual, political and judicial bureaucracies, and in which modernization forces are potent.

Personal Achievement

Status and modernization forces among the Baganda of East Africa were the subjects of a gerontological study by Nina Nahemow and Bert Adams in 1974. In this society 115 elders between the ages of 60 to 90 years were interviewed along with 1,699 secondary school students "to address the question of the salience of traditional roles for modern life and the position of the aged today" (Nahemow & Adams, 1974, p. 151). The Baganda are a particularly interesting society in which to conduct such a study, because the aged have no tradition of societal leadership, although it has been customary for them to give advice, serve as storytellers, and try to be "good grandparents" (p. 164). Nahemow and Adams relate that the Baganda system emphasizes individualism over familism, and personal achievement and change are viewed in a positive light. Rights over land are established through political affiliation and not through kinship. Interviews with secondary students indicated a general tendency toward negative stereotypes of the aged and they definitely rejected the idea that the aged should, merely because of their age, have any special position of authority.

The investigators discovered that even the traditional role of adviser-storyteller has lost its significance under the impact of modern education. Although Baganda elders appear to have lost their function as repositories of tradition, they continue to be honored and valued as good grandparents. This is possible because of the high degree of rapport between grandparents and grandchildren. This rapport results from their sharing a common traditional value system that has always revered individualism, personal achievement, neolocality, and minimal lineage ties. In other words, modern and traditional values are so much the same that grandparents and grandchildren agree on intergenerational relations and definitions of family obligations. For example, they generally agree "that it is legitimate to criticize parents and grandparents; that grandparents should not 'spoil' grandchildren; and that each individual has a responsibility to both descending and ascending generations in terms of providing for them" (Nahemow & Adams, 1974, p. 161).

The Baganda example should impress us with the value of approaching every situation in terms of the total cultural context. A superficial analysis of the Baganda situation might very well result in the conclusion that modernization has been highly detrimental to the aged, but a more holistic analysis (of values and social structure) would reveal that the present situation in which the Baganda aged find themselves is not particularly out of character with tradition.

Although the majority of the studies dealing with status and role of the aged have tended to dwell on societal conditions or cultural factors, Virginia Kerns (1980) reports on a society, the Black Carib of Belize, where elders through individual activity and appropriate interaction affect their own status. To begin with, Kerns found a great gap between the ideal and the manifest in regard to intergenerational relationships. Obligations to parents and affection for elders are values and sentiments universally espoused but not always realized, and there is a great range in societal observance. What is found is a great deal of pragmatic behavior on the part of elders to ensure their security within the kinship and village structure. Older women, for example, work at making themselves indispensable within kin relationships. Kerns (1980) explains: "The parent-child relationship is the central social bond" (p. 120), and what is significant about this relationship is its reciprocal nature. Therefore the quality of support of the elderly depends greatly on the quality of the parent-child relationship throughout life. Parents strive to establish themselves as someone to "bank on," someone to call upon for help when it is needed. Elderly parents also control their security by using potential public opinion as a source of pressure on errant adult children.

In summarizing the significance for gerontology of her Black Carib experience, Kerns (1980) writes:

There is no denying that the ideal of filial responsibility is an important one to the Black Carib, but certainly the efforts that aged parents must make to enforce this ideal are equally worthy of attention. These efforts argue against the popular conception of the elderly as passive dependents. (p. 124)

Societal Types

Another approach to the study of status in old age is that of Tom Sheehan (1976), who investigated the relationship between esteem for elders and the economic and political nature of the societies of which they were members. He studied 47 societies representing three levels of societal complexity to determine elders' decision-making authority in interpersonal relationships and over offices and material or intangible property. The types of societies compared were (a) geographically unstable, that is, semipermanent bands ranging from people who periodically relocate their villages to complete nomads; (b) various tribes inhabiting fairly large, permanent villages; and (c) nucleated peasant communities with an economic base of agriculture or animal husbandry.

Esteem for the aged, defined by Sheehan (1976) as "the intersection of decision-making role or resource control and quality of received behavior" (p. 433), was definitely found to correlate with societal type. For example, Sheehan found that the lowest esteem for the aged is found in societies with the simplest and smallest socioeconomic structures. He reasons that "they have the fewest material resources and human relationships available for control and are usually located in harsh environments favoring youth and vigor" (p. 436). The highest esteem for elders was enjoyed in large-landed peasantries with highly developed social organizations. Although Sheehan was not specifically interested in change and its effect on elders' status, he did comment that the decline in status or esteem often observed in societies involved in modernization may result from a weakening of the social structure, and it therefore represents, in effect, a return to a less complex societal level. The author explains:

> The community turns away from extended family living or kin loyalties. With different emphases, both capitalist and socialist structures replace familial orientations with other-directed individualism on a mass level. A partial return is therefore made to the ideology of the nomadic band: old age and seniors are not accorded special status. (p. 437)

Property Control

An important factor that frequently governs both status and treatment of the elderly has to do with how well they can control property. By holding and controlling property, the elderly both maintain their own independence and control the opportunities of the young. Property owners in most groups provide work and make work assignments, and therefore the community's security depends on their decisions and knowledge. This maintains the authority of the aged long after their capacity to actually work the land has ended. Leo Simmons (1962) suggests that the intergenerational process of property transfer that ensures old age security is like a game. The game involves progressively relinquishing just enough personal resources (land and other property) to make young people happy, while retaining enough to guarantee that family members will continue to render respect and personal care in exchange. He states: "Aging must be gamey up close to the end to remain good" (Simmons, 1962, p. 50).

Let us look at how successfully this game is played in a variety of cultures. The prime example of how not to play the game is King Lear, who divided up his kingdom among his daughters and found himself without support or security for his old age. As Goody (1976) suggests: "No longer able to command their obedience, he is dependent upon their love; yet their gratitude is of far less value than he anticipated" (p. 119).

Something of the King Lear situation can be observed among the Fulani of West Africa. Here middle-aged household heads give portions of their livestock to each of their children when they marry and keep only those animals that they themselves can watch after. While the father gradually experiences the depletion of his herd, the mother in like manner gives away her decorated calabashes and other household property to her daughters as they marry. When the last daughter has left the household, the mother is, in effect, out of business as a mother, as a housewife, and as a dairywoman. D. J. Stenning (1958) tells us that the old man and woman even must abandon their own homestead and reside as dependents. The mother is considered of some use in caring for infants, but

> an old man is regarded as of little use. . . . Old people in this situation spend their last days on the periphery of the household, on the male and female sides respectively. This is where men and women are buried. They sleep, as it were over their own graves, for they are already socially dead. (pp. 98-99)

Although this arrangement appears callous or even cruel, incidents in our own society occasionally occur that are not too different. In June

1981 the *Eagle-Beacon* (the Wichita, Kansas, daily newspaper) carried the story of a local elderly couple who were being evicted from their home by their son, who had acquired the deed to the house from his parents some six years earlier. Because of conflict over how the elderly couple should spend their Social Security income, the son was demanding their removal from his property (Connell, 1981).

The property game is played well in most cultures. For example, the Etalese of the Caroline Islands value land above all other property, and although most young men acquire some land from their parents, it is not until their parents are very old that the sons acquire full title. According to James Nason (1981):

> Older people also gain or lose respect in the community by the way they administer their property. . . . It is thought foolish for an old person to dispose of all property—meaning here village and agricultural lands held with full title, individual trees . . . or important objects such as canoes—because it is almost an explicit statement of intent to withdraw from active social life in the community, an inappropriate form of behavior, and leaves one even more fully dependent on others than would otherwise be the case. The continued control of property is one way for an old person to remain somewhat independent and to exert some control over the way he or she is treated. An old person who has property need not fear neglect, since if kin fail others will soon appear, hopeful of receiving the remaining property as their due reward. (pp. 167-168)

Nason found that people age 45 and older controlled 60% of all individually owned land, and approximately half the canoes on the island were owned by men over 45. Property control is for them not only a strategy for maintaining authority and respect in one's family but it is necessary for the retention of respect within the entire community. Only foolish persons give away all their property but, on the other hand, attempting to hang on to all of one's property and thereby preventing adult offspring from acquiring some measure of prestige through property ownership is equally reprehensible.

An example of this latter situation is found in Ireland, where it is reported that in the traditional rural peasant family the father would choose one of his sons to inherit the family farm. The sons were kept guessing as to which of them would be selected and often delayed marriage pending the father's decision, which not infrequently came late in life. "The 'old man' delayed both inheritance and dowry decisions for as long as possible in order to maintain control over his dependent and vulnerable sons and daughters for as long as possible" (Scheper-Hughes, 1983, p. 131). In recent decades the forces of modern change have undermined the authority of these patriarchs.

Few play the property game better than the Kirghiz, a nomadic pastoral group in Afghanistan. In this society, household heads own the yurt (felt tent) and its contents, the herds, and all other material wealth associated with the family. However, the property is used to ensure the aging household head and his wife that there will always be someone present to care for them. The Kirghiz social system provides economic and psychological security by passing the responsibility for the parents down the line of sons. As each son marries and moves out of the natal household to establish his own, the next oldest son assumes the responsibility for the parents. When only one son remains in the household, he must stay within the household until the father dies, whereupon he inherits the yurt, the herds, and the household material goods. While the youngest profits the most materially, the eldest son inherits the father's political influence and prestige. Throughout the parents' elder years all sons are expected to visit frequently and aid the parents in any way they can. This is especially true in regard to the eldest son, who must maintain a close relationship between his household and that of his father.

In the Samoan islands, chiefs not only are the heads of large extended families but their titles also guarantee their right to control family lands. These titles are held for life, and succession to a chief's title comes not through inheritance but through election by kinsmen. Candidates are judged on the basis of their record of service, hard work, loyalty, and respect rendered to the family, particularly to its head. Thus young men who wish to hold chiefly titles in the future are forced to show deference and obedience to their aging family leaders who control not only the family land but also the political future of the young men who work the land.

In 1979 Sonya Salamon and Vicki Lockhardt described research among corn-belt farm families on the effect of control of land on the quality of intergenerational relations. They found that in the tightly knit German community of Heartland the elderly held a high position. What seems to have created this situation was a kind of "carrot on a stick" arrangement in which some land was turned over to an owner's children at their marriage and there was a gradual increase in crop profit sharing, but the actual transfer of land ownership tended to be reserved for some future time. Of this modern American farm community, Salamon and Lockhardt (1979) write:

> An elder has prerogatives because she or he owns land which allows control of timing of retirement, use of land, sharing of management, and disposal of holdings. Those maintaining a future orientation and who planned for transfer of holdings tended to be well integrated with rich and respectful family relationships. (p. 21)

Not only were these parents successful in acquiring respect and establishing positive relations with their children, they also managed to exert a good deal of control over their children's future activities. The community as a whole has been described as extremely successful at binding children to families and keeping them in farming.

It has been pointed out that hunters and gatherers have a minimum of property, and this normally puts the elderly at a disadvantage. However, the !Kung Bushmen of the Kalahari have found a way to make the young dependent and responsive in spite of a lack of heritable property. According to Biesele and Howell (1981):

> Economic accumulation as we know it is not a source of power for aging !Kung. This egalitarian society keeps individuals of all ages from hoarding goods, largely through the rules of generalized reciprocity and the *hxaro*, or gift-giving system, which militate against accumulation of wealth. Older people do not generally own more goods than people in other age groups. (pp. 92-93)

These hunting and gathering people are, of course, nomadic and claim little in the way of property in the form of land. Water holes and the food resources surrounding them are owned by kin groups by virtue of tenure of use. The elderly are, in effect, the stewards of the water holes and the resource areas because the "old *k'xausi* (owners) and their spouses provide genealogical stability over time to each water hole and resource area. Kin ties to these old people—as their siblings, offspring, or cousins—are the basis for young people's camp membership" (Biesele & Howell, 1981, p. 85).

Therefore Bushmen elders do not have property that can be willed or turned over to heirs, for such ownership can only come through long-term use, but the elders do make possible the existence of community. While young people respect the wishes of the elders in regard to use of food and water resources, the old people never act without taking into consideration the wishes of the young.

Status and the Decrepit Elderly

In recent years discussions of factors that govern the status of elderly people have often raised the issue of the impact of declining physical and mental health. In other words, as long as a person is in good physical health and is mentally competent, his or her status in the family and community may be good, but will that be true if the person becomes decrepit (Foner, 1984; Glascock, 1990)? The question was investigated by Glascock and Feinman (1981) and Maxwell, Silverman, and Maxwell (1982) using a research methodology known as *holocultural* analysis, which draws upon previously collected ethnographic data found in a world sample of societies in the Human Relations Area Files. To analyze treatment of the elderly, Maxwell et al. (1982) used a sample of 95 preindustrial societies and Glascock and Feinman worked with a sample of 60. Both studies found that a considerable number of societies treat their elderly quite badly at a certain stage in their lives, but a key factor appeared to be whether the elderly were (a) the normal old, that is, intact, or (b) the "already dead," that is, decrepit.

Simmons (1960) had observed that many societies have a special category of people who have become inactive and nonproductive and refer to them as being "living liabilities," "the overaged," "at the useless stage," "the already dead," or those belonging to the "sleeping period" (p. 87). Life for such individuals can be difficult indeed in many societies. Glascock and Feinman (1981) found that 51% of the societies they analyzed practiced what they referred to as "death-hastening" behavior. Of these, approximately two thirds engaged in killing the decrepit, 38% abandoned them, 19% denied them food, and 23% denied all support. On the other hand, nearly half of the societies that they surveyed were supportive of the very old. These were, by and large, the more economically complex, sedentary agricultural societies that were located in temperate climates, had systems of social stratification, and had a "belief in active high gods" (Glascock, 1990, p. 53). Societies that engaged in death-hastening behavior, on the other hand, tended to be located in harsh climates, practiced little or no agriculture, and lacked social stratification.

Maxwell et al. (1982), using a worldwide sample of 95 societies, found the existence of some sort of negative attitudes or mistreatment in 65 of them although deliberately killing the elderly was found in only 13 (14%). Reasons for mistreatment were found to include "physical weakness," "senile deterioration," "possession of obsolete skills," "loss of wealth," and "devalued appearance" (p. 70). They did not find mistreatment present in societies that were located in harsh climates, but they did find that nomadic hunting and gathering societies were more apt to deal harshly with the very old than were the more sedentary and socially complex agricultural ones. The major conclusion, which pretty much appears to have been reached by both sets of researchers, was summed up by Maxwell et al. (1982) as follows:

> We have noted that ill and enfeebled old persons are not invariably killed or abandoned, even in those societies in which we would otherwise expect such practice to occur. Much seems to depend on circumstantial considerations, including whether or not the old person remains "useful" in some sense or other, despite his dependence on others. (p. 80)

Holocultural analysis of phenomena such as death-hastening behavior provides some important cross-cultural insights into the range of elderly directed behavior, but because facts like "killing" or "abandonment" are taken out of cultural context, it is questionable whether or not we should conclude that this kind of treatment necessarily indicates contempt for the elderly or represents a decline in their status.

Judith Barker (1990), in describing the elders of Niue in western Polynesia, states: "Decrepit elders are frequently ignored, even neglected, by kin and community, left to fend for themselves without any longer having the physical or psychological means to succeed" (pp. 300-301). But she also warns that "such behaviors cannot be understood outside their proper cultural context" (p. 303).

While from the perspective of Western ethics and values death-has-tening behavior might be considered reprehensible (although some of it does exist even in the United States), Barker asks us to be relativistic in our evaluation of this behavior and consider Niuean perspectives, particularly their ideas concerning death. She writes:

> Niuean [language] uses the same word, *mate*, to encompass several states that we distinguish as delirium, unconsciousness, and death. Thus, there are no clear distinctions, linguistic or conceptual, between being incoherent, being comatose, being dying, or being dead.... Decrepit elders, then, especially those who no longer look or behave like competent adults . . . are being actively courted by *aitu*, are *mate*, in transition. (p. 311)

Thus, according to Barker, abandonment or neglect of decrepit old people is actually a ritual activity designed to prevent contamination by spirit *(aitu)* forces from the afterworld. By treating the "nearly dead" in this way, the family and community are attempting to persuade them to go to the realm of the *aitu*, where they will no longer threaten the living but will become revered ancestors.

Defining Status

One of the criticisms of the modernization theory has been that Cowgill and Holmes (1972) did not adequately define what status is, although the authors did imply "high honor and prestige" (p. 10). While status can mean numerous things, most social scientists whose studies are described in this chapter, including Cowgill and Holmes, would no doubt tend to follow *Roget's* (1988) definitions in which *status* refers to "a person's high standing among others," the "positioning of one individual vis-à-vis others," the "level of respect at which one is regarded," or "the established position from which to operate or deal with others" (p. 950). Some, like Glascock and Feinman (1981), would question whether or not high status would also include a guarantee of special or even humane treatment, but the Cowgill and Holmes concept assumes that treatment of the elderly is a reflection of their status, although there are documented exceptions. And if one is relativistic in the analysis of such things as gerontocide among such people as the Eskimo, the action of killing an elder is to be properly understood as being a way of respecting the wishes of highly honored individuals who no longer wish to participate in a rigorous and unrewarding environment.

In an attempt to better understand what status means and how it can be manifested, Silverman and Maxwell (1983) have developed the "Deference Index," which is a device designed to measure "the degree of esteem enjoyed by the aged in a given society" (pp. 48-49). It includes the following items:

(1) Spatial deference. Examples: Being given the best seat in the theater; in Japan, having "silver seats" reserved for the elderly on public transportation; being given a place at the head banquet table; or receiving a parking permit for the VIP lot.

(2) Victual deference. Examples: Being served the choicest foods, being fed before others, or receiving a special part of game that is traditionally taboo for these of lower rank.

(3) Linguistic deference. Examples: Being addressed by an honorific title like "Your Majesty," "Your Honor," or in West Africa as "Grandfather" even though the elder is not a kinsman; or being spoken to in the "chiefs' language," which is the proper communication medium for people of high rank in Samoa.

(4) Presentational deference. Examples: Special behavior required in the presence of high-ranking persons such as kneeling before them or making sure that one's head is not above theirs if they are seated, or the requirement that West Africans must lower their gaze when speaking to a superior.

(5) Service deference. Example: Any work performed for the elderly out of respect and not just because that elder may be decrepit or handicapped.

(6) Prestative (gift-giving) deference. Example: Gifts that are given out of respect and not as part of a reciprocal exchange.

(7) Celebrative deference. Example: Where rituals are given to dramatize the worth of elders to the family or to the society; being knighted in

England, or in the United States being voted into the Baseball Hall of Fame or receiving the Medal of Freedom.

In addition to the above, the anthropological literature has documented a variety of additional forms of deferential treatment extended to the elderly. They may be honored by having children named after them, by being given special ceremonial or religious roles, by being asked by the family or the community to give advice, by being asked to arbitrate conflicts, or by being given the freedom not to work if they so choose. Deferential treatment may also include being given the right of having idiosyncrasies tolerated or the right to scold or engage in improper behavior such as using foul language or vulgar gestures.

Family, Kinship, and the Aged

The family is humankind's most basic, most vital, and most influential institution. It is the foundation of society, the molder of character and personality, and the mentor of cultural values. Ideally, it is a group where people care about and support one another in times of triumph or times of failure. Family is what makes the difference between a "house" and a "home." It is in the family where one first learns to walk, to talk, and to function as a human being. It is where one learns the values that will influence behavior throughout life in dealing with the greater society.

Leo Simmons (1945a) maintains that "throughout human history the family has been the safest haven for the aged. Its ties have been most intimate and longlasting, and on them the aged have relied for greatest security" (p. 177).

Although family is a universal institution, families exist in an almost unbelievable variety of forms. In the United States and in most of western Europe, kinship is reckoned *bilaterally* (or *bilineally*) and within that system one is equally related to the families of both parents, whereas in much of the Third World *unilineal* reckoning of kinship prevails. This system acknowledges dual biological descent but stresses a single line of kin affiliation. If a system is said to be *matrilineal*, the mother's line is stressed, and if *patrilineal*, the emphasis is placed on the father's line. Membership within such a line of descent is clear cut, and rights and obligations are carefully delineated. In such a system a man knows who it is proper for him to marry and what relationships might be considered incestuous; he knows what he will eventually inherit in regard to social position and material wealth; and he knows to whom he might look for care when he becomes old. In a *matrilineal* system, for example, mother's brother will play a much more important role in nurturing and educating a child than the biological father, who is technically not even related.

Unilineal systems trace descent through one parent and recognize kinship with the sum total of descendants from a common ancestor. This group constitutes a *lineage* and stresses *consanguine* (blood) bonds. The lineage head is often the eldest male in a three- or four-generation family and as family patriarch may have great prestige and power over the members of his kin group and their activities. Where kinship is reckoned bilaterally, the *kindred* is the significant social entity, and this involves recognition of all individuals to whom one is related through blood, marriage, or adoption. Barbara Myerhoff (1978) has suggested that lineage systems are more supportive of old people than kindred systems. She writes:

> Kindreds are more often found in the changing, industrial, and Western societies that stress individuality, achievement and mobility. Where the lineage principle is used to generate the most important groups the older members of the society accumulate great authority and status. (p. 160)

People who see themselves as kinsmen may thus be related through *consanguine* (blood) ties or *conjugal* (marriage) ties, and some systems (like those in the Western world) tend to stress marriage ties over blood ties while others (i.e., much of the rest of the world) stress lineage affiliation.

While kinship systems are important considerations for anthropologists with gerontological interests, what might be considered of greater importance is the nature of the actual domestic, or household, groups whose members live together and interact on a day-to-day basis. A household may be composed of a *nuclear* family, that is, a set of biological parents and their dependant offspring, or an *extended* family, that is, two or more nuclear families linked together through parent and child or siblings (Keesing, 1975). Biological parents are united through the bonds of marriage, but these unions may take several forms. The most common arrangement is *monogamy* (one husband, one wife) but some cultures opt for *polygyny* (one husband, more than one wife), or *polyandry* (one wife, more than one husband). The latter two arrangements are collectively classified as *polygamy*.

Another highly variable characteristic of family life has to do with residence. Where kinship reckoning is *matrilineal*, there is a pronounced tendency for residence after marriage to be with the wife's relatives (*matrilocal* or *uxorilocal* residence) whereas *patrilineal* kinship systems tend to favor living with the husband's people (*patrilocal* or *virilocal* residence). Bilateral kinship systems can feature either *patrilocal* or *matrilocal* residence but *bilocal* residence (having a choice or living alternately with both sides of the family) is also found. A common pattern in the Western world, which features small nuclear families and bilateral descent, is *neolocal* residence, where a newly married couple establishes a residence independent of either family. All of these systems can and do have ramifications for the elderly, particularly in regard to who will function as caregivers and what the role and status of widowed persons will be.

Anthropologists who study aging are very much interested in family structure and function as this can have a tremendous impact on what roles are assigned the elderly, what their authority and status might be, and how they will be cared for. In most preindustrial societies and a high percentage of developing Third World societies, kinship and family organization are much more important than in the West, and people's involvement with family determines everything they do, think, and value. A value system like this is referred to by social scientists as *familism*. Familistic values place family concerns over personal concerns, stress the centrality of family, and clearly delineate proper courses of action for all who identify with the kinship unit. Familism is primarily a characteristic of societies wherein kinship is stressed over other forms of relationship and affiliation is with larger groups such as clans, lineages, kindreds, or extended-family household groups. Familism may even have religious sanctions as in the case of prerevolutionary peasant China wherein filial piety was demanded by the teachings of Confucius.

Respect for the aged tends to be greater in societies in which the extended family is intact, particularly if it functions as the household unit. Rosow (1965) maintains that the position of the aged in a society is relatively higher when the extended family is central to the social structure because "a clan can and will act much more effectively to meet crisis and dependency of its members than a small family. Mutual obligations between blood relatives—specifically including the aged—are institutionalized as formal rights, not generous benefactions" (p. 22).

The literature provides us with abundant examples of the supportive nature of the extended family. Munsell (1972) observed that among the Pima Indians recent developments that have brought the nuclear family into prominence at the expense of the extended form have to a large extent deprived the elderly of decision-making functions and therefore resulted in loss of status and authority. Press and McKool (1972) found in Chinaulta, Guatemala, that

> loss of extended family viability goes hand in hand with low, dependent status of the aged. . . . Where the economic unit is largely coterminous with the extended family, the elder members *de facto* remain economically active and may exert considerable control over the behavior of others. (p. 303)

Frances M. Adams (1972), on the other hand, emphasizes the importance of the extended family as a socialization influence that provides family members with a positive attitude toward growing old. She writes:

> Changes in behavior expectations as a person gets older . . . are understood in advance through close association with older people who have already made the transitions. For example, a person knows how to be an old person because he has observed first his grandfather and then his father in this role. The emotional security developed in childhood in the context of the extended family is not lost in old age. (p. 110)

Shelton (1972) stresses still another aspect of extended-family organization that contributes to respect for the aged. This is the emphasis it puts on the cyclic flow of family members and spiritual forces. He notes that in West Africa:

> The dead are not buried and forgotten, but are "returners" who reappear in the patriline. The aged persons in the family, accordingly,

Samoan chief and grandchildren. (Photo by Lowell D. Holmes.)

are not simply individuals who have served their brief span on earth and are soon due to disappear forever, but indeed are getting closer to the apogee of their cycle—they are soon to be ancestral spirits, in that most powerful condition in the endless cycle of existence. (p. 35)

Sheehan (1976) points out, however, that when a community turns away from an extended-family emphasis and kinship loyalties are replaced by structures that emphasize peer allegiance and other-directed individualism, there is, in effect, a return to the less binding ties associated with peoples practicing a nomadic life. In such societies, he maintains, "social and geographic mobility become goals; individual autonomy emerges as a value" (p. 437). This is not unlike what happens with increased modernization. "As urban-industrial society increasingly technologizes, seniors ever more lose their family ties along with accompanying status, decision-making power and security" (p. 437).

Generational Reciprocity

In all societies, the prevailing values prescribe some mutual responsibility within the family between generations. Leo Simmons (1945a) has observed that "social relationships have proved the strongest securities to the individual, especially in old age. With vitality declining, the aged person has had to rely more and more upon personal relations with others, and upon reciprocal rights and obligations involved" (p. 177).

Dependency is a reality of human life during both the beginning and the concluding years of the life cycle, and people in most societies think in terms of a kind of reciprocity where care received when one is young is paid back (with respect) when one's caretakers become old and need assistance and solicitude. Prevailing societal values can greatly affect this relationship, however. For example, in America (an extremely youth-oriented society) there tends to be an attitude that youth dependency (often extending as long as 25 years when offspring acquire professional education) does not carry a mandate for reciprocity when parents become elderly and in need of help. The more common pattern found around the world, however, is that there tends to be a balance between infant care and old age care. Furthermore, there is a tendency—so common that it might also be cited as a universal—that the way the members of a society treat their aged is a reflection of the nature of child-rearing practices. Societies with warm and loving relationships between parents and their small children appear to also promote warm and loving relationships between adult children and elderly parents. de Beauvoir (1972a) suggests:

> If a child is kept short of food, protection, and loving kindness he will grow up full of resentment, fear and even hatred; as a grown man his relations with others will be aggressive—he will neglect his old parents when they are no longer able to look after themselves. (p. 80)

de Beauvoir also relates that after doing thorough research on this issue she found only one example where happy children grew into adults who were cruel to their fathers and mothers. That group was the Ojibway. Numerous ethnographic examples support de Beauvoir's generalization, however. Marie Scott Brown (1978) tells us that the Kikuyu of Kenya are "noted for their warm and permissive child-rearing practices. There are particularly warm attachments between the grandparents and the grandchildren who . . . symbolically . . . belong to the same age group. There are, in fact, warm relations between all the generations" (p. 99).

The Tiv of Nigeria also have extremely warm and supportive acculturation and socialization patterns, and, as a result, even grown children are very close emotionally to parents and grandparents, and the elderly are in general treated with respect. Similarly, de Beauvoir (1972a) reports for the Yaghan of Tierra del Fuego:

> The boys and girls are very well treated, they are deeply attached to their parents, and when they are in camp they always want to live in their parents' hut. This love persists when the parents are very old, and all the aged people are respected. (p. 59)

In a number of societies where James W. Prescott (1975) found infants provided with a great deal of "tender loving care" (p. 67), it was established that attitudes toward old people were positive and supportive. Such societies are the Andamanese, the Chuckchee, the Maori, the Trobriand Islanders, the Jivaro, and the island people of Lesu. On the other hand, in societies where children are raised under austere enculturative situations, where there is little warmth, love, and affection displayed toward them, evidence indicates that the aged will also be treated badly. de Beauvoir (1972a) writes: "The Yakut and the Ainu, who are badly treated as children, neglect the old most brutally" (p. 80). Trostchansky (1908), who lived among the Yakut of Siberia for 20 years, reports that the aged were turned into slaves by their sons, who beat them and required very hard labor of them. Landor (1893), in *Alone With the Hairy Ainu*, describes the fate of a neglected, starving, and physically ill elderly woman he encountered in an Ainu home. He reports that the woman was not "taken care of by the village or by her son, who lived in the same hut; but she was something that had been thrown away, and that was how they treated her. A fish was occasionally flung to her" (p. 55).

It is conceivable that this correlation between ill treatment of children and devaluation of the aged may serve as an explanation of the less than enthusiastic respect and support extended to the elderly in the United States. A 1953 study by John Whiting and Irving Child of child-rearing practices in a variety of cultures discovered that in regard to warmth and affection (measured in terms of nursing, timing and severity of toilet training, severity of aggression training, and sexual training) Americans were among the least affectionate and warm parents investigated.

Some societies formalize reciprocal relationships between the generations in their family or kinship obligations. A good example of this is the concept of *filial piety* found in traditional Chinese culture.

The prerevolutionary Chinese family can be described as consisting of a family patriarch (the eldest male) and his wife living together with their sons and their families (and perhaps a few collateral relatives like uncles and aunts) in a common household on land that the family may have owned for many generations. The family unit shared both the work and the resources of the farm, although the family patriarch had final authority on all family economic and social matters. As the sons married they brought their brides to live in this extended-family household. Chinese marriages were usually arranged by the parents of the bride and groom, and much more importance was attached to a prospective daughter-in-law's thrift, industry, and potential compatibility than to her beauty, charm, or romantic attraction to the groom. Although there was bilateral reckoning of kinship, the family emphasis was consanguineous, in that the most important ties were those of blood rather than those of marriage. A father-son or a mother-son relationship, for example, was much more important than a husband-wife relationship. A wife had to defer to her mother-in-law during the older woman's lifetime, and she would acquire a measure of authority only when her son would bring home a wife to be her daughter-in-law.

As long as the family patriarch lived, his sons had to obey him and work the land according to his wishes. The respect and obedience that were required of sons was based on the Confucian teachings of the *Hsiao Ching*, which outlines the concept of *filial piety*. Within this tradition, support of one's aging parents is presented not as a matter of choice but as a moral duty. According to Francis Hsu (1971):

> The son owes his father absolute obedience, support during his lifetime, mourning when he passes away, burial according to social station and financial ability, provision for the soul's needs in the other world, and glory for the father by doing well or even better than he. (p. 68)

Although filial piety directly relates to father-son relationships, the status of the aging parent is also tied to the nature of the total kinship system. The Chinese family places emphasis on the paternal line through five degrees of kinship and a select number of close relatives on the mother's and wife's side. The extended-family emphasis involves mutual obligations and privileges. Unless a couple was unfortunate enough not to have children, aged Chinese had little to worry about concerning support in their declining years. As Hsu writes (1981):

> The Chinese parent-child relationship is permanent. A father is always a father, whether or not he is loving or kind. A son is always a son; rarely is he disowned because he is not dutiful. . . . Chinese social organization is such that age, far from being a defect, is a blessing. Chinese parents have no reason to regret their children's maturity, for it assures not a lesser role but a more respected place for themselves. The Chinese pattern of mutual dependence thus forms the basis of a mutual psychological security for both the old and the young. (p. 116)

The close father-son ties involved authority on the part of the parent and filial piety on the part of the son, and the mother was also guaranteed maximum security. By the time she reached 50 or 60, she could dominate the domestic operation of the household. At this age she was relatively free of male domination, although she had to depend on her sons for future support. When the patriarch died, the eldest son inherited the authority of the father as well as management of the family economic enterprise. Because the son was often middle aged by this time, he had long observed the manner in which the household must be run and merely took over the management of its material and human resources. Neither the efficiency nor the continuity of the family was disturbed. In the traditional Chinese family, individual action was discouraged. Personal considerations had to be subordinated to family considerations, and men had to take direction from their older relatives when they themselves were middle-aged adults.

Traditional China was an age-honoring culture. The average Chinese genuinely believed that old age, which was thought to begin about age 55, marked the beginning of a higher and more respected status. It was perceived as a blessing and a period of life when a person could sit back and enjoy the fruits of his or her labors.

While the above picture of Chinese society presents an ideal that operated in peasant China for many generations, modernization, urbanization, and demographic changes in recent years have resulted in modifications in the way that generations relate in contemporary China and particularly in a place like Hong Kong. This was the focus of Charlotte Ikels's (1980) study, "The Coming of Age in Chinese Society: Traditional Patterns and Contemporary Hong Kong."

Ikels's research dealt with the ideal of filial piety and the realities of everyday family life in overcrowded Hong Kong. Here she found that the veneration of age, so often identified with Chinese culture, was mostly enjoyed by the well-to-do. One of the reasons the concept of filial piety is breaking down is that many of the supporting features—such as family property—do not exist in the urban setting. Also, the percentage of aged in Hong Kong is far greater than in rural areas. Because of increasing strain in intergenerational relations, Chinese elders have adopted a practice of carefully selecting and cultivating the child who will willingly respond when parents need support. Although Ikels's study confirms the fact that filial piety and respect for the wisdom of the aged remain paramount within the Chinese value system, she maintains that such ideas are difficult to carry out where population density approaches 400,000 per square mile.

Childlessness and Its Consequences

In a society that depends as much on generational reciprocity as did traditional China, the matter of childlessness posed a particularly serious problem. Andrea Sankar (1981) tells us that "failure to produce heirs was regarded as an affront to one's ancestors, as unfilial behavior toward one's parents, and as a serious spiritual and supernatural threat to one's own soul as well as one's family's future prosperity" (p. 66). The threat to one's soul was believed to be the danger of becoming a Hungry Ghost wandering alone in the Underworld. There were, however, ways in which childless couples or people who remained single could create special relationships that would ensure support for them in their elder years.

Childless, single women often acquired domestic employment in another household and became "free servants" and were considered somewhat like distant relatives. They were allowed to partake in the family's activities and after a lifetime of faithful service with little financial gain they were assured of a secure and comfortable old age. This is even true in modern China. There is a law in Hong Kong that states that any servant who has served more than 20 years is entitled to full support in his or her old age.

Childless spinsters and bachelors also had the option of joining Buddhist or Taoist religious orders and living in nunneries or monasteries where care in senior years was guaranteed and where the elderly were exempted from physical labor and other rigors of monastic life. There was also a secular sisterhood movement in the Canton Delta that promoted a spinster lifestyle and made provision for old age care.

Childless couples were sometimes cared for by affluent extended families, but this required considerable surplus income. Even couples who produced only girls were considered the same as childless. This was occasionally remedied by departing from the usual pattern of patrilocal residence and having a daughter remain at home and acquire a husband who would reside with her (because he was too poor to object) and serve her parents. Often he would remain only until the death of his wife's parents and then the couple would return to his natal household.

William Donner (1987) also studied the problem of childlessness in a small Polynesian community on Sikaiana atoll in the Solomon Islands. In this society, which featured patrilineal descent, lack of male offspring presented a situation that was described as "stopping up" (as in a clogged pipe) the family line. People who have no children or who only have female offspring are distrusted by other members of their patrilineage because it is assumed that, because they have no one to inherit family authority and property, they are not interested in the general welfare of the kin group.

The matter of reciprocal care obligations is solved in this society by a rather typical Polynesian pattern of fostering. Donner tells us that 48% of the children on Sikaiana at the time of his research were residing in the households of foster parents. He writes: "On Sikaiana, the social message of fosterage is that a person has many different people to whom he/she is emotionally attached, for whom he/she can expect support, and to whom he/she should feel obligation" (Donner, 1987, p. 49).

Foster children (known as *tama too*) and biological offspring were treated equally, although the former had inheritance rights only in their natal household. Foster children, however, had an obligation to support both their natural parents and their foster parents (called *tupuna*, or "grandparents"). It was considered a sign of generosity and kindness to take in a foster child, and no child was ever refused residence. Fosterage was practiced by both childless couples and couples with children but it often was the case that foster children showed more concern for elderly people than did biological offspring. This has become a particularly important fact today with the great mobility of young Sikaianans. Many elders have no children living on their atoll and must rely on their foster children.

By way of comparison, anthropology's avenue to insight, let us now turn to an analysis of childlessness in the United States by Robert L. Rubinstein (1987). He maintains that, in much of the world, care for the elderly is seen as properly a family responsibility, and children are seen as a kind of insurance against old age crises. Studies of the childless in America have revealed that such people also may ultimately turn to family for support, but development of strong kin ties tends to be with cousins, nieces, and nephews. We also know that childless unmarried individuals (never married, widowed, or divorced) differ from childless couples in that the former tend to enjoy a greater feeling of independence and a greater capacity for strategic planning for old age while the latter appear more dependent on each other and consequently more isolated and lonely.

Rubinstein believes that in the United States childlessness is generally viewed negatively, and cites studies that show that people perceive that childless people are unhappy, lonely, and unfulfilled. However, there is an increasing tendency for childlessness to be voluntary. In the United States and in many developing countries, women see childlessness as a trade-off in their desire for personal freedom and vocational success, but Rubinstein suggests that what these more liberated women gain by remaining childless must be balanced against the possible insecurity of later years. It must also be recognized that, with the protection of Social Security, adequate pensions, and Medicare, childlessness in modern America might be considered less undesirable than problems of "unwanted involvement in children's lives, lack of independence, mental aggravations of various sorts, continuing financial demands, and an inability to transcend undesired aspects of the parental role" (Rubinstein, 1987, p. 4).

Although the majority of studies of childlessness, both in the West and in non-Western cultures, have tended to deal with problems of care in old age, Rubinstein discusses a number of other studies that have dealt with lifestyle correlates of the childless situation such as low religiosity, marital disharmony, urban residence, desire to maintain a particular level of living standard, and what psychological characteristics and childhood experiences prompt people to remain childless.

SUMMARY

A *role* may be defined as the traditional patterned behavior of an individual occupying a particular position (for example, elder, father, guru, chieftain) in a family or in a society while *status* refers to the level of respect conferred upon the individual who occupies that position. Beginning with Leo Simmons's study of role and status of the elderly in preindustrial societies in 1945, anthropologists have explored this topic with considerable interest, considering the relationship of role and status to such factors as control of useful information, ecological circumstances and subsistence patterns, family and societal structure, personal achievement, ritual participation, property management, and long-term value orientations such as filial piety. More recently investigators have assessed the influence of modernization and Westernization on senior status and have described the impact of migration, population aging, technological advance, urbanization, and education.

The family is humanity's most basic and important institution, but families are varied in form and function in various parts of the world. In some societies family controls and determines nearly every aspect of human existence, and this case social scientists refer to as *familism*. Respect for the elderly tends to be greater where familism obtains, and also where the extended family is central in the social structure.

Generational reciprocity is also a topic of research for scholars interested in status and treatment of the elderly. It has been discovered that, in societies where children are treated with kindness and respect, similar attitudes and actions will characterize their relationships with their parents when the latter become old. We have also learned that childlessness is disadvantageous to the elderly in a wide range of societies, but less so in societies where the extended family is dominant or where there is an institution of fostering.

5

 Community Studies

During the 1960s a burning gerontological issue was whether old people should be segregated in age-homogeneous retirement residences or whether they should remain integrated in society and participate in activities without reference to age. Some elders are extremely happy sharing life with people of their own age, but one survey (TIAA Cref, 1974) revealed that just as many volunteer such advice as "Don't hole up in a senior citizen enclave or retirement home until you must. Stay where you can get mad at the school kids cutting across your lawn" (p. 2).

Of course, the question of what kind of community is best for the elderly is important, because such matters are often vital government policy concerns or involve private-sector capital investment. When bureaucrats and real estate developers initially turned to the social scientists for answers, the social scientists had to admit that they frankly did not know what kind of community situation would best meet the physical, psychological, and social needs of the elderly.

Although the majority of researchers in gerontology were sociologists in the 1960s, a number of anthropologists were particularly interested in this question. Community study was not new to anthropologists, because most of them had worked in small, isolated communities in preindustrial societies and had evolved a methodology appropriate to this kind of research. Also, they were especially interested in the nature of community. Robert Redfield had produced a classic study, *The Little Community and Peasant Society and Culture* (1960), and documented community characteristics in "The Folk Society" (1947). Redfield defined community in terms of distinctiveness and group consciousness, size (small enough for ongoing interaction), homogeneity (sharing common goals and values), and self-sufficiency. Arensberg and Kimball (1968) had suggested that "community" is not a thing, but a process, and that it must be understood in terms of ongoing human interactions—adjustments, compromises, and cooperation. Therefore, when anthropologists turned to an analysis of communities of old people, they were interested in an applied problem: What is the best residence for the elderly? They also addressed theoretical aspects: What is community? How does it develop? What are its functions for the elderly?

This chapter describes a variety of communities of old people where these and other questions were of primary concern to the anthropologists and sociologists who studied them. Much of this research has been done in the United States or Europe, but development of specialized housing for the aged is on the increase in non-Western countries. The examples from Asia and Africa included here illustrate cultural variation in administrative policies and reaction of aged residents to these nontraditional living situations.

One of the first social scientists to take an interest in doing ethnographic research on the retirement community question was Jerry Jacobs. Jacobs not only produced a detailed monograph on a retirement community in southern California, which he facetiously titled Fun City, but he also analyzed the characteristics of several others. In *Old Persons and Retirement Communities*, Jacobs (1975) contrasted three different kinds of retirement residences with the goal of "providing some initial insight into the question of retirement and retirement settings and a basis for a grounded theory of aging" (p. vi). Jacobs was not only interested in the quality of life for the elderly in a variety of retirement settings, he was also interested in exploring the theory of "disengagement," which holds that as old people grow older they tend to disengage from social and economic relationships and that this is beneficial to them and to their society.

Jacobs looked first at High Haven, a 21-story retirement residence of "well elderly" located on a university campus in a middle-sized eastern city. The facility was originally established under a federal grant to the university, and the school, along with the city housing authority, administered a program specially designed to promote interaction between elderly residents and university students living in adjacent dormitories. Interaction was supposed to take the form of eating together in the university dining room, sharing a snack bar, attending a film series together, and attending holiday parties. It was anticipated that this arrangement would result in greater intergenerational understanding and that the students and the elderly residents could assist one another in solving their respective personal problems.

Neither the 420 residents nor the students were informed that they were social science guinea pigs in an experiment in intergenerational living, and very little interaction took place. Segregation by age is, after all, a predominant pattern in American life. Some aspects of the experiment were put into operation, but after a time the university's grant funds ran out and the administration of High Haven became the sole responsibility of the municipal housing authority. The snack bar closed for lack of business, the elderly found the dining facility too expensive, and attendance dropped at the film series. The elderly residents, unhappy with their campus environment, began haranguing one another; cliques developed and this resulted in some people becoming recluses. Several residents attempted suicide, and alcoholism became a major problem. Thus the experiment in creating an artificial intergenerational community proved to be not only nonproductive but nearly a disaster.

Jacobs next contrasted his High Haven findings with those from Fun City, an age-homogeneous community that he studied much as he might have studied an exotic tribal society. Fun City was a specially planned tract-home town of 6,000 white middle- and upper-class elderly. It was a relatively isolated (90 miles from a metropolitan area) community located in a warm (often hot) valley in California. The name Fun City was coined by Jacobs because of the stress developers had placed on the community's many recreational opportunities. Fun City, however, had no young people (except visiting family members), no people of color, no people of less than middle-class means, no hospital, no fire department, and no security force. Jobs, for those who sought to relieve boredom with part-time employment, were limited, and shopping facilities were less than adequate. The two so-called supermarkets and a coffee shop actually had more social value than they did as a source of food and other supplies. Shopping became a valued means of meeting people and breaking the boredom. Although the people of High Haven had a multitude of problems and complaints, Jacobs believed that they fared better than the people of Fun City, because they were able to be in contact with friends and relatives constantly, while the isolation of Fun City rarely permitted its residents to maintain close ties with either family members or former friends.

The third old age residence described by Jacobs was Merrill Court, a community of 43 elderly welfare recipients living in a small apartment building in San Francisco. Most residents received rent subsidies. Merrill Court was not isolated like Fun City, but it too had no black or Jewish residents. Nearly all were widows. Although they had little in the way of planned activities, they were described as relatively happy and generally in good health. Merrill Court residents appear to have developed greater participation, reciprocal aid, and social involvement than was true of the residents of either High Haven or Fun City. Arlie Hochschild (1973), who did the original study of this community in 1966-1969, believes the study shows that old people who live among other old people make more friends than old people who live among young people (pp. 28-29).

Based on his somewhat limited but diverse sample of retirement homes, Jacobs concluded that these are not just unique examples of retirement communities and that they are important in understanding a number of basic theoretical issues. He believed, for example, that "it may be more fruitful to consider not so much the merits of this or that kind of retirement setting, but the pattern of social interaction within these various settings." Moreover, he believed that "similar settings may produce very different interaction patterns and that this is best understood not only with reference to the kind of setting, but also with respect to special characteristics of the individuals comprising it" (Jacobs, 1975, pp. 121-122).

A study of a public housing project for the elderly in Milwaukee produced results that somewhat paralleled those of the Merrill Court project. This study showed that age-homogeneous housing can have a positive influence on the mental and physical health of residents. Eunice Boyer (1980) found that residential homogeneity did not produce a ghetto of the rejected aged, but instead it allowed residents to overcome mobility limitations (thereby permitting greater social participation), gave them a greater opportunity for leadership, reduced isolation, allowed a more vigorous social life to develop, and gave greater opportunity for mutual aid and exchange of helpful services. Because they had less anxiety about need satisfaction and because they had increased social activity and opportunity to play useful community roles, the residents had a decidedly positive perception of their own physical and mental health and well-being.

Jennie Keith, a leader in the anthropological study of old age communities, has had a career-long interest in the concept of community and how it is manifested in a variety of settings involving the aged. Beginning with her doctoral dissertation, Keith has been concerned with the analysis of community formation and functioning. A comparison of eight widely varied retirement communities has resulted in her formulation of a set of characteristics common to all. They are (a) a common shared territory, which is jealously protected against encroachment by outsiders; (b) a strong sense of in-group/out-group differences; (c) shared norms and common goals; and (d) clearly defined roles and statuses, that is, a social system. Keith believes, however, that the real meaning of community rests not in models or prerequisite functions but in flesh-and-blood relationships. She writes:

> All of these old people have turned to each other for many kinds of social needs. They are friends, lovers and factional adversaries; they protect each other in illness and emergency; they laugh, dance and mourn together. They evaluate each other in terms of the life they share, rather than according to the status ladders of the outside world where they are guaranteed a place on the bottom rung. That outside world is seen as dangerous in many ways: physically, financially, socially and psychologically; the community of age-mates is a refuge from all of these threats. (Ross, 1977, p. 192)

Although anthropologists traditionally seek cross-cultural perspective in their study of human behavior, the bulk of age-homogeneous community study has been done in the United States. Cultural differences in communities comprising elderly people from a variety of class and ethnic backgrounds was the focus of a special issue of *Anthropological*

Quarterly in 1979. The included studies described styles of community participation among Cubans, blacks, Sephardim, and whites and attempted to identify factors that promote or obstruct community formation among old people. Researchers touched on such aspects of group behavior as the affective (we-feeling) and the structural (social interaction and shared norms), and an analysis of boundary (relationship of the new community to the surrounding society) (Keith, 1979).

Keith's study of Les Floralies, a retirement community located in a Paris suburb, broadened our understanding of age-homogeneous residential settings with a cross-cultural example. This study focused on community formation and maintenance in a French working-class retirement home and then compared it with what the "west end of Boston, a trailer park in northern California, and a band of Pygmies in the Congo have in common" (Ross, 1977, pp. 4-5).

Les Floralies is the cornerstone of Keith's study of community, although she goes on to compare it with a variety of retirement home settings in the United States in an attempt to understand such important gerontological issues as these: Under what conditions does "community" develop in a residence for old people? What is the relationship between patterns of social life inside and those of the wider society outside? How do people learn to participate in this new kind of community? How does this community made up exclusively of old people differ from more heterogeneous ones?

Keith's study reveals that community creation among the aged is not materially different than community creation among any other group of people, but perhaps studies of the aged reveal important factors that are taken for granted or overlooked in other groups. Keith observes:

> Friendship, love, conflict, power, laughter at "in" jokes, support in the face of common fears and sorrows, and roles to structure time and action are the stuff of everyday social life, so necessary that most of us take them profoundly for granted. To the old, they often become both scarce and precious. By preserving these possibilities for each other, older people join in a kind of communal conspiracy to continue living like human beings. (Ross, 1977, p. 198)

Thus Keith concludes that common age can become a context for community; social interaction appears to be greater in age-homogeneous groups, and this increased contact between age-mates means that morale is usually higher.

As the size of the aging population has increased, age-based residential settings have proliferated, and with this increase the types of communities have become considerably varied as well. Retirement migration has even resulted in communities of retired Americans in foreign countries. Stokes (1990) has described such a community in Mexico, called Lakeside by its residents. The "we-feeling" in this community comes from their identity as Americans in this foreign setting; age and socioeconomic status are less important. They have developed strategies for interacting with the host culture that facilitate meeting their needs while retaining the "social border" between the two groups. The Lakesiders have adopted some patterns of the Mexican community such as "timing of meals, visiting, and modified celebrations of sacred and secular rituals" (Stokes, 1990, p. 178), but the lifestyle is predominantly American. Few Lakesiders speak Spanish and all maintain numerous links with the United States. Philanthropic endeavors, focused on the children of the Mexican community, are important to Lakesiders. Although they have no real power in Mexico, some of the American retirees have been accorded the prestigious role of patrón.

Dorothy Counts and David Counts's (1992) research on RVers, retirees who live in recreational vehicles, provides an interesting example of a new type of community. While we might be tempted to assume that this would be too transient a lifestyle to have any of the characteristics associated with "community," Counts and Counts argue otherwise:

> Although retired RVers do not share a common territory or a common history, they have developed strategies that allow them to establish instant community. These strategies include the ways that they use space to define a sense of "we-ness" and the insistence on reciprocity.
>
> RVers expect to provide help and support to others in their RV community in times of crisis, to share food when there is surplus and to engage with each other in ways that assure security of person and property. Reciprocity demonstrates the equality of those who share and expresses the principle, "We're all the same here." (p. 155)

Their study of American and Canadian RVers in California and Arizona revealed that while there are variant patterns of the RV life-

Escapee RV Club members greeting new arrivals at an RV park in Arizona—a daily ritual designed to reinforce their position that all members are part of an "extended family." (Photo courtesy of David Counts and Dorothy Counts.)

style—part-timers or full-timers, degree of mobility, or types of parks—there are common cultural components of RVing. Temporarily becoming RVers themselves, the Counts compared "boondockers," who pay minimal or no fees to park on public land where no amenities are provided, with RVers who live in private resort parks. The two groups differ primarily in their preferences for these different kinds of parking or camping facilities. Boondockers desired the space and lack of restrictions associated with their setting; private park RVers liked the security and comfort features of the more planned facilities.

There are variations in income level, in the cost of "rigs" (the RV), and the nature of preretirement occupation among both boondockers and private park RVers. The similarities, however, are numerous. The common characteristics include shared values, especially about the qualities of the RV lifestyle, and "a sense of community" and valued friendships, which in some instances seem to be more meaningful than what they experienced in their preretirement settings.

This study found that "community happens" among RVers in part because of balanced reciprocity. Being retired and involved in a mobile lifestyle holds the potential for any number of difficulties—the typical problems faced by aging people with the addition of those associated with spending part of the year or more moving about the country. These latter concerns include "difficulty getting access to funds; illness far from one's own physician; mechanical breakdown; the fact that they spend much of their time among strangers" (Counts & Counts, 1992, pp. 164-165). As a consequence, RVers have become a kind of mutual aid society for each other both on the road and in the parks. One large organization, the Good Sam Club, developed in response to this need. Reciprocity is also involved in the rituals of arriving, parking, and leaving a park, during which personal information is exchanged between new arrivals and current residents. Food sharing is very important and occurs on various occasions. Participation in such activities builds trust and contributes to the sense of community.

RVers represent a unique type of retirement community, one that contributes much to our understanding of the concept of community. Counts and Counts (1992) summarize:

> Because they share no history with their RV neighbours, there is no one to fill the status of "friend" or "family," but the ideal content of these forms is shared knowledge. Therefore, when a newcomer pulls in, the strangers who are also neighbours immediately begin to perform the roles of friend and family by sharing substance and labor. They help the newcomer set up, bring food, give advice and exchange information and personal history. This sharing and exchange allows RVers, who do not have a common past, to recreate the structure of history from one park to another and to embed themselves in a familiar social structure given substance. (p. 179)

Another recent phenomenon described by Hunt (1988) is what he labels the Naturally Occurring Retirement Community (NORC). The NORC is found in an apartment complex, for example, not planned for a special population but one that has become attractive to older persons, often due to accessibility to services and prior friendship with other residents. They are not age homogeneous but are predominantly occupied by older persons. Most of the data available on NORCs to date seem to be limited to demographic characteristics, but such settings hold potential for future research on community formation.

Retirement Communities as Age-Graded Phenomena

Retirement communities, we have noted, are often called age homogeneous, although they may include people who range in age from 60 to 100 years. *Age homogeneous* is an adjectival phrase that could better be used to describe the elderly in some non-Western cultures, because many such societies have what is known as an age-grade or age-set system.

While anthropologists have long been interested in age-graded societies, only recently have anthropological perspectives focused on age stratification in our own society. Of particular note is the work of Asmarom Legesse (1979), who looks at the American retirement community as a kind of age grade and compares its social structure with that found in African societies.

Although African age grades and retirement communities differ in many ways, they have a number of common features. First, Legesse (1979) points out that a process of resocialization is inevitable as an age group enters each new age status, and he maintains that this is clearly observable in American elderly as they become assimilated into retirement communities. He writes: "The intolerance toward noisy children, the heightened intolerance toward authority figures, the elimination of pre-retirement status distinctions or symbols, and the establishment of egalitarian peer relationships are all examples of behavior changes" (Legesse, 1979, p. 63).

Second, Legesse suggests that initiation rituals that are frequently found in non-Western age-graded societies have a parallel in American retirement residences in

> the seductive advertising, the encounter with the manager, the screening procedures, admission into the community, the purchase of a lot, the taboos attendant on membership. . . . All these steps strike one as fairly elaborate role induction procedures and are perhaps the modern functional equivalents of rites of transition. (p. 63)

Several years ago, S. N. Eisenstadt (1956) postulated that "age-homogeneous groups tend to arise in those societies in which the allocation of roles, facilities and rewards is not based on membership in kinship units and criteria" (p. 54). Legesse wonders if, according to this idea, the strength of ties within the retirement community and the strength of ties with people outside the community are related. Cross-cultural data cast doubt on the Eisenstadt hypothesis, however, and data from other gerontological studies show that "the more friends an individual has among the elderly, the more likely he or she is to maintain family ties outside the community" (Legesse, 1979, p. 63).

Legesse also contends that age-set systems universally seem to be marked by egalitarianism in their organization and values, but that the relationship between age sets is that of a pecking order. Within the age set, peers support one another but tend to be intolerant of outside authority figures. Similarly, our age-homogeneous retirement communities "lack in internal hierarchical organization and are extremely intolerant of bosses of any kind . . . who supervise the communities. Even the informal governments that emerge in retirement communities are fairly broad based and democratically recruited" (Legesse, 1979, p. 65).

Another similarity between age sets and age-homogeneous communities is that members of both behave like novices when entering a new phase of the life cycle. Legesse (1979) writes of our age-homogeneous group residents:

> They behave like novices who are not entirely sure as to how to form the communities and what rules should govern their new lives. They are supervised in this process not by their elders but by a younger group of men and women who hold positions of authority because of their expertise. (p. 66)

This reversal of what is normally found in age-graded societies the world over—elders being initiated by younger people—is unnatural at least in age-grade terms and may be responsible for many of the problems encountered by residents and administrators alike.

Legesse's comparison of age grades and retirement communities also calls attention to the subject of group competition. The retirement community, on the one hand, exists within a pluralistic society and therefore may include a variety of racial and ethnic representatives. Data concerning age-grade societies, on the other hand, reveal that they have much less sociocultural diversity and therefore little or no deviance that can threaten the structure. One wonders if American ethnic variations can be successfully reconciled or if the normal age-grade tendency toward forcing members into a narrow mold will prevail, perhaps to the destruction of the group. Although these questions pique our academic interest, comparisons of retirement communities with age-grade systems may also prove to be a fruitful approach to understanding the dynamics of age-homogeneous living. Regardless of where we look in the world, all societies tend to have a number of common organization and transition problems. Unlike families, both age grades and retirement communities are transitory and must draw on a different method of achieving unity and cooperation. Age-grade analysis is a good example of how the findings of anthropologists in non-Western societies can be brought to bear in promoting a clearer understanding of the nature and functioning of our own social institutions.

Non-Western Homes for the Aged

Descriptions of retirement residences in other cultures are relatively scarce in the anthropological literature. To a certain extent, this is because the traditional pattern among nonliterate peoples has been that the elderly were invariably cared for in the home by the family. One of the earliest surveys, "Trends in Old Age Homes and Housing for the Aged in Various Parts of the World" (Abrams, 1951), is a New York legislative report on aging. This study by Albert Abrams (1951) of 68 countries revealed that "the old age home is common in most of the western world" but "is uncommon or completely unknown in some near Eastern and small Central American countries" (p. 268).

Examples of societies where old age homes were completely unknown in 1951 included Iran, Lebanon, Pakistan, Thailand, Liberia, Ethiopia, Nicaragua, and Costa Rica. Generally he found a positive correlation throughout the world between high industrialization and urbanization and the existence of old age homes. On the other hand, he found an inverse relationship between cultures stressing family responsibility and the existence of homes for the aged. There were, however, a few notable exceptions to this. Cultures that stress family responsibility but are in the process of changing from an agricultural-based to an industry-based economy are beginning to find a need for old age homes. Such has been the case in Japan, Korea, Burma, Ceylon, China, Saudi Arabia, and Mexico. Some countries where life expectancy was low had relatively little need for old age residences because only a small percentage achieved elderly status.

Abrams also discovered that relatively long life spans and a scarcity of inexpensive domestic help were consistently associated with the existence of homes for the elderly in non-Western cultures. Apparently, inexpensive and readily available domestic help takes some of the strain off the family, who can hire people to help them meet their obligations to elders.

Gerontologists generally believe that, as societies become more modern, responsibility for the aged shifts from the family or clan to the society as a whole, with specific responsibility being placed on either the local or the national government. While this is generally true, many of the homes for the aged in developing, non-Western countries are church, industry, or philanthropic group supported. If the homes are supported by national or local governments, they are financed through general taxation or lotteries.

The examples of non-Western homes for the aged discussed below are residential, not nursing, homes, although one occasionally finds a facility that also takes people in need of nursing care. We find considerable variation in type of accommodations, management, services provided, activities, and personal freedom in non-Western age-segregated residences. Conditions that typically lead to residence in these homes are poverty, being childless, problems in intergenerational relationships, and social change (Delaney, 1981; Holmes & Holmes, 1987; Ikels, 1975, 1983; Nyanguru, 1987; Rhoads & Holmes, 1981). The nature of relationships between residents is also variable and may be influenced not only by the social environment but sometimes by the reasons people came to live there.

Hong Kong

Ikels (1983) describes two kinds of housing for the elderly in Hong Kong. Wah Hong Hostel was the first government-sponsored residential facility for old people. It consists of apartmentlike units, each of which houses four people who are responsible for housekeeping and cooking for their unit. Social events are scheduled by the hostel and occasional entertainment provided by other organizations. Residents may go out into the surrounding community for shopping or other activities, but do face some limitations on overnight or longer visits away from the hostel.

In contrast to the hostels, homes for the aged in Hong Kong tend to be religious-sponsored facilities. The elderly residents are expected to be "reasonably healthy, mobile, and relatively independent in daily living activities" (Ikels, 1983, p. 120). In these homes there is more communal sharing of facilities; meals are served in a dining room and sleeping quarters may be quite crowded. Some Buddhist homes are very restrictive, requiring residents to eat a vegetarian diet and pray regularly. Those who are not Buddhists but who are placed in such a home are unhappy with this arrangement (Ikels, 1975).

While some residents of these homes or hostels for the aged in Hong Kong consider themselves fortunate to have a place to live, others are "humiliated" about their circumstances. Ikels (1975) indicates that there were a few who even "ceased writing letters to relatives in China because they did not want them to know of their situation—it was better to be presumed dead" (p. 234). Such feelings may inhibit formation of friendships in these homes.

Africa

In comparing two homes for the aged in Zimbabwe, Nyanguru (1987) reveals some significant factors related to planning residential environments for the aged. He indicates that the changing societal conditions in Zimbabwe have resulted in the impoverishment of many of the elderly, leading to a need for special housing facilities for this population. Two facilities are described that are designed to provide "meals, laundry service and general care."

Kudzai Old People's Home, operated by a church group, has better accommodations for housing and health care. Here they have indoor sanitary facilities, a dining room, and rooms furnished with beds (usually two residents per room). Services are provided by a trained staff, including nurses. It is a restrictive environment, however, with the staff clearly in control of activities, even visits away from the home. There is no apparent input from residents. Nyanguru (1987) "observed fewer active friendships at Kudzai. Rather, individuals appear to be 'alone together' " (p. 351).

Dambudzo Old People's Cooperative is situated on farmland. It houses fewer residents and offers very basic facilities and much more limited health care than at Kudzai. Residents live about five to a room, which have mattresses, but no beds; an inadequate supply of serving ware results in meals eaten in shifts. There is only one staff person employed; residents do their own housekeeping and cooking and even produce some of their food. "A residential committee sets policy for the cooperative and rules on admissions and expulsions" (Nyanguru, 1987, p. 350). They are free to leave for visits and most do so on weekends.

In interviews with most of the residents of both homes (51 out of 56 at Kudzai and 33 out of 34 at Dambudzo), it was determined that in spite of their more meager physical facilities, 91% of the Dambudzo residents were content to live there; at Kudzai, on the other hand, 76% were dissatisfied. Nyanguru (1987) believes that the social environment is crucial in homes for the aged; provision of first-class facilities is not enough. What is most important is "continuity in the conditions of life, opportunities for self-help, participation in the day to day running of the home and democratic decision-making, all of which are needed to enhance the individual's sense of dignity and self-worth" (p. 356).

Japan

Filial support of parents has long been the norm in Japan and strong interpersonal relations have been almost solely confined to the family group, but industrialization, modernization, and urbanization have created conditions that threaten traditional patterns of intergenerational support. Although 50% of children have parents living in their home at the present time, this percentage has been declining about 1½% per year, and most children who have live-in parents do not expect their own offspring to take them in. Add to this the rapidly swelling population of elderly and one would expect that there would have to be a movement toward development of housing for independent living for Japan's elderly. While the idea is repugnant to most, the more realistic have begun to support construction of retirement communities such as Fuji-no-Sato. This facility is located in a resort-type setting within the national park that includes Mt. Fuji. Tokyo is two hours away by high-speed express train. Established in 1979, it was among the first alternative independent living communities built in Japan to serve the elderly. The facility consists of 10 two-story residential buildings with studio, one- and two-bedroom apartments (all with cooking facilities), a community center that houses activity rooms, hot spring baths for men and women, a dining hall for those who prefer not to cook, a small shop for sundries, and a large meeting room. There is also an administrative building that houses a clinic, and there is a nearby nursing home that is supposed to care for Fuji-no-Sato residents when they reach the point when they can no longer care for themselves.

Fuji-no-Sato is one of four retirement communities run by a private enterprise corporation. They charge a reasonable entrance fee and monthly fees commensurate with a middle-income worker's retirement income. The community has 372 residents occupying 288 residential units. Residents must be 60 years old or older, and the average age is approximately 70. It is a young-old population, well educated, and largely with business executive, managerial, or professional backgrounds. They are described as upper middle class.

Kinoshita and Kiefer (1992) write:

> The age and class homogeneity of Fuji-no-Sato makes it a more or less egalitarian community and as such very unusual for Japan, where interpersonal relations are usually vertically organized. Like most other Japanese, the residents of this community have not been socialized to cultivate the unstructured, voluntary social relationships one usually finds in this kind of peer group-oriented setting. (p. 154)

Sociability at Fuji-no-Sato has its own unique flavor with informal activities consisting primarily of hobby groups (chess, golf, choral singing, artwork), Christian groups (Bible study, prayer meetings, and hymn singing), volunteer groups (visiting nursing home residents and folding and sorting their laundry), and, most important of all, gardening (flowers and trees but not vegetables).

In spite of the activities that bring people together, Fuji-no-Sato is somewhat lacking in characteristics normally associated with community—interpersonal interaction, group consciousness, shared values, and common goals. Kinoshita and Kiefer (1992) describe the lack of informal interaction of residents and report:

Many spontaneously commented that they didn't want deep or close relations with their neighbors. One typical way of justifying their lack of close friendships was to say, "My relations with other people here are strictly *tatemae*" [that is, according to cultural norms rather than private feelings]. (p. 173)

Having had very little previous experience developing close and intimate relations with peers, the residents of Fuji-no-Sato appeared to be cautiously attempting to establish guidelines for appropriate behavior. A few key norms regulating behavior have emerged. Three that best illustrate patterns of shared behavior are cited by Kinoshita and Kiefer (1992) as (a) "Don't cause trouble to others," (b) "Exchange Respect," and (c) "Dress to Impress."

The first relates to respecting the independence of other residents and not imposing upon their comfort or freedom. "Exchange Respect" refers to the expectation that residents greet one another formally at each and every encounter, thus symbolically verifying community affiliation. Greeting is described "as especially important for older people in Japan, and it generally signifies that the greeter recognizes the identity of the other. Strangers are rarely greeted in casual situations" (Kinoshita & Kiefer, 1992, p. 180). "Dress to Impress" is described as involving the requirement that "personal preference in clothes and grooming is generally subordinated to a strong set of norms that regulate one's impression on others" (p. 184). This norm allowed residents to be less conscious of age-appropriate clothes, and as a result they did not "look much like typical Japanese elderly" (p. 184).

Perhaps the greatest threat to community at Fuji-no-Sato is gossip, an evil that is described as resulting from

(1) the absence of privacy, leading to their inability to control their public image, (2) the lack of a system of social control, whereby gossips and rumor mongers could be called into account, and (3) the lack of a system of information control, whereby false public belief could be corrected. (p. 186)

Kinoshita and Kiefer's (1992) study of Fuji-no-Sato is the first ethnographic description of a retirement community in Japan. It is a description of an institution and its residents attempting to deal with unfamiliar roles and hierarchical relationships and with methods of need satisfaction without precedent in their cultural system. They are described as "the explorers of the new social frontier" (p. 208) and as such they may well discover new formulas for creating and maintaining community in a rapidly changing world.

Social Networks

Anthropologists can no longer expect the communities they study to have clearly defined boundaries, particularly if they are working in their own society. When research sites were mainly in preindustrial societies, they observed people who lived together in a limited area (usually a village) and who interacted in daily face-to-face relationships. Many communities composed of the aged are still like this, but in areas where old people do not live in special segregated housing, their communities are not always clearly defined. Because of this, anthropologists have had to resort to analysis of social networks to identify communities, because sometimes viable communities exist only as chains of social and economic linkages, or cliques, of interacting individuals. According to Barnes (1972): "The study of networks calls for information about a plurality of persons who are in contact with one another, and consequently the traditional methods of selecting respondents individually are inadequate" (p. 23).

Network analysis has been used effectively by Sokolovsky and Cohen (1978, 1987) and Eckert (1983) in analyzing degrees of isolation of inner-city elderly, particularly those living in single room occupancy (SRO) hotels. Studies of elderly living in such environments have stressed their isolation, anonymity, normlessness, and lack of communication resources. Sokolovsky and Cohen (1978) contend that this perception is incorrect and is "distorted by a tendency to study social linkages within the context of formal institutional structures rather than viewing the social matrix as culturally significant in itself" (p. 324). Their work in New York, as well as research on SROs in San Diego (Eckert, 1980; Erickson & Eckert, 1977) (also using network analysis), reveals that considerable social interaction takes place within and outside SRO hotels. One study (Cantor, 1975) reports that 80% of the hotel residents sit and talk with neighbors in front of the building or in nearby parks, and two thirds of them have a visiting relationship with neighbors. Some investigators have found a real sense of community within these inner-city hotels, although personal networks may be temporary. Extensive personal networks operate during the day, but there is a drastic curtailment of interpersonal contact at night. This is, of course, due to fear of street crimes and assaults. This threat has resulted in an increase of neurotic symptoms associated with the night in both SRO hotel and inner-city tenement dwellers.

SRO residents are often called loners, but Sokolovsky and Cohen believe that such designations do not accurately describe SRO behavior, because many of these "loners" have larger than average personal networks. *Loner* does, however, describe a worldview that appears to have adaptive utility in a difficult inner-city milieu.

Van Willigen (1989) found network analysis useful in studying the social interactional channels and mutual aid configurations of the elderly in a rural area in Kentucky. The method was also used by Linda Cool (1980) to identify and analyze a community of elderly Corsican migrants living in Paris. She found a very effective structure of kinship and friendship bonds being used to combat feelings of loneliness and homesickness and to solve a variety of personal problems. Cool (1980) writes:

All but a few elderly Niolans can find the assistance they need in special situations—someone to talk to about difficult problems and someone on whom they can rely in an emergency. Sixty-nine of the 74 sample members report that they have a confidante, either relative or friend. All but one of the elderly Niolans feel they have someone to call on in case of an emergency. Seventy individuals know of people on whom they could rely if they were sick, even for an extended period of time. (p. 158)

Network analysis also has its uses in discovering channels of interaction and interdependence within an age-homogeneous community. Jonas and Wellin (1980) found the method valuable in studying ways in which problems of transportation, health care, and household maintenance were solved by elderly living in a public housing project in Milwaukee. Although the housing unit itself represented a kind of community, the investigators were particularly concerned with who does what for whom, why, and how often. In discovering this kind of data, Jonas and Wellin learned how social and mutual aid networks develop and function and to what extent they serve as effective ways to meet old people's needs. They found that peer responsibility for long-term support of disabled friends greatly relieved pressures on relatives, deferred institutionalization, and reduced demands on public assistance programs. Not only did reciprocal aid by peers meet physical needs, it also permitted the aged a degree of independence because it allowed them to continue living in their own apartments and gave them a measure of self-esteem because they could contribute to the needs of others.

A great deal of the information available about support networks for the aged relates to kin-based support systems, especially in ethnic populations in the United States. We will consider this topic in that context in Chapter 7.

SUMMARY

Anthropologists have always been comfortable studying small homogeneous communities (particularly in non-Western societies); it is not surprising therefore that they have been partial to research on retirement residences and communities. In the many studies that have been undertaken, researchers' interests have centered on such questions as (a) what community is, (b) under what conditions does community develop, (c) how do people learn to relate to the age-homogeneous situation, (d) what is the quality of life in a variety of institutional settings, and (e) the more basic question of whether elders should live in a community of their age peers or in the society at large. The study of community in complex urban America has, however, presented researchers with methodological problems, and in many cases they have been forced to turn to network analysis to locate "community" and study its patterns of interaction and interdependence.

Retirement communities have often been termed *age-homogeneous* groupings, and some theorists have compared them with age-graded societies in other parts of the world (primarily Africa). Actually, age-graded societies and age-homogeneous communities have much in common in regard to attitudes and interaction patterns of members. In spite of these behavior similarities, the retirement home is a uniquely

Western phenomenon. A few nursing homes and senior citizen residences have been established in non-Western locales such as Zimbabwe (Kudzai and Dambudzo), Hong Kong, and Japan (Fuji-no-Sato), which are experiencing the disorganizing influences of modernization, but some of these establishments have been initiated by people from outside the culture, such as missionaries or religious orders. Most developing countries still vehemently insist that the family or clan can take care of its own elderly.

6

🔲 Varieties of Aging Experience

To understand fully the rationale for the ways a society copes with the problems of aging and the aged, we must approach that society holistically—in terms of the physical environment, the economic or subsistence patterns that support it, the social structure that binds its citizens together, and the traditional values and procedures that have evolved throughout its cultural history.

This chapter presents three such analyses. These case studies in human aging present information on three very different societies in three very different physical environments with diverse subsistence patterns and distinctive traditions regarding the proper roles and status of old people.

The first group, the Eskimos of North America, represent a particular kind of hunting society—one located in a very rigorous climate where there are great environmental limitations in regard to natural resources and the choice of ways of getting a living. These people are nomadic and this imposes hardships, particularly on the aged. But life is difficult for everyone in this society, and each and every family member is expected to contribute his or her share of effort and cooperation to the common welfare. The question of what happens when people are too old to make these contributions is an important consideration in this analysis.

The second society—the Samoan Islanders of the South Pacific—is one with a simple agricultural economy. These people live in sedentary seaside villages where nutritional requirements can be met with a minimum of physical exertion and where food sharing practices ensure the well-being of children, the handicapped, and the aged. A benign climate guarantees a reasonably comfortable and secure old age, and traditional societal values and extended family solicitude make old age a rather pleasant time of life.

The third society—the United States—is industrial, capitalistic, technologically complex, and essentially urban. It is a culture with great wealth and intellectual capacity, but it is an individualistic, youth-oriented society and as such is philosophically unable to honor its elders. The value system places great emphasis on independence, self-reliance, and freedom of choice, and the society confers status on the basis of production and achievement. Although this society has great sedentary cities, its citizens are highly nomadic, moving from city to city. Families are small and self-centered; there is neither room nor desire for extended family organization. Although this industrial society is the most capable economically of supporting the elderly, the old of this society are no doubt the most anxious and apprehensive of any of the three.

Growing Old in a Hunting Society: Eskimos

The Eskimo people occupy one of the largest culture areas in the western hemisphere. They share a common language and physical type and essentially a common culture within an arctic region stretching some 3,000 miles east and west and extending north and south from 60° to 72° north latitude. The word *Eskimo* was not found originally in the vocabularies of any of these people but is instead an Algonquian word meaning *raw meat eater*. Anthropologically, this culture area is traditionally subdivided into a western and a central-eastern zone. The people of the western portion live in northwest Canada and Alaska, and the central-eastern people inhabit an area from Mackenzie Bay (Canada) to Greenland. The Eskimo population today numbers approximately 35,000 to 40,000—about half their precontact total. White men's diseases (measles, influenza, and tuberculosis) have seriously reduced their numbers.

The region the Eskimos occupy is essentially a harsh environment, with long winters and temperatures reaching as low as –65°F and short, mosquito-plagued summers. The treeless landscape, called *tundra*, supports a minimum of plant and animal life, and this tends to impose a cultural homogeneity throughout the entire culture area.

The major subsistence activities in most areas are sea-mammal hunting (mostly seals) in the winter, when the people camp near the sea, and caribou hunting in the summer, when they move inland. Alaskan Eskimos engage in whaling operations in spring and summer. Common traditional weapons include the harpoon and bow and arrow, with the rifle being added after contact by white traders.

Although some Eskimos (particularly in the east) retain fairly traditional subsistence activities, western Eskimos today are often engaged in trapping-trading operations, commercial fishing, and wage employment. Most Eskimos live in relatively permanent settlements in winter and then set up temporary hunting and fishing camps during the summer. Skin tents were traditional with all Eskimos during summer months but in winter Alaskan Eskimos lived in earth-covered homes, and eastern groups lived in igloos. Much of this traditional housing has disappeared in modern times. James VanStone (1962) described the settlement at Point Hope, Alaska (population 265), as follows:

> The village consists of some fifty houses, all of which are of frame construction although there are a few that closely approximate old, semisubterranean type. . . . Many of the frame houses have a covering of sod around them so that they give the appearance of old-style houses. (p. 11)

The village also contains two schools, an Episcopal church, a store, and a National Guard drill hall.

Certain objects of traditional material culture—kayaks, women's knives, bow drills, snow goggles, and dog sleds (fan hitch in the east and tandem hitch in Alaska)—are pan-Eskimo features. Men are dominant in subsistence activities, but women are essential to the household routine, because they dress hides, make clothes, and prepare the food. It would be difficult for a man to survive on a hunting trip without a woman supporting his activities. Women were often loaned to single hunters who were about to embark on a hunting trip.

The Eskimo family is typically monogamous, but wife hospitality and wife lending are known. The immediate family is the significant social unit, and kinship, emphasizing ties to both male and female lines, is similar to that found in the modern American family. Formal political organization until very recently (when elected village councils have appeared) was nonexistent, and group activities involving leadership were confined to such events as whaling expeditions or communal seal hunts.

Eskimos believe that all animate and inanimate objects have souls, and they also believe in an impersonal supernatural force known as *sila* that somewhat resembles the *manitou* concept of American Indians or the *mana* concept of Pacific Islanders. Mythology is not elaborate and centers on tales of Sedna, the goddess of whales, seals, walrus, and all that lives in the sea. Shamans (part-time religious practitioners) are prominent, but the ritualistic ceremonies involving groups of people consist of yearly gatherings in which masked men impersonate the gods.

Although contact with the white people has brought many modernizing influences, we will turn to early accounts of the traditional system in investigating the role and status of the elderly in Eskimo culture.

Among the Eskimo, the aged were accorded great respect. They were treated with considerable deference and their words were regarded as final. Murdock (1887-1888) reports that, among the Eskimo of Point Barrow, "respect for the opinion of the elders is so great that the people may be said to be practically under what is called 'simple elder rule' " (p. 427). Hughes (1960) records that among the St. Lawrence Island people informants maintained: "Oldest is boss for everything. Eskimos always ask first our oldest one, when we do something" (p. 265). Van-Stone (1962) observes that

> the transition to old age is not clear-cut. Parents whose children are grown, married, and have moved away from home are not necessarily old by Point Hope standards. Eskimo men seem to age early in terms of appearance, but remain active until relatively advanced years. (p. 93)

Guemple (1974) found among the Qiqiktamiut Eskimos in Hudson Bay that physical appearance was less important in determining old age than physical capability. He states:

When a man cannot hunt in mid-winter, when the work is most rigorous, and when the need for food is most pressing, then he will be called "old" by his fellows. Old age comes to a man suddenly; the transition can take place in a single year. . . . Because women's work is less demanding . . . the decreasing physical capability of a woman does not appear so obviously or so dramatically. (p. 205)

But physical capability is only part of the criteria for defining "old age." One is "old" in this society when one has grandchildren who have reached the time "when they begin to learn basic work skills in earnest, in other words by age 8 years" (Guemple, 1974, p. 204).

Within the Eskimo family the grandparent-grandchild relationship is one of extreme affection and support, with emphasis on mutual helpfulness and kindness. Eskimos believe that knowledge increases with age and teaching children is seen as an appropriate and valuable function of the aged. Instructing children in games, rituals, taboos, and other ancient lore is carried out by grandparents, who are considered repositories of songs, stories, and tribal history as well as monitors of proper behavior. The elderly are considered great storytellers, and stories are told for both education and entertainment. Rasmussen (1908) reports of the Polar Eskimo that almost every question was answered and every problem explained by a tale. His informants reported: "Our tales are men's experiences. . . . The experience of the older generations contains truth" (p. 97). Turner (1894) writes that Eskimos were extremely fond of these narrative sessions, and young people sat "with staring eyes and countenances which show their wondering interest in the narration" (pp. 260-261). Old people also function as "village newspapers," making it their business to know and tell all of the recent happenings.

Family members always consult their elderly members about choice of marriage partners, division of material wealth, and settlement of family disputes. Elders are directly involved in the naming of children because of their involvement with name-souls. After death the soul associated with the name of the deceased is believed to hover around waiting to be reincarnated in a newborn child. Old people are believed to have special knowledge of the spiritual world, and they inform the child's father if a particular name-soul is agreeable to be given to the new infant.

The elderly play an important role in educating children and even adults in economic skills. Old men are often consulted by their sons as

Eskimo elderly are always consulted on such issues as choice of marriage partner or division of material wealth as well as in the settlement of family disputes. (Photo courtesy of Lee Guemple; used by permission.)

to the proper time to go hunting, how to care for a boat or other equipment, and how to apportion goods or game. Burch (1975) relates that

> if some of these [elders] were wiser and more skillful than others, an ambitious young man might undertake to recruit these people to his own local group, or he might go to live with them. In return for food, shelter and protection, they could provide instruction and advice of a kind few of his same-generation kin could offer. (p. 219)

Among most Eskimo groups, elders are seldom idle. If men can no longer hunt, they fish or help snare birds. Ray (1885) writes that among the Point Barrow people old men made seal spears and nets and old women worked on clothing, boats, and the dressing of skins. Elderly and feeble Labrador Eskimo women plaited straw hats and baskets and cared for the family clothes. Old men in this group had special medical skills and old women were in charge of childbirth and the rituals following, which were performed to safeguard the newborn. Concerning the Eskimos of northwest Alaska, Burch (1975) observes:

> Parents gradually gave over the heavier work to their sons and daughters as they began to age, busying themselves in the lighter activities of logistic support. Aging fathers tended to stay home and spend their days making and repairing tools, nets, and other equipment, while their sons hunted. Similarly, mothers increasingly limited themselves to watching over infant grandchildren for their daughters, and assisting them with lighter tasks, such as sewing. (pp. 138-139)

Elderly Eskimos are believed to have considerable magical or spiritual power. Among the special supernatural capacities supposed to be possessed by the elderly are (a) the ability to foretell the future, (b) the ability to change one's future just by willing it, (c) the ability to interpret dreams and receive magical formulas in dreams, (d) the ability to "talk up" winds that will drive the ice offshore, and (e) the ability to ward off evil spirits. The supernatural power of all old people is believed to be considerable, and it was held that neglect of or offenses against an old person could cripple or sicken one's children. According to Burch (1975), magical ability was not restricted to old people, but they were believed to have more of it than others. In northwest Alaska, magical songs, charms, and techniques are passed on from grandparent to grandchild and not from parent to offspring.

Old age is not only glorified in the folklore of most Eskimo groups, but many of the gods, heroes, and demons found in the tales are elderly. For example, the Polar Eskimos believe the goddess Nerivik is an old woman who lives beneath the water and will not let seal hunters succeed until the village shamans visit her and groom her matted hair. Another myth tells of an old man who was transfigured into a luminous body and shot up into the sky, where he now exists as a bright star. Labrador Eskimos claim that an extremely old woman lives beneath the sea and controls the tides and the fortunes of fishermen. Another aged goddess lives inland and controls the caribou.

Although not always, the shamans are frequently elderly. Rasmussen (1908) describes the influence they exerted over the community:

> We believe our *angakut,* our magicians, . . . because we wish to live long, and because we do not wish to expose ourselves to the danger of famine and starvation. . . . If we do not follow their advice we shall fall ill and die. (p. 16)

The special functions shamans perform include drawing out dangerous foreign matter from the body and contacting the spirit world to counteract bad luck in hunting or to determine the cause of illness or barrenness. Public performances often include miraculous feats, such as drawing blood through a self-inflicted knife wound but then later revealing the lack of a wound. Spirits often possess the shaman and bring on hysterical behavior greatly resembling an epileptic seizure. The spirits often speak through the religious practitioner during these trance states.

Given the harshness of the arctic environment, the lot of the aged might be assumed to be a relatively difficult one. In some respects this is true, but Eskimo societies appear to be structured to provide as much support for the elderly as their precarious lifestyle would allow. As is often the case among hunting peoples, the Eskimo have developed food sharing practices that ensure that widows, orphans, and the elderly are provided for. In some cases the elderly men are in charge of food distribution, and therefore they can make sure that young and old all receive adequate commissary. Graburn (1969) reports that in 1959 when

> one band returned from a hunt near Charles Island with thirty-six large bearded seals some of the younger members did not want to share these with the other more than two-hundred Sallumiut, but the will of the older men prevailed and every household received considerable amounts of meat. (p. 176)

In traditional culture, the honor of being the successful hunter was only slightly greater than that associated with the generosity involved in sharing the kill. Graburn (1969) records that after a successful hunt there were often feasts where everyone was invited and "the male host basked in the prestige of being able to provide for so many *tujurngminat*, 'guests, invited strangers' " (p. 72). Another custom required men to send special food gifts at the end of their first successful hunt of the season to the elderly women who acted as midwives.

One method that ensures the elderly ample food is to make certain kinds of food taboo for everyone except those who cannot hunt for themselves. Polar Eskimos reserve eggs, entrails, hearts, lungs, livers, and certain small animals and birds (hares and ptarmigans) for old men who in turn are permitted to share with women who have given birth to more than five children. Aged women among the Labrador Eskimos are guaranteed food for caring for men's boots. In spite of the fact that Eskimo societies are structured to be supportive, Graburn (1969) maintains that if the fall hunting had been poor, resulting in a great shortage of food during the winter, the patterns of food sharing often broke down.

A great deal has been said about the custom of gerontocide among Eskimo peoples, but it should be noted that not all groups resorted to such extreme measures. VanStone (1962) reports that exposing the aged to die was never practiced at Point Hope, Alaska, and Burch (1975) writes of northwest Alaska:

> Aged parents were abandoned only under conditions of the most extreme hardships, and it was rare even then. . . . Abandonment occurred in situations in which old people had to be sacrificed or everyone would have starved to death. In the exceptional case, the individuals did abandon their parents; they came to be regarded as deviants as a consequence, and were subsequently treated as outcasts. . . . Old people were not left behind at all; it was so that the younger, more active members of the family could travel more quickly to where food could be procured, and *then return*. (p. 149)

The situation seems to be somewhat different for central-eastern Eskimos. Graburn (1969) reports that "often the old people would ask to be left behind or even killed if they felt they were useless, for those who died a violent death were thought to go to the highest of the Eskimos' 'three heavens' " (p. 73). In paradise they would spend their time, with the spirits who died in the same way, playing football with a walrus head.

Most authorities agree that Eskimos show little concern for death, and Freuchen (1961) writes: "Fear of death is unknown to them, they know only love of life" (p. 145). There no doubt are more cases of suicide among the aged than there are of abandonment. This might occur, according to Freuchen (1961), with

> old men and women who are burdened with the memories of their youth, and who can no longer meet the demands of their own reputation. . . . When an old man sees the young men go out hunting and cannot himself go along, he is sorry. When he has to ask other people for skins for his clothing, when he cannot ever again be the one to invite the neighbors to eat his game, life is of no value to him. Rheumatism and other ills may plague him, and he wants to die. (p. 145)

Freuchen describes numerous cases of which he had personal knowledge, maintaining that in some tribes an eldest son or a favorite daughter was asked to put a skin rope around the elder's neck and hoist him to his death. This was supposed to be done at the height of a party or feast when everyone (including the old person) was in high spirits. All the guests were supposed to assist in the hanging by pulling on the rope, for it was a great honor to be asked to help end the suffering of an old one who wanted the comfort and peace of the Eskimo hereafter. Old women, it is said, sometimes preferred to be stabbed in the heart with a dagger by a son or daughter. Particularly revealing of the attitude toward deliberately ending one's life is the following account by Freuchen (1961):

> In the Hudson Bay area, I once arrived at a village at Wager Inlet in the midst of great commotion. Just before my arrival, an old man called Oomilialik had been found hanging from the ceiling of an igloo. He had climbed up on top of the snowhouse, drilled a hole in the roof, and lowered a rope down to serve his purpose. Fortunately, just after he had hanged himself, the eldest of his four sons returned home from the hunt and came in in time to cut him down. The old man was furious.
>
> All four sons assured me and their father that they did not consider him a nuisance or burden at all. They had plenty of meat and good game, and they wanted to see his face among them for a long time yet and take advantage of his renowned experience. . . .

The old man said that he had been the greatest caribou hunter ever known, and now his knees were too weak to walk across the hills. So life had no more to offer him. Besides, he had no more tobacco, and without that he found it too hard to sit at home instead of accompanying his sons out hunting.

The next year I passed by Wager Inlet again, and I went to visit Oomilialik's house. I found only his sons at home, and I asked them how their father was. They answered me that he was all right, doing well, because he was now dead. He had hanged himself again, and this time with greater success. (pp. 153-154)

Cultural Change

With the coming of the Europeans and the trappings of their modern world, some things have improved for the Eskimo elderly but many things have worsened. On Holman Island in Arctic Canada, Condon (1987) tells us that

adults in the community who were born in snowhouses and who spent most of the first part of their lives out on the land now watch color televisions in the comfort of heated homes equipped with running water and electricity. The elderly, who have vivid memories of starvation and frostbite, now receive government pensions to ensure their welfare and comfort. (p. 5)

On the other hand, Graburn (1969) reports for the Hudson Bay area that the elderly men and women are losing their influence and decision-making function in community affairs. Councils of elderly that once directed civic activities are how being replaced by elected community organizations in which young men have a great deal of authority. The old patterns of community food sharing are giving way to a commercial attitude toward hunting.

At Point Hope the traditional functional definition of when old age begins (when men are too old to hunt) has been superseded by a chronological one (65—when old age assistance checks begin). Old age assistance and pension checks have, of course, provided a new source of value and recognition for the aged. Burch (1975) writes:

> After the advent of old age pensions, elderly Eskimos were able to make another major contribution to the welfare of the family. In the 1960s, for example, many a son obtained cash for ammunition and other items from the aged parents, supplying them with food in return. (p. 139)

This new source of status is, however, a poor substitute for the respect and admiration they once enjoyed. Education, once largely in the hands of the elderly, has since World War II been transferred more and more to the government-supported school. This has brought, among other things, significant changes in grandparent-grandchild relationships. Traditionally, grandchildren not only learned much of the culture from grandparents but also helped the aging relatives in many ways. Burch (1975) reveals that when a grandchild was

> five or six, it had begun to perform many chores for the grandparent, particularly if the latter was getting on in years or else was an invalid. Aged grandparents always had one grandchild more or less "in tow," following them around or playing in their immediate vicinity so as to be readily available should their assistance be required. This grandchild would help the grandparent check the net or snares, assist them over rough spots in the path, run errands for them or do innumerable other chores. (pp. 156-157)

In the Northwest Territories of Arctic Canada, the Inuit of Holman Island still find security and support for the elderly in the traditional practice of adoption. Adoption here as well as in a number of other Inuit groups is an informal affair involving verbal agreements between households. According to Condon (1987): "A large number of adoptions in the community are grandparental adoptions. . . . One such form . . . involves sending an older child, usually a young girl between nine and sixteen years of age, to live with and care for an elderly grandparent" (pp. 96-97).

In the villages of Wainwright and Unalakleet near the Bering Strait in northwest Alaska, Jorgensen (1990) found that the elderly not only were well cared for but they had found a role in promoting family welfare. He writes that grandparents

> are looked after by their children, grandchildren, nieces, nephews, grandnieces, and grandnephews. As spouses die, or as couples age,

more distant relatives and friends in the village join in looking after these people. Yet even with advancing age, most of the older people maintain considerable physical activity and continue to give from their end. . . . Their houses are always open, they have their adult children and grandchildren stay with them, they take their young children to raise, and they give financial help when they can manage. (p. 245)

In many villages today, however, a language barrier has developed between the old (who speak Eskimo) and grandchildren (who are taught and urged to speak English in school). The result is very little intergenerational communication or learning. However, much of the knowledge the old people traditionally have imparted is now largely irrelevant anyway, and both grandparents and grandchildren know it.

The elderly have also lost other traditional functions. Store-bought goods have eliminated the need for old people to make such things as weapons or clothing, and maintaining new mechanical and electrical gadgets requires skills they have never acquired. The elderly at one time performed magical services and taught young people magic songs, formulas, and techniques, but the coming of Christianity has done much to destroy belief in or use of such phenomena. In the larger communities, curing activities and midwife duties have been taken over by trained medical personnel.

Life in a Simple Agricultural Society: Samoa

The islands of the Samoan archipelago lie in the southwest Pacific midway between Hawaii and New Zealand at 14° latitude and between 168° and 173° west longitude. Politically, its nine inhabited islands are divided into Western Samoa (an independent nation) and American Samoa (a territory of the United States), but culturally, racially, and linguistically, they are one. Of the 214,800 people who inhabit the archipelago, 90% are classified as full-blooded Polynesians. It is a young population. For example, the 1990 census reports that 44% of the American Samoan population is under 18; people 65 and over make up 3.4% (U.S. Bureau of the Census, 1993d).

The Samoan islands are located in the western part of the Polynesian culture area and share many traditional cultural traits with the Fiji and Tonga Island groups. Among them is a way of life that is based on simple slash-and-burn agriculture, supplemented by some deep-sea and reef fishing. Food plants consist of taro, breadfruit, coconuts, yams, bananas, papayas, and mangos. Domesticated animals are mainly chickens and pigs but a few horses and cattle have been raised in recent times. The land is rich and green, the climate warm and humid but pleasant, and, with the exception of hurricanes or other disasters, it is a land of plenty, requiring only a moderate expenditure of energy to maintain an adequate if not abundant subsistence.

The majority of Samoan communities, with the exception of port towns of Apia and Pago Pago, are seaside villages varying in population from 200 to 600 people. Villages consist of series of houses strung along a sandy beach (see Figure 6.1) with a mixture of traditional *fale* (beehive shaped thatch-roof houses) and European-style houses (resembling summer or beach cottages). Most villages have a school, a church (usually Congregational, formerly called London Missionary Society), and a *malae* (village green). Some have medical dispensaries, and most have general stores and copra sheds, where the kernel of the coconut is stored until marketed. All Samoan villages on the major islands of Tutuila and Upolu are connected by paved or graveled roads with the urban centers, which have shops, hotels, theaters, hospitals, and commercial houses and banks. Some villages on islands such as Manono in Western Samoa or Ta'ū in American Samoa are relatively isolated and culture remains somewhat more traditional. Most Samoans are farmers, and they work lands that are relatively small in acreage and located on the mountainous slopes behind the seaside villages.

People in Samoa are said to be old when they are no longer able to do heavy agricultural work or the more strenuous domestic tasks. It is at this time that men are referred to as *toeaina* or *matuaali'i* and women are referred to as *lo'omatua* or *olomatua*. These labels are usually applied sometime between ages 50 and 60 but, of course, there is a good deal of variation, depending on the health and strength of given individuals. After occupying the status of "old" for several years, the term *vaivai* (weak in the body) is often added, although in many cases it might not accurately describe the physical condition of the old person. Senility, as we know it in America, is extremely rare in Samoa.

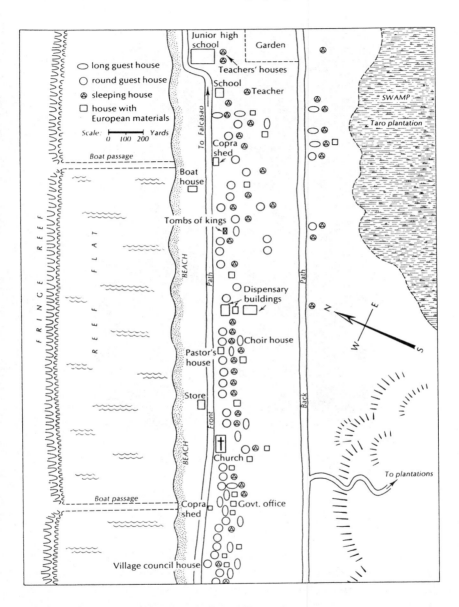

Figure 6.1 Ta'ū Village: A Typical Samoan Community
SOURCE: Map by Lowell D. Holmes.

In Samoa, old men sometimes "retire" to tasks that can be done sitting down. (Photo by Lowell D. Holmes.)

Until very recently, most Samoans, young or old, have agreed that old age is "the finest time of life." The elders do not have to rise before dawn and go to the plantations high on the mountain slopes. They have the option of working or resting, depending on their inclination. During the day, they are free to sit for hours and chat with other elders of the village without feeling guilty about not carrying their full load of activities. When villagers pass by the *fale* (which is open on all sides), no one fails to wave and give the elderly a friendly greeting. Only the elders have time to observe fully the activities of the villagers, and they are often the most informed about the current events of the community.

Even though old people are excused from the heavier tasks, they all feel that it is important to be productive in some way. Most older Samoans explain their longevity by the fact that they keep busy every day. Generally, the young take care of the strenuous labor and the old account for the tedious labor—the kind you can do sitting down. Old men sew units of sugarcane thatch for roofs and braid sennit, the coconut fiber twine so important in traditional house and canoe building. They weed the yard and help the women prepare pandanus leaf for mat weaving. In the afternoon when the tide is low and reef flat exposed, old men often set their globe-shaped fish traps in shallow pools with hopes of snaring brightly colored reef fish. They also scavenge the reef for small eels and shellfish.

Elderly men are in many cases the titled heads of families and as such are referred to as *matai*, who are either *ali'i* (chiefs) or *tulafale* (talking chiefs). They are elected to these positions relatively late in life by the members of their extended family. Whether one is a chief or a talking chief (orator) is a matter of family and village tradition. Various titles with various designations were created for (or bestowed by indigenous rulers on) families at different times throughout Samoan history. Such titles have traditionally been awarded to men who are intelligent, knowledgeable of Samoan tradition and ceremonial life, and hardworking (on family enterprises). There are a few female *matai*, but the majority are men. *Matai* are elected for life, although it is not uncommon for a very old family head to step down and request that the family select a younger man. They coordinate family work activities and control family expenditures. In some families, even people working at wage employment contribute heavily to family welfare by giving a portion of their income to the *matai*. At marriages, funerals, and title installations, it is the *matai* who must collect money and gifts from his family; these will be used in the ceremonial property exchanges that take place on such occasions. Because generosity is a principal avenue to status, the *matai* is responsible for maintaining his family's prestige by collecting substantial sums of money and goods.

Although some chiefs are middle aged, there is a tendency to equate being a chief with being old. The behavior expected of a chief is described by one of Margaret Mead's (1928) informants:

I have been a chief only four years and look, my hair is grey, although in Samoa grey hair comes very slowly, not in youth, as it comes to the white man. But always I must act as if I were old. I must walk gravely and with measured step. . . . Old men of sixty are my companions and watch my every word, lest I make a mistake. Thirty-one people live in my household. For them I must plan. I must find them food and clothing, settle their disputes, arrange their marriages. There is no one in my whole family who dares to scold me or even to address me familiarly by my first name. It is hard to be so young and yet to be a chief. (p. 36)

The *matai* represent their families in the village council (known as the *fono*), which meets periodically to discuss village business. It is presided over by the village paramount chief, and to a large extent much of the business is controlled by the talking chiefs. Because all decisions must be unanimous, discussions are often long and drawn out. A role of considerable importance in the *fono* is that of *tu'ua*, or elder statesman. Grattan (1948) describes the position as follows:

As a mark of respect and dignity, the village may choose one of their orators to fill a position known as *tu'ua*. Not every village chooses a *tu'ua*. Such a person must enjoy high personal rank as an orator and have a degree of knowledge relating to the village and perhaps district affairs which fits him for the position. Considerable deference is paid to him and it is to him that the village looks thereafter for pronouncements on any disputed point. The *tu'ua* is the one entitled to sit in the middle post of the front of a house and if he should arrive late or unexpectedly at the village meeting and that post is already occupied, the place will be vacated at once and left open to him. (p. 19)

Two other honorific positions are reserved for elderly men in Samoan society. One is that of *tapuaiga* (the one who prays for the work) and the other, mentor at *fa'asausauga* (night assemblies for discussion of family and village traditions). A *tapuaiga* is considered to be an essential ingredient in any successful house-building venture. The old man who functions in this role does not actually pray but merely sits and serves as a conversationalist for the workers, many of whom are young men and enjoy the tales of old Samoa. The *tapuaiga* is not permitted to be critical

Elderly Samoan women weave floor mats, baskets, fans, and fine mats. (Photo by Lowell D. Holmes.)

of the quality of the work, but in carrying out his symbolic role of support, his very presence no doubt means that the workmen are somewhat more careful about their work. *Fa'asausauga,* on the other hand, provide the elderly chiefs with an opportunity to pass on important traditional and ceremonial knowledge. Although participation in these meetings is theoretically restricted to chiefs, they actually provide an excellent opportunity for young untitled men to come and sit outside the meetinghouse and listen and learn.

Older women also play ceremonial roles and are consulted on political issues. Every village has a Women's Committee, and this organization mirrors the village council in structure and family representation. It is often concerned with village welfare issues such as the adequacy of church or dispensary facilities, and its members are responsible for providing hospitality to visiting parties *(malaga)* from other villages and support for the village council on village ceremonial occasions or at district political conferences.

Although men tend to be most visible politically and ceremonially, Women's Committees are very influential in determining village and interisland social and political events. Elderly women often have important positions in these organizations, but the major contribution of old women in Samoa is economic. Women in this society produce a category of goods known as *toga*. This includes all varieties of weaving—floor and sleeping mats, baskets, fans, house blinds, fine mats, and bark cloth tapestries, known as *siapo*. Many of these articles are used in the home, and all serve as wealth to be exchanged between families for *oloa*—pigs, food, and money—at weddings, matai installations, funerals, or church dedications. All women produce *toga*, but the bulk of the production is in the hands of elderly women who can devote long hours to this tedious labor, because they no longer are required to join their men in the cultivation of their agricultural plots. Much like elderly women in the United States engage in quilting or "fancy work," Samoan elders produce the heirlooms of the future while they tend the small children left behind by the mothers spending the day in the gardens.

They are often assisted in their work by teenage girls or young women, and there is nothing of the segregation of age groups that is so characteristic of America. In Samoa no old person ever complains of being "lonely," for it is difficult to be lonely or even alone in the average household, which numbers between 8 and 12 people and can include at least three and probably four generations who eat together, work together, and often sleep together in one large unpartitioned room.

Old men are often found assisting their wives or female relatives in some of the activities that might be considered woman's work, but in old age there is great freedom of choice. Young people who are siblings or cousins (the latter are referred to with the same kin terms as siblings) must observe a brother-sister taboo beginning at the time of puberty, but once they have attained old age there are no longer any social restrictions.

Old people also have the privilege of violating many of the standards of decorum. They often perform bawdy songs and dances at *fiafia* (parties), and they are politely tolerated when they give long, tedious, and irrelevant speeches in the village council.

One job completely reserved for older women is burning candlenut and collecting its soot, which is used as a pigment in tattooing. At one time, every young man underwent the ordeal of tattooing, but then the practice fell off. In recent years, interest in this rite has revived. Although old women once delivered all the babies in the village, this function has now been taken over by Samoan medical practitioners and locally trained nurses. On rare occasions, elderly midwives are called on. Even today old women continue to be storehouses of knowledge concerning the medicinal properties of herbs and many of them are specialists in *fofo* and *lomilomi* (forms of massage).

Gerontocide

Although abandonment or murder of the aged has been observed in hunting cultures in harsh environments, a custom such as live burial of the aged seems strangely out of place in a society of sedentary horticulturalists living in a hospitable environment. Yet such a custom did exist in earlier times in Samoa and has been reported by a number of European observers. To understand this rather bizarre custom, we need to consider three things: (a) the Samoan belief system, (b) the Samoan concept of honorable death, and (c) the importance of status and respect within the society.

Of the belief system, Leo Simmons (1945a) writes:

> Belief in a future life . . . has been generally so firm and matter-of-fact that it is difficult for modern man to appreciate it fully; and with the consequence that death has often been regarded as a welcome release from the fetters of age and a direct means of enhancing one's personal interests. (p. 224)

In addition to this promise of a joyful afterlife, assured by the Samoan belief system, there was also the attraction that great honor and prestige could be acquired for oneself and family if one died a noble and courageous death. Before the colonial and territorial governments of white men did away with interisland warfare and extended voyaging, it was considered desirable for elderly men whom fate had robbed of a glorious and honorific death in battle or on the sea to request being put to death by members of their own family. This was done through suffocation in a live burial following a normal ceremony of interment where large amounts of property were exchanged (the greater the amount, the more important the deceased) and eulogies presented. Turner (1884) describes such an event:

> When an old man felt sick and infirm, and thought he was dying, he deliberately told his children and friends to get ready to bury him. They yielded to his wishes, dug a round, deep pit, wound a number of fine mats around his body, and lowered down the old man into his grave in a sitting position. Live pigs were then brought, and tied, each with a separate cord, the one end of the cord to the pig, and the other end to the arm of the old man. The cords were cut in the middle, leaving the one half hanging at the arm of the old man, and off the pigs were taken to be killed and baked for the burial feast. . . .
> The greater the chief the more numerous the pigs. . . . The poor old man thus wound up, furnished with his pig strings, and covered over with some more mats, was all ready. His grave was then filled up, and his dying groans drowned amid the weeping and the wailing of the living. (pp. 335-336)

Thus live burial was an honor and not an act of cruelty, allowing an old and ailing chief an honorable way out of life, amid the acclaim of his family and community.

Cultural Change

Samoan families have always taken great pride in supporting their elderly, but today they have problems. Changing times, involving greater emphasis on a money economy and greater emphasis on educational needs of children (which every family has in abundance), have sometimes resulted in a shift of priorities from an emphasis on age to an emphasis on youth.

Although modernization in the islands has often created conditions that make it more difficult for families to care for their elderly, it has brought new programs for the old, particularly in American Samoa, where its nationals are eligible for many of the federal programs enjoyed by elderly in the United States.

The Territorial Administration on Aging, with an office in Pago Pago, has been surveying the needs of the elderly since about 1975. There is a nutritional program, a program that assists the elderly with purchase of eyeglasses and hearing aids, and a clinic at the LBJ Tropical Medical Center that serves seniors virtually without charge. There is also a program that provides the aged with passbooks to ride on busses on Tutuila (the only island with such transportation); Manu'a elders are entitled to one trip per month to Tutuila on a local airline. Transportation is a much valued benefit in this society because of its traditional pattern of visiting relatives, often for extended periods. An employment program for senior citizens provides some remuneration to low-income elders for part-time work. In Manu'a this program emphasizes handicraft production; on Tutuila employment is more difficult to find because the jobs available often are more physically demanding than many aged Samoans can manage. Some do teach crafts in the schools, however.

In spite of numerous changes in Samoan lifestyle in recent years, there is still a strong emphasis on extended-family living, and there is great concern and support for aged relatives. In a 1976 study conducted in American Samoa by Rhoads and Holmes (Rhoads, 1981), 71% of the aged interviewed maintained that they received better food and care than other family members; 98% believed that young people both respect and obey old people; and 97% spoke of special favors and kindnesses accorded them because of their age. Although 93% volunteered that they were still consulted about such matters as family problems, funerals, weddings, and titles, about 86% did not think that their words were heeded as much by the young as in the past. A study carried out in the islands in 1986-1987 by J. D. Pearson (1992) found the status of old people and their relationship to the family virtually unchanged. The remarkable thing about modern Samoan culture is the tenacity of the Samoan family both in the islands and in migrant communities in the United States and New Zealand. Approximately 88% of the elders interviewed by Rhoads and Holmes in 1976 maintained that the extended family continued to be as important and influential in Samoan lives as it was 10 years earlier, and this is seen by Rhoads (1981) as a prime factor in ensuring the welfare of the aged. Pearson's 1986-1987 data, however, indicate that although the traditional Samoan family system is still relatively strong in American Samoa and Honolulu, there are definite signs of change and conflict. Multi-generation households are less prevalent, and service to *matai* is declining (Fitzgerald & Howard, 1990). These changes may be reflected to some extent in the responses of the subjects to the question about the "best time of life." Traditionally, both young and old Samoans "almost universally" referred to old age as the best time of life (Holmes, 1972). However, less than 15% of these samples report that old age is the best time of life. (Pearson, 1992, p. 80)

Aging in an Industrial Economy: The United States

According to the human geographer J. H. G. Lebon (1969), an Occidental industrial economy is one in which there is widespread use of mechanical power in mass production industry and extensive exploitation of oil, natural gas, minerals, water, and timber resources. Efficient production and management techniques in all facets of agriculture and industry create abundance and a high standard of living. Because of mechanization and advanced scientific knowledge of plant and animal production, a small percentage of agriculturalists can support large urban populations who engage in highly specialized occupations in industry, commerce, and the arts and sciences. Societies of this type have a highly mobile, achievement-oriented workforce of individuals who are highly materialistic in their economic values and are peer-oriented in their social affiliations.

The Cultural Setting

As a nation, the United States has long been thought of as a melting pot, but this is not entirely correct, because all the constituent national ingredients remain clearly recognizable. People of many nationalities have come to our portion of North America, and the social fabric of America is characterized by class, ethnic, racial, regional, and even occupational differences, all of which influence attitudes and behavioral patterns. But in spite of this heterogeneity, social scientists generally agree that Americans have a recognizable, predictable way of life. This is a lifestyle that by and large tends to be associated with middle-class America—a social category to which a substantial majority of Americans claim they belong. The culture of this "establishment" dominates the educational curriculum and dictates the behavioral norms that most Americans, regardless of race or national origin, strive to emulate. This set of values and behavioral characteristics has been well documented by scores of skilled observers from Alexis de Tocqueville (1899) in the 1830s to Margaret Mead. Generally, the postulates of this American cultural system include the following:

1. An individual's most important concern is self interest and this involves self-expression, self-development, self-gratification, and independence.
2. The privacy of the individual is an inalienable right: intrusion into it by others is permitted only by invitation.
3. All forms of authority, including government, are suspect; but the government and its symbols should be respected. Patriotism is good.
4. An individual's success in life depends on his acceptance among his peers.
5. Men and women are equal.
6. All human beings are equal.
7. Progress is good and inevitable. (Hsu, 1969, p. 63)

How Old Is Old?

In the United States, old age is defined chronologically. One is old in America at age 65—an arbitrary figure that has been selected by representatives of government and industry as the time when it is appropriate for men and women to withdraw from productive labor and permit younger workers to take over. The figure 65 has very little to do with physical or mental capacity of Americans, but because it has been so universally accepted as the threshold of decrepitude, few would challenge its validity. In the United States there is also a tendency for age 65 to be considered the terminal point for all efficiency, creativity, and productivity. In most cases, people of this age are expected to retire and there is little opportunity for reemployment on either a part- or full-time basis should they so desire. Some individuals have managed to establish successful postretirement businesses, but this is relatively rare. For some, retirement means increased time for travel or for pursuing neglected hobbies, but for many it is a time of unwanted idleness, boredom, and stagnation.

The Aged Population

Nearly 32 million men and women in America are over the age of 65. This group, which represents 12.6% of the total population and is rapidly increasing, is, contrary to popular belief, extremely heterogeneous. In 1900 only slightly more than 3 million were elderly and they represented only 4% of the whole. This expansion in the proportion of the elderly is the result of two factors: a decline in the birthrate and an increase in life expectancy from 47 years in 1900 to 75.5 in 1991 (American Association of Retired Persons & Administration on Aging, 1993). The majority of the aged in America are women. As is true of most countries, American women outlive their men by several years. By age 65 there are only 67.5 men to every 100 women, and by age 80 the number of men per 100 women shrinks to 46 (Kinsella & Taeuber, 1992).

Residence Patterns

In recent decades many elderly Americans have moved to the sun-belt states of the South and West. The aged constitute 18.3% of Florida's population, with the Sarasota area having a median age of 49. While California as a whole has a fairly low median age, some places such as Santa Barbara have a population that is more than 21% elderly. And distribution within all states is erratic. Inner-city areas have increased proportions of elderly, because the young are moving away and leaving the old behind. For example, Pittsburgh's elderly population is growing progressively older and now constitutes 17.6% of the total (U.S. Bureau of the Census, 1992c). Some rural areas also have a preponderance of senior citizens, again because young people have moved away. Nearly half of the counties in the state of Kansas, for example, have populations where 20% or more of their numbers are seniors (U.S. Bureau of the Census, 1992a).

Of the elderly in the United States, 5.5% (or 1,772,032) are institutionalized. There are 16,000 nursing homes of various types in America

(*Directory of Nursing Homes*, 1991). The skilled nursing facility provides 24-hour nursing care for the chronically ill, whereas the intermediate care facility has registered nurses in attendance only eight hours a day. They offer more limited nursing care but do provide considerable personal assistance to patients. Residential care facilities serve functional, independent old people, providing mainly recreational and nutritional services. There are also adult day-care facilities that serve essentially as social and/or therapy centers for those elderly who live at home but who cannot be left alone and/or require supervision or medical services.

Early History

In colonial and frontier America, the aged were relatively scarce. In 1790, 50% of the population was under the age of 16, and people 65 and older made up a scant 2%. If people did survive to old age in those days, they received considerable respect and honor, although not necessarily a great deal of love and affection. Puritan belief, which dominated much of early social thought, held that old age was a sign of God's pleasure and that old people most closely resembled the image of God, who was usually thought of as grandfatherly and with a long white beard. Because so few people in colonial America were literate, respect for elders often stemmed from the fact that they were repositories and teachers of traditional knowledge and values. In the slowly changing society of eighteenth-century America, their experience and wisdom were ever relevant, and they were seen as important agents of communication. At public gatherings, such as New England town meetings, the places of honor were reserved for the elderly rather than the rich. Wealth made a difference, though, as far as respect was concerned; aged paupers were treated cruelly. Fischer (1978) records that

> a New Jersey law of 1720 instructed justices of the peace to search arriving ships for "old persons" as well as "maimed, lunatic, or any vagabond or vagrant persons" and send them away in order to prevent the growth of pauperism in the colony. (p. 61)

Widows are said to have fared badly because few were very well provided for by their husband's estate. Some were actually driven away by neighbors who were afraid that their presence would result in increased poor taxes.

The fact that there were a considerable number of poor and homeless old people in colonial America contradicts the commonly held belief that extended families were the rule in America before industrialization and urbanization. It is now believed, however, that nuclear families were the norm in western Europe as far back as the Reformation. Certainly the emphasis on political and religious freedom that marked the social thought of colonial America would not have provided a very fertile environment for the existence of larger multigenerational extended families. Even in rural areas, related nuclear families often lived close to one another and cooperated on agricultural projects, but the three-generation household was probably a rarity. Fischer (1978) describes the pattern of family life before the twentieth century:

> The responsibilities of child-rearing normally continued to the end of life. Normally the first baby was born within a year of the marriage; the last came when the wife was thirty-eight and her husband was forty-two. As a rule, the youngest child did not marry until the parents were sixty-four and sixty. Men and women continued to live with their unmarried children nearly until the end of their lives. Very few old people lived alone; most remained in nuclear families with their own children still around them. Scarcely any of them lived in extended, three generational households. Those who did usually had taken in a married daughter or son who had lost a spouse. When three generations lived together, it was more often the young who were in some way dependent upon the old than the old upon the young. (p. 56)

The only people who had a concept of retirement were New England ministers, but few of them voluntarily chose this option because they rarely received financial support during retirement. Some, however, were forced to retire by dissatisfied congregations. In early America very few families were able to save a great deal for old age during their lifetimes, and old age pensions were unknown until after the Civil War, when military pensions were awarded to nearly 1 million veterans. In regard to compulsory old age pension plans for industry, Fischer (1978) writes that they

> were denounced by clergymen as hostile to the morals of the Republic. They were condemned by economists as destructive to

the spirit of enterprise. They were attacked by politicians as dangerous to American liberty, and capitalists called them a corrupt form of socialism. Labor leaders denounced them as "deferred wages." (p. 168)

Not until the twentieth century did private corporations establish pension plans. Railroads led the way; the Baltimore and Ohio Railroad initiated the practice in 1884. Various states—Ohio, Pennsylvania, Wisconsin, and Massachusetts—maintained pauper institutions for destitute elderly, but as late as 1922 no state in the union had enacted a satisfactory old age pension system. Aged Americans had to wait until the Social Security legislation of 1935 for any form of government-sponsored plan of old age assistance. While programs for the elderly in America lag far behind those in other European countries, today elderly Americans have access to Social Security, Supplemental Security Income (which ensures a reasonably adequate minimum monthly income for low-income elderly), Medicare (a health insurance program that helps the aged meet the high cost of health care), Medicaid (a program for low-income persons regardless of age), and many other local, state, and national programs.

Ceremonial Life

In America there are few ceremonies associated with aging. Aside from half-hearted recognition of the significance of 16th, 21st, and 40th birthdays, there is little observance of age milestones. The media tend to pay special attention to people who manage to celebrate their 100th year of life, and there is some recognition of 50th, 60th, and 70th wedding anniversaries, but there is nothing to match the excitement and prestige associated with completing the fifth 12-year cycle of life in Japan or Thailand. Retirement, which takes place for most at age 65 in the United States, is sometimes marked by a special ceremony at which the retiree is given a gift (often a watch or a piece of hobby or sports equipment), eulogized with humorous speeches from coworkers, and told to "drop by any time and see us."

Religion

The religious tradition observed in the United States has little effect on attitudes toward the aged. While the Bible urges believers to "Honor thy father and mother that thy days may be long," this commandment has never had the impact on behavior that the filial piety principle has had in Oriental religions. It states an ideal but does not represent a guarantee of respect and responsibility. Like American society in general, American religion is youth oriented and for every congregation with a minister to the elderly there are 100 with youth ministers. Nearly every congregation has a young people's organization (e.g., Christian Endeavor, Canterbury Club, Christian Youth Fellowship, Catholic Youth Organization), but very few maintain special organizations for the elderly. Some denominations do, however, operate retirement or nursing facilities for the aged, and the Catholic order, Little Sisters of the Poor, has established homes for old people in a variety of foreign cultures.

The Value Environment

America is a difficult society in which to grow old—in many respects more difficult than those of the Eskimo or the Samoan. It is a society where people anticipate old age with "sorrow or rebellion. It fills men with more aversion than does death itself" (de Beauvoir, 1972a, p. 539). To be old in the United States is to be a member of the country's least visible minority, and, in general, it involves being less healthy, less mobile, and less financially secure than most Americans. This dismal situation is the result of a combination of (a) a particular set of values, (b) a particular level of technological development, and (c) a particular form of social organization. Specifically, Americans' attitudes toward the aged and their own aging result from the fact that the United States as a culture ideally

(a) places a high value on self-reliance, independence, and success;
(b) is characterized by social alienation;
(c) is youth oriented;
(d) associates physical beauty with youth;
(e) is future oriented;
(f) is precision and time oriented;
(g) views the universe as mechanistic and conceives of man as its master;
(h) is a wasteful, throw-away culture; and
(i) is democratic and egalitarian.

Self-Reliance and Success. Anthropologist Francis Hsu (1961), a China-born analyst of American culture, maintains that

> the American core value is self-reliance. . . . Every individual is his own master, in control of his own destiny, and will advance and regress in society only according to his own efforts. . . . In American society the fear of dependency is so great that an individual who is not self-reliant is an object of hostility. . . . "Dependent character" is a highly derogatory term, and a person so described is thought to be in need of psychiatric help. (pp. 216-219)

Self-reliance is seen not only as the key to mental health but also as the prerequisite to personal success. Having rejected nearly all forms of dependence on fellow human beings, the American finds that "security must come from personal success, personal superiority, and personal triumph. Those who are fortunate enough to achieve success, superiority, and triumph will, of course, bask in the sunshine" (Hsu, 1961, p. 228). In America the game is not played for the sake of playing; it is played to be won, and every activity of value represents an arena for competition. It is inconceivable in America that status-conferring tasks should be reserved for elderly people as they are in Samoa, because in America winning is too important for rewards to be conferred without a struggle.

Most aged Americans are by definition dependent—dependent on Social Security, on pensions, on family goodwill and interest, or on government health and welfare programs. Some are more dependent than others, but very few are productive members of the labor force. Furthermore, these elderly individuals have been ruled out of the personal achievement competition by societal laws that actually prohibit their participation. While economic achievement is ruled out by forced retirement, it is important for elders to hold their own. Not becoming a burden has become of ultimate importance. By way of contrast, Sylvia Vatuk (1990) reports that India's elderly think in terms of "legitimate and hard-earned rights to support and care in old age. To accept such aid from adult sons and their wives is a pleasure and a source of pride. . . . It certainly does not threaten their self esteem" (p. 84). In the United States such support tends to produce feelings of shame and guilt for the elderly recipients. This has led to insistence on separate residences for old people until physical or mental health problems necessitate institutionalization. This rather complete segregation of generations imposes problems not only on the aged but on children as well. It deprives the aged of the companionship of grandchildren and other family members and separates them from young ideas and intergenerational perspectives. Young people, on the other hand, are robbed of a source through which they might better understand and prepare for their own old age.

Social Alienation. In the book *Man Alone,* Eric Josephson and Mary Josephson (1962) write that

> alienation has been used by philosophers, psychologists, and sociologists to refer to an extraordinary variety of psychosocial disorders, including loss of self, anxiety states, anomie, despair, depersonalization, rootlessness, apathy, social disorganization, loneliness, atomization, powerlessness, meaninglessness, isolation, pessimism and the loss of beliefs or values. (pp. 12-13)

When societies become large, mechanized, secular, and bureaucratic, individuals tend to become alienated in the routinization and automation so necessary to maintaining a complex system. The United States is such a society; there is abundant evidence that it has become callous to personal needs and has found it convenient to treat individuals like faceless statistics. Most businesses, universities, and government agencies keep track of people through numbers rather than through names. Not to know one's Social Security number renders an individual beyond the help of most agencies.

The dehumanization and consequential loss of community that appears to be a by-product of our civilization in the closing decades of the twentieth century is a form of oppression affecting all human beings, but especially elderly ones. In a society characterized by anonymous beings, the aged are the most invisible, least valued of all. When asked, "What is the relationship of fellow human beings to one another?" Erich Fromm (1962) answered that they are "two living machines who use each other" (p. 68). The employer uses his employees; the salesman uses him customers; everyone is, to everyone else, a commodity. It is a marketing orientation, says Fromm. Modern humans in the United States see themselves as things to be employed successfully on the market; it is one's job to sell oneself effectively. It can readily be seen that the elderly do not fit into this scheme of things, because they have nothing to sell. Retired men and women have been deprived of the one thing that gave them value—their world of work. The reason they are not saleable commodities is that the market is only buying new models. Simone de Beauvoir (1972b) sums up the alienation dilemma:

> Old age exposes the failure of our entire civilization. It is the whole man that must be remade; it is the whole relationship between man and man that must be recast if we wish the old person's state to be acceptable. A man should not start his last years alone and empty-handed. . . . If he were not atomized from his childhood, shut away and isolated among other atoms, and if he shared in a collective life . . . [t]hen he would never experience banishment. (p. 264)

Youth, Beauty, and the Promise of the Future. In the United States, the emphasis is on what is young and what is new. To keep up with new trends and new ideas is to be young in spirit, and no one in America ever really looks forward to growing old. The American accent is on youth because the future belongs to the youth of the nation, and America is future oriented. In such a society, the people with the least value are those with the least future. Euphemisms such as *senior citizens, sunset years, golden age* attempt to hide the truth about growing old, and frequently "middle age" extends right up to senility or death. In America most people will not reveal their age unless forced to, on the grounds that it might incriminate them. This is especially true for women, because aging is profoundly more painful for them than for men. Being physically attractive has traditionally counted for more in a woman's life than in a man's in the United States. Men can age and still remain attractive and desirable, but women cannot. Nora Scott Kinzer (1974) writes:

> Woman is a sexual object. Woman must use her sexual wiles to succeed in life. Success means having a man and keeping him. A body beautiful guarantees that the rent will be paid, the children will have shoes, there will be food on the table, and he won't walk out. (p. 4)

Although in reality there is an abundance of beautiful old people, the association of beauty with youth seems unshakable. On the other hand, the things that are often admired in men—competence, autonomy, and self-control—are not necessarily associated with age, and masculinity does not depend on youth or physical appearance. The fact that men can be considered attractive and desirable in spite of gray hair and wrinkles is well documented by the fact that men of power and influence often have wives 30 or more years their junior. Witness the marriages of Frank and Kathie Lee Gifford (23 years' difference), Senator Strom and Nancy Thurmond (45 years' difference), and Johnny and Alex Carson (26 years' difference). Of course, it is the men who make the proposals in American society, and these men in particular had considerable wealth, but no doubt other attractions led their wives to consent to marriage. When the situation is reversed and a very wealthy woman marries a much younger man, the general public is less accepting. While the things that make a man masculine often are enhanced by the years, the things that have traditionally been associated with femininity—passivity, helplessness, dependence, noncompetitiveness—are not.

It would be ridiculous to assume that aging men have no anxiety at the prospect of aging, however. The middle-class American male's problems during the years of "middle age" are linked to the extreme pressure of having to be successful. It is terribly important in our society that men achieve the goals society has set for them and, indeed, they have set for themselves. One's career accomplishments define one's membership in the middle class, and failure to meet societal and personal expectations is the root of the social and psychological pathology known as the "male menopause." This phenomenon, also related to the value of youth and the tyranny of time, is most common in men in their late forties and early fifties who suddenly realize that time is running out, that younger men are standing by to take their place, that retirement is in the offing, and that one's goals have not been realized.

In spite of the general fear of aging in America, most of its citizens are wishing their lives away looking toward a rosier tomorrow. Americans seem to need something to look forward to. They are definitely future oriented. The whole credit system operates on a tomorrow concept. Buy today and pay later. The fact that elderly people often have trouble getting credit probably involves the perception that their future (when the payments will be made) is limited.

Compare these attitudes with those of groups that honor the past. In such societies the worth of individuals is measured in terms of past experience and not future potential—the older, the wiser, and consequently the more respect due. In traditional China, offspring took pride in their parents' accomplishments and boasted about their ancestors (Hsu, 1981), whereas in America, Christmas letters immodestly describe the triumphs of offspring, and Little League games and dance recitals are events where proud parents come to bask in their children's accomplishments. One of the most popular of special events at some universities is Dad's Day at the football stadium. Here dozens of fathers line up on the field with their son's numbers on their backs and receive special recognition through identification with their sons. Although American culture gives young people few legal rights, they exert great control in families and are the recipients of great amounts of attention. Emphasis on the value of youth as opposed to old age is so great in America that the majority of citizens seldom question why parents are expected to support a child for as many as 22 to 25 years (if professional educations are involved) but have no guarantee that they will receive even a few years of financial support when they become old.

It would also appear that this downward trend in financial support continues long after college. A study carried out in 1988 of 6,524 households by Martha Hill of the University of Michigan's Institute for Social Research found that household heads aged 25-34 gave an average of only $25 a year to their parents in gifts and various kinds of financial support but received an average of $525. In the 35- to 44-year-old group, parents received an average of $100 annually while giving $500. Children in the 65-74 age group contributed approximately $25 a year to their aged parents but received nothing in return ("Older Parents," 1993).

Precision and the Tyranny of Time. America is a nation whose industrial enterprise and commitment to science demand precision. Television and radio programs begin exactly on the hour and half hour and the accuracy of the nation's time pieces is monitored by Western Union. The society's artifacts—for example, cars, planes, and household appliances—are produced on assembly lines and their parts are interchangeable because they are identical to the hundredth of a centimeter. Lives are lived on rigid schedules—8 a.m. to 5 p.m. workdays and 7, 12, and 6 o'clock mealtimes; one soft-drink producer recommends drinking the product (Dr. Pepper) precisely at 10 a.m., 2 p.m., and 4 p.m.

In America actuarial tables predict life expectancy with brutal accuracy. While some will live longer than the life expectancy figure (which is an average) and some will live less long, all will be retired precisely at the age established by the employer—65 for most, in some cases 70. While preindustrial societies judge old age functionally and therefore recognize that it comes to some earlier than others, in the United States old age comes to all precisely on their 65th birthday.

In a society that values precision as highly as America, people are constantly aware of the unrelenting movement of time. Old age and retirement come at 65 and death comes (on average) 15 (for men) to 19 (for women) years later. The aged retired American has no alternative but to sit idly at home observing his or her superbly accurate gold watch (which the company presented on retirement) tick off the minutes and the days the life insurance company table maintains are remaining. In contrast, people in preindustrial societies like those of the Eskimo and Samoan think of the life cycle not in terms of years but in terms of hunting seasons or planting and harvest times. Few feel it is important to record or even recall how many such seasons they have lived. Ultimately they know they will grow too old to hunt or harvest and someday they will die, but they see no constructive purpose in accurately predicting and monitoring the eventuality. The American system guarantees that most old people will spend about two thirds of their lives worrying about getting old.

In the society of the United States where time is measured, spent, saved, squandered, budgeted, used to best advantage, and generally equated with money, temporal emphasis can be depressing for the elderly in still another way. Robert Smith (1961) suggests:

> An individual in his later years . . . used to being active, . . . may now find that an absence of scheduling poses problems for him. It no longer matters that he is on time for anything. He may, indeed, find that he is not required to arise at a certain hour or that he may eat at any time he chooses, in short, that his days are now stretches of time which an earlier discipline will not fill up. (p. 86)

A Mechanistic Universe With Man as Its Master. In describing one aspect of the American value system, Arensberg and Niehoff (1964) state:

> For many Americans the natural environment is something to overcome, to improve, or to tear down and rebuild in a better way.

... This conquering attitude toward nature appears to rest on two assumptions: that the universe is mechanistic and man is its master. (p. 224)

This ability to control nature has become a major source of pride for Americans. American scientific know-how can accomplish almost anything. If Americans want a recreation lake, they have the U.S. Army Corps of Engineers dam a stream; if they need rain, they "seed" the clouds with silver iodide; if they need snow at a ski resort, they merely bring in a snowmaking machine; if a bone disintegrates or an organ ceases to function, medical science provides an artificial one. There is, however, one natural phenomenon that Americans seem powerless to do anything about, and that is the process of aging. In spite of a constant search for "fountains of youth," modern America has clearly failed to halt or reverse this dreaded natural process. Therefore we consciously or unconsciously punish the messenger—the elderly population that is constantly before us telling us by way of their white hair and wrinkled faces that all of our science has failed. The elderly are reprehensible symbols of failure in our quest for mastery over nature. Old people are not only loathed for their dependency (forced on them by society), they are equally loathed for their failure to triumph over the physical degeneration of old age (forced on them by nature).

Democracy and Egalitarianism. The democratic, egalitarian nature of American society is, by and large, most laudable, but we must realize that elders do not fare as well in such societies as they do in authoritarian, collectivistic, totalitarian, and static ones. An examination of the cross-cultural data found in Leo Simmons's *The Role of the Aged in Primitive Society* (1945a) reveals that those societies where old people have the highest prestige and the greatest security tend to be those governed by autocratic monarchs, despotic chiefs, or restrictive councils of oligarchs. These societies usually feature hereditary castes and classes, and important life decisions, such as choice of a mate or disposition of property, are made by the society or by the family and not by the individual.

Democracies permit individuals to operate free from traditional restraints, but they are societies impatient with the restrictions of convention. There is a hunger for new ideas and new ways of doing things. They are throw-away societies that would rather create than preserve. In a memorable television series dealing with an interplanetary visitor, Mork from Ork, the alien was perplexed by the fact that in America furniture becomes more valuable with time (as antiques), but people do not.

Democracies are societies on the move, and they have little time for ceremony or convention. Traditional lore, old families, and old people do not automatically command respect. It is probably no coincidence that our model of democratic government (Greece) was one where the prevailing attitude toward old age was contained in the proverb, "Whom the gods love die young."

SUMMARY

In this chapter we have been exposed to three cultural solutions for meeting the problems, challenges, and rewards of growing old. The three cultures vary greatly in ways of getting a living, family structure and interaction, and technological development. The Eskimo function in a rigorous climate where their nomadic way of life imposes hardships on all but especially the elderly, and gerontocide was a traditional practice often carried out at the request of the elderly. In this culture the aged were regarded as sages, teachers, and repositories of tradition. Their status was extremely high.

Samoa, with its agricultural economy, sedentary lifestyle, and benign climate, allows for a much less challenging and problematic aging experience. Here the large extended family is very solicitous of its old people, and old age was traditionally considered the best time of life. Family chieftainship is held only by mature men and occasionally women, and the elderly are revered for their wisdom, judgment, and knowledge of *fa'aSamoa*, the Samoan way of life.

The United States is a modern industrial nation, technologically advanced, materialistic, and individualistic. It is a society that welcomes change, is not particularly family oriented, covets a high standard of living, honors youth, and devalues its elderly. Many of the key American values such as future and progress orientation, association of beauty with youth, social alienation, self-reliance, precise time orientation, and egalitarianism do not favor the elderly. America is a society on the move and it has little time for ceremony or convention, which are cherished domains of the elderly.

7

◉ Ethnic Aged in America

The United States is a nation of immigrants. With the exception of the Native Americans who were already here when the first European settlers arrived, all of us have ancestral roots in some other country. Historically, the early arrivals—Anglo-Saxon groups—shaped much of what has come to be referred to as the dominant culture of the United States, but the stream of immigrants continues and has become increasingly diverse. In the early 1900s a play titled *The Melting Pot* apparently gave rise to the idea of America being such a phenomenon. The premise was that, if various ethnic groups combined as metals do in the smelting process, the result would be a unique but better society. In this view, assimilation was seen as best for all concerned (Kalish, 1986). Over time the emphasis changed from assimilation to acculturation, "with its support of accommodation to the larger society and functioning effectively within it but without losing the positive aspects of ethnic identity" (p. 23). According to Kalish, in recent years cultural pluralism has become the acceptable approach with "acceptance of numerous cultures that function side by side in some contexts and retain their individual uniqueness in other contexts" (p. 23).

The old melting pot idea has not worked; we have not produced a cultural fondue but something like chow mein, with distinctly identifiable ingredients and flavors. Throughout this book we have noted how aging is influenced by culture, and when numerous cultural groups, each with increasing proportions of aged persons, live side by side in a society, an understanding of the concept of ethnicity is critical.

In this chapter we first discuss and differentiate the concepts of ethnicity and minority and emphasize the great cultural diversity masked by the labels most commonly used in referring to ethnic minority populations in the United States. We present examples of several ethnic groups to illustrate some of the cultural variation affecting the ethnic aged. The groups chosen are African American, American Indian (Navajo), Mexican American, Asian American (Chinese and Japanese), and Italian American.

The terms *ethnicity* and *minority* are often used interchangeably or even together—ethnic/minority group, for example. There are differences in these concepts that need to be considered. Richard Kalish (1986) has offered the following explanation of *ethnicity*:

> *Ethnicity* refers to (a) group membership based on (b) the integration of (c) values and feelings and (d) practices and behavior that (e) arise though historical roots in the family of origin and (f) through common cultural, religious, national, and/or linguistic background, and (g) culminate in a shared symbol system and (h) a sense of shared identity. This approach suggests that ethnicity is a living reality, a way of life. (p. 17)

Subsumed under this definition could be a wide array of customs with which members of an ethnic group would identify—food preferences; patterns of dress; musical styles; family configurations; beliefs about education, work, health, and illness; strategies for solving problems; and, of course, ideas and attitudes about aging.

> A *minority*, as defined by Wirth (1945), is a group of people who, because of their physical or cultural characteristics, are singled out from the others in the society in which they live for differential and unequal treatment, and who therefore regard themselves as objects of collective discrimination. (p. 347)

He further describes the status of minorities relative to the dominant group as "disadvantageous," with restricted access to "opportunities," and therefore little "freedom of choice." "The members of minority groups are held in lower esteem and may even be objects of contempt, hatred, ridicule, and violence. They are generally socially isolated and frequently spatially segregated" (Wirth, 1945, p. 348).

It should be noted that *minority* is not used here as a numerical term, meaning a smaller number, although most minorities are in fact outnumbered by the white population in most of the United States. In Wirth's terms, the black population in South Africa has clearly had minority status even though it is much larger than the dominant white population.

Ethnicity, then, is based in cultural heritage, while minority status as defined is characterized by inequality and discrimination. When one speaks of minority groups in the United States, the reference is generally to African American, Asian/Pacific Islander Americans, Hispanic, and Native Americans. It is also common to describe them, including minority aged, in terms of social problems associated with membership in these groups—poverty, limited education, housing problems, and lower life expectancy, for example. Any of these groups can also be described in terms of ethnic characteristics. It is these cultural characteristics that we want to emphasize in this book although some consideration of problem issues is necessary to understanding the ethnic elderly.

It is important to recognize that the labels used above to identify various groups are simplistic and may mask a great deal of cultural diversity. The Hispanic population, for example, includes people from Mexico, Cuba, Puerto Rico, Spain, various Central and South American countries, and the Caribbean islands. While there may be some underlying cultural commonalities, there is still great variation. The "Asian Pacific" label covers even greater diversity. Major Asian groups found in the United States are Japanese, Chinese, Filipino, Korean, Vietnamese, Thai, Laotian, and Cambodian; Pacific Islanders include Samoans, Tongans, Guamanians, to name only a few. The largest island populations tend to be from territories of the United States. There is great linguistic variation as well as very different political histories, belief systems, and value orientations represented among these peoples. The designation "Native Americans" now includes American Indians, Eskimos, and Aleuts. Historically, American Indians may have had very similar experiences over the past few centuries at the hands of white settlers and government officials but the dozens of different tribes in this country represent considerable variation in other aspects of their cultural heritage.

To this mix of ethnic groups, we must add the many white ethnic populations in the United States. These are the Euro-American peoples listed by Guttmann (1986) as

> Albanians, Armenians, Basques, Belgians, Bulgarians, Byelorussians, Carpatho-Ruthenians, Croatians, Cypriots, Czechoslovaks, Danes, Dutch, Estonians, Finns, French, Germans, Greeks, Hungarians, Italians, Jews, Latvians, Lithuanians, Luxembourgers, Maltese, Norwegians, Poles, Portuguese, Romanians, Russians, Serbians, Slovaks, Slovenians, Spanish, Swedish, Ukrainians, and Yugoslavs. One could also add the English, Irish, Welsh, and Scots, as these ethnic groups also originate in Europe. However, they are not usually included in this designation because English is the common language. (p. 6)

In other words, the representatives of the non-English-speaking countries of Europe are those typically categorized as white ethnics. Their numbers are many and their history in the United States extends back into the nineteenth century, and yet as ethnics they are to some extent invisible. It may be assumed, incorrectly, that all whites in the United States are the same (Kalish, 1986) when compared with the previously mentioned minority ethnic groups. It may also be assumed that Euro-Americans are more assimilated into the mainstream culture, but this, too, is a mistaken belief.

In the metropolitan areas of the Midwest and the northeastern states, these Euro-Americans are often more visible in ethnic residential and/or business enclaves within the cities, but outsiders still may be unaware of the cultural patterns that structure life in these neighborhoods. According to Guttmann (1986), recognition of Euro-American elderly as distinctive groups with needs/problems requiring sensitivity to cultural variation is a recent phenomenon. As with other ethnic groups, the aged may feel more allegiance to traditional customs and values. Kalish (1986) explains this situation: "Since the elderly are more likely than their younger counterparts to have been socialized in a family setting in which ethnic values permeated everything that went on, Euro-American elderly are frequently more influenced by traditional values than the non-elderly" (p. 27).

These comments refer specifically to Euro-American elderly, but the same statement would apply to many other ethnic populations as well.

We should expect to find variation in the particular cultural values that are meaningful in different groups. It should be noted that there are also social class differentiations within any given ethnic group.

We do not mean to suggest that there are no changes in the culture of ethnic groups after immigration. Cool (1987) indicates that change does occur but without necessarily "damaging the group's viability as an ongoing collective identity" (p. 265). Kalish (1986) speaks of this persistence of ethnic identity "for over a century. Although undoubtedly the form has altered . . . the customs, rituals, language, values, and a sense of group belongingness have continued" (p. 20). And this is possible even when a group becomes dispersed geographically and people have extensive involvement with outsiders (Kalish, 1986).

Individual members of an ethnic group may alternately emphasize or sublimate their ethnicity in some situations or at different points in their lives. In the workplace or when dealing with casual acquaintances, ethnic attributes may not be apparent. At home, with friends from within the ethnic group, or in old age, ethnic identity may be activated and even accentuated. And there is evidence (Amoss, 1981; Cool, 1981) that ethnic identity may function as a source of prestige for elders. The aged often provide a link to the past history of a people that has been obscured as the result of social and cultural change. In her work with Coast Salish Indians, Pamela Amoss (1981) found just such a situation:

> They now find themselves in a period when people want to affirm their Indian identity and need the old to legitimize their claim to an exclusive cultural tradition. . . . So although many of the active old people are developing new solutions out of old ideas, both they and their younger relatives emphasize orthodoxy, not innovation. The contemporary aged are taking advantage of the current enthusiasm for the old ways both to perpetuate what is most central in the old values and to improve their own position in the social group. (p. 229)

African American Aged

For many years the influence of African roots on the behavior of African Americans has been controversial. Glazer and Moynihan (1963) staunchly maintain that "the Negro is only an American and nothing else. He has no values and culture to guard and protect" (p. 51). E. Franklin Frazier (1939), in *The Negro Family in the United States,* argues that images of the African past are merely "forgotten memories" and that in regard to "the Negro family, there is no reliable evidence that African culture has had any influence on its development" (p. 12).

Opposing this point of view are a number of social scientists and historians (Billingsley, 1968; Hentoff, 1966; Herskovits, 1941; Pollard, 1978; Wylie, 1971) who believe that African Americans represent an ethnic subculture with a unique cultural history involving the following circumstances: (a) blacks came from Africa and not Europe; (b) they came as slaves and therefore were separated from their family systems and cultural orientations in which they had been enculturated; and (c) blacks have been excluded from meaningful participation in major institutions of the United States from slavery days until the present (Billingsley, 1968).

While these circumstances do not lead us to conclude that the value orientation and behavioral patterns of African Americans are markedly African, neither can we see justification for assuming that African Americans are carriers of the same cultural traditions as whites. One need only look to the literature on elderly black Americans to realize that life is quite different for them compared with their white counterparts. For example, Messer (1968), Wylie (1971), Jackson (1982), Manton (1982), George (1988), Taylor (1988), and Groger (1992) have established the following model differences between black and white senior citizens' lifestyles. Although there are class and socioeconomic differences within groups, in comparison with whites, it is possible to generalize that African Americans

(a) see old age more as a reward than a disaster;
(b) have fewer anxieties about old age, and therefore higher morale;
(c) are less likely to deny their actual age;
(d) tend to remain part of their family structure to a greater degree, and consequently are more respected and better treated;
(e) are strongly supported by bonds of mutual assistance (with friends, neighbors, and family);
(f) are more likely to maintain useful and acceptable family functions;
(g) are more likely to be tolerated by their families in spite of behavioral peculiarities;

(h) are generally more religious but less involved in economic and political institutions;

(i) feel less integrated into the society at large;

(j) have a life expectancy at birth of approximately 8 years less for men (64.8) and 5½ years less for women (73.5);

(k) live longer once they reach the age of 75;

(l) tend to be in poorer health; and

(m) are considerably less prone to commit suicide.

While a case could possibly be made that blacks have had a different enough history of events in the United States to account for most of these differences, many believe that African patterns modified during slavery and postslavery days account for the bulk of the variance.

Critics of the idea that African traditional influences can be discovered in New World family forms and various aspects of black social behavior often point to the immensity of the African continent and the multiplicity of cultural systems found there. Therefore one questions how one can narrow down this diversity to a single model of African behavior. However, Africans came to the United States as slaves, and the overwhelming majority came from a number of tribal societies located along the coastal area of West Africa between the Senegal and Congo Rivers, with the bulk of the captives coming from regions known today as Nigeria, Ghana, Benin, Ivory Coast, and Sierra Leone. Although the cultural traditions of West African tribal societies varied considerably, Melville J. Herskovits (1967) has cited numerous common denominators that could conceivably represent a baseline for the New World black culture. The following are traits shared throughout the West or Guinea Coast of Africa:

1. The people lived in large kingdoms with complex economic, social, and political institutions.

2. Societies were essentially agricultural but were marked by a considerable degree of labor specialization (in trading, crafts, religion, and art), and cooperative labor and mutual self-help was the norm.

3. The extended family was well recognized, with kinship traced legally though one line (matrilineal or patrilineal).

4. Although monogamous marriage was most common, polygyny was sanctioned and in many cases preferred. In such marriages

the mother was the most important family influence in the children's lives, because a child had to share a father (who lived in a separate house) with many half-siblings, but lived with a mother who only had to be shared with a few siblings.

5. The fundamental sanction of the kinship system was the ancestral cult that tended to deify dead kinsmen. Elderly people were known as "almost ancestors."

6. In addition to ancestor veneration, the basic religious pattern featured a pantheon of gods, each with its own special groups of worshippers (cults) and its own elaborate rituals.

The attitudes and patterns of behavior that West African societies evolved in relating to their elderly are notable. In Dahomey a popular proverb declared, "Respect the elders, for they are our fathers," and according to Herskovits (1938), Dahomeans believed that

with age comes considerable judgment, but more important, with age comes a closer affinity to the ancestral dead, and it is injudicious to act rashly with one who may any day have the opportunity to carry a grievance to the world of the dead. (p. 351)

In most groups, the elderly served as political leaders and counselors, and Rattray (1923) maintains that, among the Ashanti, elderly men and women were the ones who had accurate knowledge, and the people's respect for their wisdom was expressed in the proverb, "The words from the mouth of an old man are better than an amulet." Old men and women were, in fact, thought of as the coiners and keepers of proverbs.

In much of West Africa, elderly men and women were referred to as "grandfather" and "grandmother" as a mark of respect even by nonkin, and the word *grandfather* is reported by Wylie (1971) to be a general term used by the Hausa of Nigeria to refer to the members of the village advisory groups. Among the Ashanti, *grandfather* and *grandmother* were terms used to address local deities (Ellis, 1887, pp. 53-54).

The use of these kinship terms to convey respect gives some indication of what grandparents represented in the West African family systems. Herskovits (1938) relates that, in Dahomey (today called Benin), "the relationship between grandparents and grandchildren is very close, and the young children often live with their grandparents by preference. There is, indeed, the saying that a man's grandchildren are his true children" (p. 155). Not only were young people taught in the home to respect the elderly in general and their aged kin in particular, but secret societies such as the Beri and Sande among the Vai prepared youth for the duties of adulthood and trained them "to respect their parents and elders" (Ellis, 1914, pp. 126-127).

When the Africans (mostly young and mostly male) were taken from their homeland and shipped in overcrowded, squalid slave ships to ports in the Caribbean and the American South, the captives brought nothing except the clothes on their backs and the cultural traditions that they carried in their heads. While there were no doubt few if any slaves over 65 shipped out of Africa, there is evidence that age seniority was honored even if it only involved showing deference to fellow slaves just a few years senior.

Historians and social scientists who hold that slavery conditions were such that African heritages were soon forgotten in the New World are apparently not familiar with a wealth of evidence that indicates that certain aspects of culture can be tremendously tenacious even in the face of forced change. Felix Keesing (1953), for example, found that the area of "primary group relations," involving ascribed statuses of age and sex and intimate rights and responsibilities of household and immediate family kin groups, is extremely persistent. An equally conservative area of culture is found to be "status maintenance" (conserving established superior status and entrenched authority). It is also notable that those aspects of culture learned through conditioning as a child (as respect for elders was in Africa) tend to be more resistant to change than those learned as an adult.

It is not unreasonable to expect blacks to have retained various aspects of African family behavior, certain ideas about respect for the aged, and positive attitudes toward one's own aging. Importing slaves from Africa continued as late as 1808, and it is commonplace for particular values and culture patterns to persist among a people for periods much greater than 200 years even in the face of adversity. An example is the Jews, who in spite of a history of slavery, persecution, and even genocide have preserved many of their religious and cultural traditions for hundreds of years. Persistence of cultural values is also noted in Alexis de Tocqueville's *Democracy in America*. This book, written in 1835, describes a value system not greatly different than what is found in America today, in spite of the fact that since its writing we have moved from an agricultural society to an industrial one and from a rural society to an urban one.

Herskovits (1941) devotes two entire chapters of *Myth of the Negro Past* to Africanisms in contemporary African American culture, citing such aspects as motor behavior, religious fervor, etiquette, cooperative work patterns, folklore motifs, and musical styles, and, most significant for our purpose, the importance of the extended family, a respect for age, and a special feeling for the mother and grandmother. Recalling that kin terms like *grandfather* and *grandmother* were often used as respect titles in West Africa, it is interesting to note that Frederick Douglass recorded in 1855 that slaves used terms of address such as *uncle* and *aunty* to show respect, even for people who were not relatives. Douglass also stated that "there is not to be found, among my people, a more rigid enforcement of the law of respect to elders, than they maintain" (p. 69). Equally interesting is the idea among slaves, just before Emancipation, that

> it is considered bad luck to "sass" the old folks. This latter idea may have at one time had a real meaning, since the old folks were "almost ghosts," and hence worthy of good treatment lest their spirits avenge the disrespect and actually cause bad luck to the offender. (Douglass, 1855, p. 23)

Mintz and Price (1976) documented the fact that even in slavery the obligations that grew out of the quality of kinship ties were very strong and the tendency to use kin-reliance as a coping method prevailed. They write:

> The aggregate of newly arrived slaves, though they had been torn from their own local kinship networks, would have continued to view kinship as the normal idiom of social relations. Faced with the absence of real kinsmen, they nevertheless modeled their new social ties upon those of their masters to label their relationships with their contemporaries and with those older than themselves— "bro," "uncle," "auntie," "gran." (pp. 34-35)

The role of "grandmother" was particularly important on the plantation. Elderly women were often placed in charge of the small children during the day, while their parents labored in the fields. The older woman's role as nurturer and educator of the young has been well documented. Within the actual family context (what little there was), the mother remained the most dependable and stabilizing element in children's lives. While the concept of fatherhood was of little importance to many slaveholders, and while fathers were often sold away, most masters kept mothers and children together at least until adolescence. The mother was devoted to her children, made tremendous sacrifices for them, and was generally considered the head of the family. In many respects she functioned as mothers do in polygynous households in West Africa.

Conditions were little better for the black family during the Emancipation and Reconstruction periods. At this time blacks had the *freedom* to die of starvation or illness. In some communities it is estimated that one out of four succumbed. The impact of this postslavery era is described by Frazier (1959):

> The disorder and confusion were the test of the strength and character of family ties. In many cases the family ties which were supported only by habit and custom were broken. . . . Through this chaotic situation, the Negro mother held the family group together and supported her children. This devotion was based upon her traditional role and partly upon the deep emotional attachment to her young that was evoked in the face of danger. (p. 72)

The matrifocal family still exists in the United States and Eshleman (1988) reports that slightly over half of black families have a woman as household head. In many cases, these heads are grandmothers whose authority is partly based on age and partly on the role of "granny" (midwife and repository of folk wisdom). Hortense Powdermaker (1936) comments on the grandmother role as she observed it in a small Mississippi town in 1932-1934:

> Grandmothers are present in many households, and are likely to loom larger than mothers on the child's horizon, even when the real mother retains the chief authority. . . . When an elderly woman is head of a household including a married daughter, she carries authority with the children; even where her position is less dominant, she is likely to take a share of responsibility for their welfare and behavior. (pp. 200-201)

As a result of economic circumstances as well as cultural proclivities, there also appears to be greater emphasis on the extended family in the African American community than can be found in the Anglo. Linda George (1988) writes:

> Older blacks are more likely to live with their children (i.e., children of any age) and to live in households in which at least one member is less than 18 years old. Thus the proportion of intergenerational households is significantly larger among aged blacks. (p. 113)

Not only are intergenerational families more common among blacks but it is very common for elderly African Americans to take children, grandchildren, nieces, nephews, or even friends' children into their households to raise. Considerable reciprocity characterizes the familial interaction in these households, however. Strom, Collinsworth, Strom, and Griswold (1992-1993) report that

> when compared to Anglos, Black parents were more likely to give money to grandparents, take them places, shop and run errands, repair things, and provide care during times of illness. In a recip- rocal way, Black grandparents were more likely than Anglo grand- parents to assist sons and daughters by taking grandchildren into their homes and caring for them. (p. 256)

Without question the black family cherishes its elderly and consid- ers them a powerful influence in the lives of its children. Mutran (1985) found that black elderly received more aid from their families than did white elders even when socioeconomic differences were taken into con- sideration. Shanas (1979) records that she found, while there was a pattern of white grandparents providing aid to their children and grand- children, in black families children and grandchildren were more likely to aid the grandparents.

Even if grandparents and grandchildren do not live in the same household, there is still a great deal of contact and interaction. Taylor and Chatters (1991) record that "elderly Black adults . . . reported frequent contact with family members, close affective bonds with family, satisfac- tion with family life, and relatively close residential proximity to imme- diate and extended family" (p. S213).

While the black family remains the principal agent of socialization and economic support for the black elderly, neighborhoods also play an important role in sustaining not only the childless but elderly African Americans in general. Neighborhoods often feature strong networks of mutual aid, particularly in urban areas where the aged are often neighborhood-bound (Jayakody, 1993). Friendship networks that develop within neighborhoods sometimes resemble kin configurations. Taylor (1988) describes how these relationships—operative since slavery days—function.

> It is not uncommon for unrelated older individuals to be given the appellation "aunt" or "uncle" or to be referred as a "play mother or father." Friends referred to in kinship terms tend to intensify bonds of mutual obligation in a normally casual relationship. Persons designated as fictive or pseudo-kin, though unrelated by either blood or marriage, are regarded in kinship terms and accorded many of the associated rights and statuses. Generally, pseudo-kin fully participated in the informal support network. (p. 274)

Another supportive resource for elderly blacks is the church, for religion has always been a powerful force in the lives of African Americans. Taylor (1993) writes: "Aged black adults report participating in religious activities more frequently than aged whites and are more likely to attend religious services, pray regularly, listen to religious programs and read the Bible" (p. 102).

In addition to social spiritual fulfillment, a considerable number of elderly blacks find economic support from their congregation, although Catholics are less likely to receive aid than Protestants. Also, those with higher incomes and those from rural areas were less dependent on the church for assistance.

While elderly blacks far exceed their Anglo counterparts in their participation in religious activities, the opposite is true in regard to political participation, although considering the road blocks to such activity that they have experienced throughout American history it is surprising that elderly African Americans are political at all. It is the elderly, however, who have the greatest faith in the power of the ballot, as many young blacks have been disillusioned with the democratic process. Older blacks, who have experienced great change in civil rights over their lifetime, still believe that their vote can have a positive effect on the political climate (Brown & Brown-Nacoste, 1993).

Retirement appears to be less of a goal for elderly blacks than whites, and it is not unusual to find blacks still working well into their sixties and seventies. Coleman (1993) found in her research on African American retirement practices that "a large number of older blacks said they would continue to work even if they were financially secure. Perhaps older blacks have internalized the work norm and have an intrinsic desire to work" (p. 274).

On the other hand, working past retirement age is no doubt a necessity for a large number of elderly African Americans who may have no social security or pension income. Two thirds of Coleman's sample of black women 60 years of age and above continued to work even though they were earning less than $3,000 a year, and 17% were bringing in less than $1,000. She also found more elderly black women working than black men, but many of them were widowed. Many continued to work despite debilitating health problems.

American Indian Aged

Describing *the* heritage of the American Indian is not possible, for there are some 307 officially recognized political entities—tribes, bands, nations, and other group designations (O'Leary & Levinson, 1991)—speaking approximately 149 separate languages (Voegelin, 1941) in the United States alone. While the average American tends to think of the American Indian as a buffalo hunter who excelled in horsemanship, wore a feathered war bonnet, and once fought U.S. cavalrymen, this image is hardly representative of Indians in general. In fact, the cultural variety in North America is so complex that anthropologists have been forced to use a classification device known as *culture areas* to conceptualize the mass of cultural data relating to Native Americans. A culture area is a region within which the inhabitants exhibit a greater similarity in cultural behavior with each other than they do with people in other regions. Various culture area schemes have been used featuring anywhere between 7 (Kroeber, 1948) and 17 (Driver, 1969) regions of common culture in North America.

Within these areas, traditional Indian subsistence patterns include such ways of getting a living as caribou hunting in the subarctic regions, salmon fishing on the Northwest Coast, acorn and pine nut collecting in the Great Basin region of California, bison hunting on the Plains, and intensive agriculture in the Southwest and Southeast Woodlands. In the area of social organization, we find kinship to be traced through the mother's line (matrilineal) among many Southeast and Northeast Woodlands groups, through the father's line (patrilineal) among many Plains tribes, and through both lines (bilineal) among Plateau and subarctic region groups. Emphasis in some places is on the nuclear family (Chippewyan and other subarctic peoples), but on large household, extended families, and even clans in most other regions. Political units vary from band (Plains and Western subarctic) to autonomous villages (Northwest Coast and Southwest) to tribes and tribal confederations (Southeast and Northeast Woodlands).

Just as variable as the economic and political traits of North American Indians were the attitudes toward and treatment of the elderly. Simmons (1945a) records that among the Pomo decrepit aged were sometimes strangled, that among the Hopi the death of old people was often hastened by lack of care and by the "meanness" of daughters-in-law, and that the aged among the Chippewa might be killed by their sons or left to starve on a barren island. On the other hand, Simmons records that elderly Haida enjoyed great authority and respect and received exceptional care from their relatives. Aged Iroquois were often "rulers of the house," and Crow Indians were expected to provide their aged relatives with the best food—stripped tenderloin, dried, pounded, and mixed with bone marrow (p. 184).

With all this cultural diversity, it is tremendously difficult to state exactly how "Indianness" affects the aging process of this ethnic category. Most anthropologists are reluctant to generalize about what all these people hold in common and what could be used as a baseline to begin our discussion of what it means to grow old as an American Indian. However, J. Richard Connelly (1980) cautiously suggests that the following values and cultural characteristics tend (with qualifications) to be consistent among all American Indian groups; that is, they are *pan-Indian*:

(a) respect for individual freedom and autonomy;
(b) a tendency to seek group consensus, not majority rule;
(c) respect for the land and all living things, and an appreciation for their contributions to Native American lifestyle;

(d) a propensity for "demonstrations of hospitality" and respect;
(e) a dictum that "one should avoid bringing shame on oneself, family, clan or tribe" (p. VI-19); and
(f) a belief in a supreme being and life after death (p. VI-19).

In addition, most Native Americans have always had great respect for the family, for the elderly, and for the sharing of resources with friends, kin, and community (Weibel-Orlando, 1989). Most groups featured large extended-family interaction, and often single households were composed of an assortment of nuclear family members plus grandparents, aunts, uncles, and cousins. Within these family networks, the elders were responsible for preserving traditional cultural values and knowledge.

Perhaps as important as any set of universal traditional values in understanding the situation of the aging Indian today is the nearly four-century-old history of contact with whites, which included successive periods that were directed at (a) extermination, (b) expulsion, (c) exclusion, and (d) assimilation (Connelly, 1980).

Extermination. The desire of whites to eliminate the competition began with devout Puritans in New England thanking God for sending smallpox epidemics to decimate local tribes, and was perpetuated on the frontier with the sentiment that "the only good Indian is a dead Indian."

Expulsion. During the years of America's western expansion, a series of treaties and laws removed Indians from their lands whenever a region became sufficiently populated by settlers. When no more open land remained, Indians were rounded up and placed on reservations, which were generally undesirable parcels of land in places like Oklahoma, the Dakotas, New Mexico, and Montana.

Exclusion. With their placement on reservations, the Indians lost forever any hope of achieving equality with whites. Not only were they denied access to the white world, but the whites came onto their reservations and tried to do away with anything that was Indian, particularly the language and religious ceremonies. Not only did the government in Washington not want these people to be Indians, after World War I Congress decided that Indians were not really citizens and that they had no basis for equality with whites. Indians were not permitted to use their own land for whatever purpose they chose without securing permission from the Bureau of Indian Affairs.

Assimilation. From the very beginning, government policy toward American Indians has been to make them disappear as a recognizable ethnic group. Public schools in Indian areas forbade the use of native tongues because "real Indians must speak English." The Bureau of Indian Affairs' relocation program encouraged Indians to leave the reservation by giving them a one-way bus or train ticket and a small adjustment allowance. Returning home was regarded as unforgivable and was referred to as going "back to the blanket." Cahn (1969) maintains that "the Indian is rewarded for rejecting the approval or disapproval of his elders and his peers" and for rejecting "his people's standard of achievement, performance and contribution" (p. 136).

Given the diversity of Native American cultures and given the history of oppression and discrimination to which Indian people have been subjected, it is difficult indeed to make any general statement about the influence of Native American tradition on the status of Indian aged as a whole. Perhaps the circumstances in which elderly Native Americans find themselves may be more influential in shaping their lifestyle than their traditional culture.

Of all the facts relating to the state of Native Americans as an ethnic group, the most debilitating and oppressive is their poverty. As a people they have for many generations experienced the worst poverty known to any ethnic group in the United States. About one fourth of Native Americans have incomes below the poverty level, and the number increases to about 40% for those who live on reservations (Utter, 1993). According to Cook (1990), Social Security is a source of income for only 50% of American Indians; "fewer than 51% receive Medicare benefits, and fewer than 40% receive Medicaid" (p. 140). Their numbers are negligible in nutrition programs, and less than 12% of reservation Indians benefit from Title VI of the Older Americans Act, which provides grants specifically for American Indians (Cook, 1990). Block (1979) writes:

> For most, the poverty of old age is the result of a lifetime of deprivation. American Indians from the time of birth, have experienced substandard housing, limited education, inadequate income,

poor health, malnutrition, a lack of urgently needed services, and the emotional problems inherent in a changing culture. With advancing age, the severity of these conditions is intensified. (p. 184)

By 1988 life expectancy had increased to 72 years (67 for men, 75 for women) but remained lower than for the general population. Indians are also

more likely . . . to suffer and die from a variety of causes, including all types of accidents (2.3 times as likely), liver disease (3.4 times), diabetes (2.6 times), pneumonia and influenza (1.3 times), suicide (1.3 times), homicide (1.6 times), and tuberculosis (5 times). (Utter, 1993, p. 187)

Death rates from alcoholism, although significantly reduced in recent years, remain 5.3 times that of the population as a whole (Utter, 1993).

The Reservation

The problems of American Indians are generally more critical on reservations than in urban areas. Economic, health, and education services are less adequate; the people are more isolated; and they have less freedom or opportunity to act independently in helping themselves. Their only source of help is a less than enthusiastic bureaucratic structure, the Bureau of Indian Affairs. Block (1979) writes of the reservation:

Younger Indians are often forced to leave the reservation if they are to realize any sort of job opportunity. Wages are often minimal, barely covering basic needs. Unable to support additional family members, and equally unable to send money back to the reservation, the young Indian leaves his aging parents with no economic base. Older family members sometimes receive welfare grants, but these are usually inadequate to cover basic needs. The traditional kinship support system of the family structure is unfeasible when the family has no resources, and the tribe is unable to assume the responsibility and care of the elderly because economically it is no better off. (p. 188)

To obtain a clearer understanding of the nature of American Indian aging, we will describe one reservation population, the Navajo, in the American Southwest.

The Navajo

The Navajo today (numbering 128,338) live on the largest reservation in the United States, an area in New Mexico, Arizona, and Utah about the size of the state of West Virginia. Like many other reservations it has become home for the very young and the very old. There are approximately 5,000 elderly. Many of the young adults have left to seek economic opportunities in nearby urban communities or in industrial metropolises such as Los Angeles, Dallas-Fort Worth, Denver, or Chicago.

Traditionally, the Navajo were a hunting and agricultural people, but they have been sheep raisers since 1680. Their social system features matrilineal descent and matrilocal residence, and consequently women play an influential role, partly because of their contributions to social and economic life and partly because of their control of a large share of family property.

The basic social unit is the nuclear family of a woman, her husband, and their unmarried offspring. This entity interacts with other related nuclear families "within shouting distance of each other" in a multi-household residence group that is referred to as a camp (Kunitz & Levy, 1991, p. 40). These social units, which cooperate in both domestic and economic activities, remain the preferred residence unit in spite of the decline of the traditional herding economy and the growth of wage labor.

The Navajo have perhaps been more fortunate than most Native Americans because they were able to continue their agricultural and herding activities with success until the 1930s, when overgrazing, soil erosion, and the decline of the wool and lamb markets resulted in government action to curtail these subsistence activities. According to Kunitz and Levy (1991): "After livestock reduction, there were no longer any wealthy families, only the poor and the very poor" (p. 17). Fifty percent of Navajo families have incomes below the poverty level. While the economic impact of this event on the Navajo lifestyle was pronounced, elderly Navajos were particularly disadvantaged.

The elderly had always been held in high esteem, and the phrase *My Father* was a generic term of respect accorded an old man. The address *Grandfather* was used in referring to deities. Much of the deference conferred on Navajo elderly was connected with their control of property, and Reichard (1928) tells us that aged Navajo owned large numbers of horses, sheep, cattle, and goats as well as intangible property such as songs, dances, medical knowledge, and formulas for increasing flocks. "Knowledge wealth" was seen as more valuable than material wealth, and the elderly pretty much controlled both.

When government agents began the stock reduction program and also put pressure on the older owners of stock to give substantial numbers of animals to their heirs for support of the younger generation's larger families, the prestige of the elderly declined in several ways. Kunitz and Levy (1991) record that

> Crooked Finger and his wives decided to transfer their sheep permits to some of their children and grandchildren. . . . This event marked Crooked Finger's transition from leader to dependent aged, and coincidently it was during this year that the health status of the trio began to decline. (p. 21)

With limits on the number of animals that could be owned, "knowledge wealth" (particularly information about how to care for and increase flocks) had no value, because the government would not permit flocks to grow in size. Other traditional sources of prestige for the aged were threatened as well. According to Reichard (1928), in former times young men trained in the use of therapeutic magic were required to give their aged teachers large gifts, and "certain old men could make a good living by the performance of healing rites" (pp. 90-91). Now, because young men cannot increase their flocks, it is impossible for them to pay for years of apprenticeship to a ceremonial healer, and, anyway, free medical services on the reservation are competing with the expensive and time-consuming traditional healing rituals.

Recent literature having to do with caregiving for elderly Navajo relates that these people still follow age-old patterns of assigning daughters, or preferably 8- to 10-year-old grandchildren, to function "as eyes and ears, hands and feet, herding sheep, chopping wood, hauling water and generally helping out. They are referred to as 'little sheep herders' " (Shomaker, 1990, p. 22). This relationship is seen as mutually beneficial because the "little sheep herders . . . enjoy the warm, loving relationship with their grandparents, and the socializing process of learning the things a Navajo should know by this apprenticeship with their grandparents" (p. 22).

Reciprocity is an important consideration in the intergenerational relationships, and many grandmothers maintain that if they will not be cared for in their declining years it is their fault, because they should have

The elderly Navajo artist is well attended by a granddaughter. (Photo
courtesy of Arthur H. Rohn; used by permission.)

taught their children and grandchildren that "good Navajos" care for
children and old people.

In spite of adverse economic conditions in the last 60 years, there
remains a considerable amount of respect for the elderly. Shomaker
(1990) reports that long life and the elderly are highly valued but that the
people are very realistic about it all. She describes the attitude as follows:

> To be old is desirable, and inevitable, but should be put off as long
> as possible. Old people who are capable have considerable power,
> but those that have begun to dissolve, become frail and incapable
> of contributing, stand a good chance of being ignored. (p. 26)

On the other hand, "if one is old and powerful such as a healing
'singer', there is a strong possibility that that person will be accused of
using witchcraft to attain longevity" (Shomaker, 1990, pp. 26-27).

Present day attitudes are quite different than some that used to prevail in regard to dependent aged. Shomaker (1990) reports that at one time when people became too frail to be productive "the older person surveyed his condition and burden on the resources, and decided it was time to be taken out and left to die" (p. 30). Today such people, with Social Security checks and a welfare system, no longer must face such a decision.

While the Navajo pride themselves on caring for their own frail elderly, caretaking has generated many strategies. Placing the elderly in nursing homes is not one of them, however, except in the most extreme circumstances. The only "skilled" care facility in Navajo country is located in Chinle and has only 29 beds, although these have a 95% to 100% occupancy rate. While this establishment is managed by the Navajo tribe, the Navajos would much prefer to move entirely into home care programs because (a) they believe it is the younger generation's responsibility to care for their own elderly relatives and (b) such services would cost less and more effectively serve the needs of their old people.

Concerning the Navajo prejudice against nursing homes, Shomaker (1990) writes:

> Nursing homes are looked upon with great disfavor by the Navajo because many have died there, and spirits may still be in the building. For that reason the Navajo avoid going into buildings where someone has died. Hogans are boarded up after a death to warn others to stay away. (p. 31)

Intergenerational problems persist in spite of a generally supportive kinship system. Young people are now encouraged to shift from traditional economic pursuits to wage work, and old people are a burden in this cash-oriented economy, unless of course they get a welfare check. The traditional domestic skills of the aged are of less importance in the more modern homes that the young people prefer, and young people who have managed to become educated do not always appreciate the old way of doing things. Levy writes (1967): "Young mothers complain that their parents do not care for the infant grandchildren properly. They are said to be unsanitary, careless and do not 'discipline' the children" (pp. 232-233). Present attitudes obviously have changed considerably if we can believe Reichard when she wrote in 1928, that "old people usually have a large pile of sheepskins and blankets upon which to recline—the other members of the family have one or two—they occupy the warmest place in the hogan and they are patiently waited on" (p. 57). They were the recipients of the best the family could offer—good food, a place by the fire, and, most important, great respect.

Urban Aged Native Americans

The Relocation Act of 1952 was designed to force assimilation of Native Americans by moving them off the reservations with promises of occupational training and jobs. By 1968 nearly 68,000 Indians had moved to town, and today more American Indians live in urban areas than in rural areas (1,057,906 compared with 820,379) (U.S. Bureau of the Census, 1992b). Of these urban dwellers, 5.5% are 65 or older. Native Americans have not really migrated to the city voluntarily, even though the relocation program was first called the "Voluntary Relocation Program." Indians have come to cities because of lack of employment opportunities and because of overwhelming educational, social, and health problems on reservations. The Native Americans who have migrated come from a great variety of backgrounds, but they share the fact that they have all come from a small, rural community with a cultural heritage very different than that of white America, and from a situation of dependency and often a distasteful association with the Bureau of Indian Affairs. They arrive carrying many of the problems that plagued them on the reservation—lack of education, alcoholism, and poor health, for example—and are often confronted with a whole set of new ones growing out of their unfamiliarity with white manners, the anonymity of the urban area, their darker skin, which may invite discrimination, their lack of occupational skills, and, in some cases, their inadequate use of the English language.

They may find some encouragement and assistance. Many are able to live with relatives until they find work and a place to live permanently. Indian elderly are twice as likely as Anglos to live within extended families and 9% of urban households are three or four generations deep. Ablon (1964) writes:

> In general all Indians . . . tend to feel the responsibility of helping their kinsmen or tribesmen when asked, and will give money, food or lodging to a needy family. The flexibility of the Indian household often seems to be infinite and most Indian families assume that there is

Indian mothers and grandmothers often assume a major family-care role. (Photo courtesy of "Photographic Narrative, Indians of Kansas Exhibition," Mid-American All-Indian Center Museum; Photographer, Ken Engquist; used by permission.)

always room for five or six additional persons at their table or for lodging, no matter how small the actual living quarters may be. (p. 298)

Elderly Native Americans tend to remain on the reservation when their children migrate to the city, but when they do move, their economic situation is seldom improved. Where all food must be purchased and where high rents must be paid, any funds available for support of old people do not go as far as they did on the reservation. Some of these aged Native Americans get small amounts of "land claim money" (for land leased to cattle ranchers or oil companies), but these checks are often not enough to live on and, in addition, may render the recipients ineligible for public welfare.

The plight of the urban-dwelling Native American is a depressing one. A National Indian Conference on Aging report (1978) summarizes the condition of many of these individuals:

They suffer from arthritis, tuberculosis, alcoholism, heart attacks and strokes, loneliness and depression. They do not receive a broad range of medical and dental care; most medical care is of an emergency nature only. Their depressed state goes untreated. Many drink to mask their loneliness and fear. (p. 133)

Considering the problems Indians of all ages encounter in the city, it is not surprising that the matrifocal family also is found with some frequency in this setting. Moore (1979) tells us that "as tribal life has eroded, and husbands and fathers have fallen in battle or have died of accidents, suicides, tuberculosis or alcoholism, Indian mothers and grandmothers have assumed the major family-care role" (p. 458). Some have found that elderly people in general have been very important in holding the urban Indian family together. Schweitzer (1983) has pointed out that federal guidelines for participation in programs or services for the aged, particularly the age-segregated nature of most such activities, are often at odds with the realities of life for Indian elders. The Indian grandmothers and grandfathers who have responsibility for the care of grandchildren, for example, cannot take the young ones to a nutrition site where participation is restricted to senior citizens. They must either neglect their child-care duties or reject the program for which they are otherwise eligible; most choose the latter option.

This sense of obligation has generally been rewarded with respect, but in some cases this pattern is eroding. Although some researchers have reported a rise in elderly Indian status brought on by a desire on the part of some young people to recover their cultural heritage, the forces of acculturation to Anglo standards have been great. Federal programs tend to emphasize assisting younger Indians, and the pressure on these young people to adapt to a materialistic ethic has been highly detrimental to traditional Indian ideas about the importance of kin reliance and obligations to family members, particularly elderly ones.

Mexican American Aged

Of all the ethnic groups in the United States, the Mexican Americans have been among the most successful in retaining their culture and language. In part this is due to patterns of segregation. Most urban communities in the Southwest contain barrios where Mexican Americans speak their own language, read Spanish language newspapers, hear Latin music, buy ethnic food, and attend Catholic churches with congregations almost exclusively made up of Spanish-speaking worshippers. Lifestyle retention can also be explained by the fact that Mexican Americans are constantly being reinforced culturally by people arriving from Mexico. An estimated 51% of the Mexican American elderly were born in Mexico as well as about 90% of those arrived in the United States prior to 1980 (U.S. Bureau of the Census, 1993b), many of them long before that date.

To understand the role and status of Mexican American elderly, we must trace their cultural roots to Mexico and investigate how the family and its members function in relation to one another and in relation to the community. Although the village of Santo Tomás Mazaltepec in Oaxaca is not representative of all Mexico, it does give us some idea of familial patterns and value orientation in a small agricultural Indian community. It is from villages such as this that many of our Mexican Americans have come. The people of Santo Tomás Mazaltepec are corn farmers who live primarily in three-generational family households. Household heads are usually elderly men who live with their spouse and their sons' families or, in lieu of sons, the families of their daughters and sons-in-law. The isolated nuclear family is almost unknown here, and even when elderly couples live apart from other relatives, visitation by the latter takes place every day.

The elderly make up less than 4% of the population as this is generally a young population. Old people do not retire but instead continue to work at the same kinds of tasks as younger men and women as long as they are able. In time, the older men are not capable of handling the heavy agricultural work and must settle for lighter chores, often indistinguishable from those of children. Adams (1972) maintains the "deference to old people includes, in theory, not only respectful behavior toward them but also absolute obedience to their commands" (p. 108). Old people also enjoy greater freedom of action than the average individual, and greater tolerance of idiosyncratic behavior. Although the family pattern is definitely one of male dominance, women tend to become more outgoing and domineering as they get older, often to the point that they lord it over their husbands. The society, however, does not think this is proper behavior. Both old men and women function in the role of teachers, delineating proper conduct, relating historical events, and explaining the origin of things. While both sexes remain influential within the decision-making process of the household, a kind of public disengagement pattern is forced on elderly men.

After the age of 60, men are referred to as *afuera de la ley* (outside the law). They no longer vote or pay taxes, and they cease their involvement in community politics. Their opinions may influence the action their young relatives take politically, but they are expected to retire from political action themselves. The community has a kind of advisory board made up of past mayors of the village. This group of aging men is collectively known as the *representantes*, and while their opinions are solicited, they have no veto power.

A good deal of the indigenous Mexican pattern has been carried over in Mexican American families today, although about 80% of the families live in cities. To understand the Mexican American system and its impact on aging, we shall draw upon the insights of David Maldonado Jr. (1979), a Hispanic professor of social work. He writes:

> Most students of Chicano life tend to agree that the family holds the key to Chicano culture. . . . In spite of variations in interpretation, there is considerable consensus that the following are key characteristics of the Chicano family: (1) familism, (2) age hierarchy, (3) male leadership, and (4) mutual aid and support. (p. 178)

Familism. This is the term that refers to the centrality of family. Self-identity cannot be separated from family identity, and social status is derived from family status. Family welfare is usually considered more important than individual welfare. Kin networks figure greatly in daily living. Valle and Mendoza (1978) found that in San Diego 88% of their sample had family in the immediate neighborhood and reported frequent contact. While Mexican American familism involves a maximum of extended family interaction and exchange of mutual aid, in urban areas it does not necessarily involve three-generational residence. Thus these families have been labeled "modified extended families" (Litwak, 1965).

A study by Hurtado, Hayes-Bautista, Valdez, and Hernandez (1992) in southern California revealed that "the proportion of nuclear families living with extended kin falls from the first generation (26%) to the second and third generations (12% and 9% respectively)" (p. 16). Another study of 48 households carried out by Camilo Garcia (1993) in 1987 in a

Hispanic community in southern California found that only one in five households involved three-generational living, although all of them were "extended families" in functional terms; that is, they interacted on a daily basis with other related households in the vicinity. No grandparents lived alone, but only 8 out of 40 nuclear family units had live-in parents. There simply were not enough parents to go around, although all of the households would have gladly taken them in.

Familism appears to have both a positive and a negative aspect in regard to care for the elderly. Purdy and Arguello (1992) maintain that, while Hispanic families hold their elderly in extremely high regard and believe that it is their sacred duty to care for all their elderly relative's needs, they are so committed to meeting their filial obligations that they actually withhold information concerning the availability of valuable formal services that their elderly and, for that matter, the caregivers themselves desperately need. They also found that many of the Hispanic elders were not greatly different than their Anglo counterparts. While they wanted strong ties with their families, they also coveted a degree of independence, which their families were not always willing to grant.

Age Hierarchy. On this point Maldonado (1979) comments:

> As an individual matures, he/she increases in status. The young children must respect and obey the older siblings, who at times play parent roles. Adults are always to be respected, especially the elderly. To a large extent respect was associated with the authority that rested in the older person, but was also related to the continuing functional role that the elders played in the extended family. (p. 179)

Male Leadership. Although the machismo concept has been overemphasized, Mexican American culture does support the role of male family head as one who directs its activities, controls its behavior, arbitrates its disputes, and represents the family in the community and in the society. Ideally, the woman's role is one of subordination, but the woman who is too submissive is thought to be a fool. Actually, she has a good deal of decision-making authority on domestic issues.

Mutual Aid and Support. Not only is there a strong pattern of reciprocity and cooperation within the family but this willingness to help others extends also to friends and neighbors. Offspring are expected to provide support in their parents' old age, and traditional Mexican American parents have been secure in their anticipation that in old age they will be respected and wanted by their children. The elderly consider themselves vital members of the family because they perform important enculturative functions and because they view themselves as important links to the past. Therefore they do not feel useless or burdensome and are not embarrassed by support from their children or other family members. Although more than 70% of respondents in a San Diego study (Valle & Mendoza, 1978) stated that when in difficulty they would turn first to family for help, a number of investigators (Cuellar, 1978; Leonard, 1967; Valle & Mendoza, 1978) have reported that most Mexican Americans believe that the responsibility for meeting health, housing, transportation, and economic needs growing out of retirement belongs to the government (primarily federal). Leonard (1967) explains:

> Spanish tradition and custom impose rigid class differences that include a set of rights and duties concerning the needy. Aging rural people expect their landlords and other employers to provide them with a minimum level of subsistence in old age. This is not considered charity but rather a type of deferred payment for services. Obviously, it is not a major transfer to shift this attitude to the state. (pp. 247-248)

The Mexican American community also has a strong pattern of mutual aid, which is known as the *servidor* system. Valle and Mendoza (1978) found that in San Diego 74% of their sample of aged were providing neighborhood assistance to needy elderly. This included assisting neighbors with day-to-day needs such as food, temporary housing, and transportation.

Ideally, the Mexican American family is devoted to its elderly. They are seldom left alone, they are given the best of the family's food, the most comfortable of its chairs, and great affection. Maldonado (1975) writes:

> It is common to see a very old man bedridden at home, but surrounded daily by his children and grandchildren. And it is equally common to see a very old woman in such a situation. In a

way, that bedridden person even becomes the center of the family's life. (p. 214)

Mexican Americans rarely institutionalize their elderly, and the poorer families who are least able to support ailing old people are often the most insistent on keeping them at home.

Grandparents are revered by their children and grandchildren alike, but the father remains the prime decision maker. Grandchildren often go to grandparents with questions they are afraid to ask their fathers, but any important decisions regarding the children have to be referred to the father. Grandmothers seem to command greater attention than grandfathers, and Murillo (1971) maintains that "the mother continues to be close and warm, serving and nurturing even when her children are grown, married and have children of their own" (p. 104).

The Changing Scene

As noted earlier, 80% of Mexican Americans live in urban areas, where they tend to occupy ghettolike enclaves known as *barrios*. This movement from farms and small towns in the Southwest or directly to cities from Mexico has taken place since World War II and has been associated with the growth of industry in the West, particularly California.

The extended-family concept traditionally associated with Mexican Americans is showing signs of being replaced by nuclear family structures. If this is true, then we might expect major changes in the role and status of the aged. While extended families usually confer high status and ensure maximum security for the elderly, this form of family tends to be incompatible with urban life.

The Mexican American family, like that of many other ethnic groups, is succumbing to pressure to conform to the dominant American norms. As young people have migrated from rural to urban areas, they have often brought their aged with them. Extended-family living in rural areas allows elderly to perform useful, productive roles, but city life usually leaves them with little to do except menial domestic tasks and baby-sitting. Out of their element and surpassed in education by younger generations, the elderly find little that they can contribute in the way of knowledge or skill that is meaningful in the urban environment. The dilemma of the urban-dwelling elderly Mexican American was described in a Senate hearing by the Reverend Lawrence Matula (1969):

> In addition to the economic difficulties which are encountered by the aged Mexican American, they find themselves in a world apart. They are for the most part a lonesome group. They get sick rather easily, they lack good neighbor relationships, and their thinking is very different. They have difficulty getting their food and medical care because of distance and ambulatory problems. They feel themselves an imposition upon relatives and friends if they ask for help. (p. 234)

Young and old alike feel the tension and anxiety of a lifestyle in the process of transition. Although Mexican Americans cling to the ideal of extended-family living, urban circumstances make it impossible. The young continue to respect and cherish the elderly of their families, but their inability to care for them in traditional ways has produced guilt and a tendency to conceal their problems. Human-service delivery people often continue to labor under the misconception that the Hispanic extended family cares for its own and therefore move on to the needs of other minorities, content with the belief that the Mexican American aged are being well-attended by their families.

Asian American Aged

The term *Asian American* technically includes Chinese, Filipino, Japanese, Asian Indian, Korean, Vietnamese, Laotian, Cambodian, Hmong, and Thai people. This discussion, however, will deal with only two major groups, the Chinese and Japanese, who have the longest history of migration and settlement in the United States, a history that began at least as early as 1850 for Chinese and 1880 for Japanese. They are also present in greater numbers in the United States than are other Asians. The people of Korea and southeast Asia are, by comparison, relative newcomers. Although Chinese and Japanese are quite different in traditions, language, and religion, they have a number of things in common that set them apart from white Americans. Both peoples come from countries with very old and very highly developed civilizations. They followed one another in successive waves of migration to the United States and Canada, where they occupied a low occupational status as farmworkers or common laborers. They settled in Hawaii and in West Coast states, and the bulk of them remain in these parts of the country today. Both groups are racially distinct from other Americans, and both have encountered considerable racial discrimination. Theirs has been a common experience that has resulted in a tendency to take pride in the achievements of Asian peoples and a shared resentment at their treatment in America. The fact that both identify strongly with their lands of origin and the fact that human-service delivery personnel and scientists alike often lump them under a common category should not suggest that all Asian elderly are homogeneous. Let us instead review the separate histories and separate contemporary circumstances of Chinese and Japanese Americans.

Chinese Americans

The Chinese began their migration to America in the 1850s, when they came as coolie labor to work in California gold mines, at railroad building, and in domestic service. Later they became laundrymen, cooks, busboys, kitchen helpers, and porters. The high point in their population growth occurred about 1890, but then the population steadily declined until the 1930s when immigration restrictions were enacted. At this time, a considerable number of Chinese returned to their homeland.

The elderly constitute approximately 8% of the total Chinese American population, and while the sex ratio in the past was heavily weighted toward men due to immigration restrictions, a shift has now occurred and there are more women than men age 65 and over. As 83% of Chinese elderly were born abroad (U.S. Bureau of the Census, 1993a), the greater share of them have problems with the English language. These old Chinese have spent most of their lives living in a culture they do not understand and one they have not been able to influence.

In the United States most Chinese live on the Pacific coast, and about 95% live in cities; San Francisco, for example, has a Chinese population of approximately 131,000, and about 18,000 of them are aged (U.S. Bureau of the Census, 1993c; Van Steenberg, Ansak, & Chin-Hansen, 1993). Chinese American elderly live in urban neighborhoods and, because of the many cultural anomalies, many experience great insecurity and isolation. If they had remained in China, they would now be enjoying leisure, much attention, and great respect. The elderly who were reared in China were enculturated in a system in which children were expected to be subservient and dependent, and it must be difficult for them to understand the ways of American-educated youth. Most of their own children (now middle aged) were able to acquire a better education, more saleable skills, and therefore greater earning power than their parents, and this must be seen as very abnormal for traditional-minded Chinese who never experienced such upward mobility in their Chinese homeland.

Much of the isolation that elderly Chinese feel is associated with their inability to communicate with Anglo Americans. A San Diego study (Cheng, 1978) found that 80% of the sample indicated Chinese as their first language preference and 30% maintained they could speak no English at all. The 1990 census reveals that about three fourths of Chinese aged 65 or older do not speak English well, and 46% live in a "linguistically isolated household," which the Bureau of the Census defines as a situation where no one age 14 or over speaks only English or even speaks English "very well" (U.S. Bureau of the Census, 1993a).

Most Chinese American elderly expect help and support to come from family, friends, and community. In San Diego, Cheng (1978) found that only 28% of Chinese American elderly live with children. This study revealed, however, that 70% belonged to a friendship club made up solely of Chinese, and other communities have reported the existence of benevolent aid societies and ethnic clubs. These supplied help and a sense of identity.

Given that the American experience has been one of exclusion from community participation and government benefits, and less than marginal political influence, elderly Chinese Americans tend to refrain from seeking legal advice, health care, or financial assistance from government sources until their difficulties become critical.

Both problems and lifestyles vary according to whether elders live with their children or live independently, but regardless of the variety of circumstances encountered by old Chinese Americans, Wu (1975) believes that their adjustment as senior citizens in this country has been remarkable. He explains:

First of all, endurance, another Chinese virtue, seems to be at work. The Chinese have been trained to accept reality. . . . Second, Old

Age Assistance has enabled many of them to live independently without becoming a burden to their children. Their frugality, another Chinese virtue, further helps them live on Old Age Assistance income without undue hardship. Third, and above all, their faith in God gives them strength to cope with many of the problems. (p. 274)

Japanese Americans

The 60th year of life has traditionally been observed as the beginning of old age among Japanese. This is the time that it takes the signs of the East Asian zodiac to complete one full cycle. In old Japan this was the occasion when samurai retired from office and peasants were no longer required to perform a full day's labor on collective village enterprises.

Japanese culture has long involved a concept of respect for seniors and elders, and in old Japan, communities hold annual ceremonies honoring the elderly. This tradition has been revived in recent years into a national holiday known as Respect-the-Aged Day (September 15). Most writers on traditional Japan stress the fact that the relationship with elderly in the family grew out of the Confucian concept of filial piety and respect for hierarchy. Masako Osako (1979), however, points out that adherence to Confucian ideals varied a great deal, depending on class status. While samurai families rigidly followed the dictates of filial piety, within peasant families (the kind that made up the bulk of emigrants to North America) the emphasis was on corporateness. Osako explains that "the family as a corporate entity owns and manages property to ensure the survival of its members and to perpetuate the family occupation" (p. 451). Within this context, Osako suggests that as elderly family members' contributions declined so did their status and influence. David Plath and other scholars support this idea, although they believe that, by and large, the premodern ethic called for sacrifice for one's parents, support for them in their declining years, and respect for elders in general. *The Encyclopedia of Japan* (1983) records:

Old people who were hale or judicious, those who were wise or who could act as guardians of life's mysteries, probably could command respect or attention. This may not have been true for the frail, the senile, the incapacitated, or those with no living kin. There long have been traditions about "sudden death temples" (*pokkuri ojo*) in which old, feeble, or desperately ill can pray for a quick and painless demise. Many tales and dramas have recounted the story of *obasute* in which useless old people are taken to a mountain (*yama*) and left to die. (A mountain in Nagano bears the name *obasuteyama* today.) There is no evidence that the senile ever have been routinely abandoned in Japan. But the lesson is that even elders might not merit unconditional support when they ceased to be an asset to community or family. (p. 99)

The pattern of family in traditional Japan was the patrilineal, patrilocal, extended family based on the principle of primogeniture. The ideal was that old people would live in the same household with their eldest son and his family. Aging women were expected to dominate their daughters-in-law with the sanction of their sons. Men held the position of head of household until the age of 60, but even after that they expected to be relied upon for guidance. Kiefer (1974) maintains that

old people were ideally indulged by their juniors. They were allowed greater freedom in dress, speech and comportment, and were encouraged to enjoy themselves within their means. . . . Among humbler folk, they were rewarded with gratitude for such tasks as babysitting, caring for animals, tending fires and floodgates, mending tools, sewing, cooking, providing home medicine, and dispensing their store of knowledge concerning nature and human events. (p. 171)

To understand the role and status of Japanese Americans, it is important to review the relationship of Issei and Nisei generations with each other and with the majority culture of the United States. The term *Issei* means first generation and is used to identify the original migrants to the United States. This group, which began arriving in this country in the late 1880s through early 1900s, is described by Osako (1979) as having been

born and raised in Japan, emigrated to the U.S. in their youth, worked hard, and raised their families in a climate of racial discrimination. Any Issei can recollect the dire hardships they experienced in pre-World War II days. Working twelve hours a day for seven days a week was not unusual. Farmers, in particular, toiled in the face of insecurity generated by anti-Japanese legislation and a boycott of their products. (p. 449)

The Issei were barred from citizenship, property ownership, and inter-marriage. The intermarriage prohibition gave rise to the practice of importing "picture brides." These young women, often only teenagers, were selected on the basis of snapshots sent from Japan. Although this arrangement left much to be desired by American standards, it probably was no less personal than traditional family-arranged marriages, and it did allow the migrants to establish permanent families in this country.

Racial attitudes toward Japanese Americans resulted in the Immigration Exclusion Act of 1924, which ended all immigration until 1965. Fear and prejudice also resulted in the executive order during World War II that Japanese Americans be rounded up and placed in concentration camps (euphemistically called "relocation camps"), where they remained imprisoned for the duration of the hostilities. For middle-aged men, enculturated in a tradition that honored age, the relocation camp experience was no doubt emotionally crippling for a number of reasons. Kiefer (1974) writes:

The authority of the men was largely replaced by that of the War Relocation Authority, who favored the American-born children of the Issei in their dealings with the prisoners. The men lost their jobs and their businesses, and with these the economic basis of their authority within the family. Even the communal rituals which had functioned to dramatize the values and authority patterns of the prewar communities became all but impossible in the camps. (p. 175)

Upon their release, these middle-aged Japanese Americans found employment again on farms, in factories, or in stores, but many felt themselves too old to try to reestablish the businesses that they had lost because of the internment. Most of their children were still too young to support them, and they could not return to the country of origin because it now was a vanquished nation.

The *Nisei* (second generation) were all born and educated in America. Although they had experienced the destructive effects of prejudice and discrimination themselves and had seen the struggle that the Issei had undergone in America, they had been protected from many of the economic hardships by their parents. They were urged by their parents to educate themselves, and often the Issei made great economic sacrifices to make it possible for their offspring to manage the tuition. As a result, the Nisei group is highly educated, with at least one third of them engaged in professional or highly skilled occupations (Kitano, 1969). The Nisei are truly bicultural and bilingual and are familiar with most facets of American culture. Of their relations with Issei, Kiefer (1974) writes:

> Most Nisei have felt a certain embarrassment about their parents' "Japaneseyness" even though they took their responsibilities toward these parents seriously. While they do not openly oppose many of the Issei's ideas and customs, they are prone to ignore them when it is expedient to do so. (p. 177)

Partly because of the loyalty and sense of responsibility of their children, the Issei have fewer problems and are relatively better off than the majority of ethnic groups in regard to income, health level, quality of housing, and transportation.

Japanese Americans, in spite of their educational level and degree of acculturation to American lifestyle, remain physically and emotionally close to their aged. A Chicago study (Osako, 1979) reported that the majority of the Issei sample lived very close to their children; 35% shared the same household, 17% lived within the same apartment building, and 10% had children living in the immediate neighborhood.

Although Nisei are strongly supportive of their elders, when the two generations live together, minor frictions are not uncommon, and relationships are never quite what traditional Japanese culture holds up as the ideal. Osako (1979) maintains that the

> most often mentioned sources of disagreement are differences in opinion about the rearing of the third generation (*Sansei*) grandchildren. The Sansei's clothing styles, dating, and school performance may turn into a focus of brief, but heated argument. Minor frictions come and go, often without leaving permanent traces. Yet, the parents realize sooner or later that they can no longer interfere with their offspring's business without creating animosity. (p. 450)

In some respects, the relationship between the Issei and the Sansei (their grandchildren) is very good. The latter often look to their grandparents as models of traditional culture and "attribute to the old folks the Japanese equivalent of 'soul' " (Kiefer, 1974, p. 178). But there are also problems. In many cases the grandchildren cannot communicate with their grandparents because few Sansei speak Japanese and many Issei speak very little English. They therefore have no way of acquiring an understanding of the way their elderly relatives view the world even though traditions have recently become an object of intellectual curiosity in a search for cultural identity. In regard to Japanese culture, Osako (1979) maintains that "Issei cling to the tradition, the Nisei shy away from it, and the Sansei, despite their extensive acculturation, rediscover it" (p. 454).

While no doubt there are strains between the several Japanese American generations, Osako (1979) believes that a basic compatibility between traditional Japanese and middle-class American values (in regard to diligence, thrift, and politeness) has aided the Issei in their adjustment to American culture.

Italian Americans

One of the more detailed studies of a European American ethnic population is the study of 66 elderly Italian Americans and their families carried out by Colleen L. Johnson (1985) in "Easton," a community of 180,000 in the northeastern part of the United States. Of the 414 individuals interviewed in Easton, 56 were white Protestant non-Italians who were used as a control group to highlight Italian cultural and social differences. The "Italian American" sample also included out-married Italians (those with mixed marriages) to assess variability. The individuals queried were predominantly upper-lower-class and lower-middle-class individuals who had blue-collar or white-collar jobs or, in a few cases, were owners of small businesses.

Over half of the Italian Americans in the study were born in Italy and had come to America as children or as young adults, and most had spent most of their lives sequestered in a "Little Italy" where their families and lifestyle were described as representing "the old fashioned way." However, 75% of the elderly were fluent in English.

The key to understanding the value system of this population rests in the word *family*. It is the only unit of importance in their lives, and it is the key to the problems of growing old. Although slightly less than a quarter of the elderly share a home with offspring, a third of them live within walking distance of a child and there is frequent interaction if only by numerous phone calls. Grandchildren also represent important social contacts, and three of the elderly respondents lived with grandchildren whose parents lived elsewhere. Nearly one third of these grandparents see a grandchild daily and 89% are visited at least weekly.

The more socially isolated appear to be the "old-old," that is, those over 75. The reason for this is that the Italians in this category are more likely to be widowed. However, no one in this population is without someone who can provide support. There is, however, some conscious effort on the part of the elderly to maintain some independence, but they still appreciate the dutiful child who sees the parent's needs as having equal priority with those of their nuclear family. Johnson (1985) tells us that "when the children have internalized the values of respect and affection, elderly parents can afford to become staunch defenders of their own independence" (p. 156). Respect is said to have a reciprocal aspect, and "one respects parents in order to gain their respect in turn" (Johnson, 1983, p. 99). Guilt is also a powerful weapon in maintaining parental control. Parents often delineate the sacrifices they have made for their children—the ultimate, of course, being bringing them into the world—and there is an implied message that repayment for one's existence should require an equal sacrifice on the part of children in support of the parent. Johnson notes that sons' or daughters' perceived neglect is frequently met with "sighs of despair" by the offended parent.

In spite of the emphasis on preserving traditional family values, Johnson maintains that the more acculturated parents have greater social interaction with their offspring because their relaxation of traditional values results in a reduction of the generation gap. Acculturation that has increased with intermarriage has not destroyed those aspects of the "Italian way" in regard to love and respect for elderly parents, but it has promoted a more active family life. The elderly consequently are rarely excluded from the social events of nuclear families such as birthdays, showers, christenings, weddings, and holiday get-togethers. These family social activities are vital to the well-being of the elderly because these Italian Americans have a tendency to shun organizations such as clubs or lodges and community senior citizen activities such as lunch programs. There is also a marked pattern of disengagement from friends and church, which must be compensated for by family involvement.

Particularly notable is the godparent relationship, which supplements family relationships. Of these respondents, 69% maintained that godchildren represented an important social contact for them and a major source of gifts, money, and services. These fictive relatives often assume a role equal to one's own offspring when the latter neglect their filial duties.

While inclusion of elderly parents and grandparents in family social events is normal and expected, bringing parents into the home to live is the ultimate filial responsibility. At the time of Johnson's study, only 22% of the Italian Americans were sharing a home with a parent, but a majority had lived in such a family at one time or another. There appears to be a traditional expectation that, when the youngest son marries, he and his wife are to remain with the parents. Such arrangements are not without problems, however. In such situations, divisions of labor often become a problem. Elderly mothers have a tendency to dominate the kitchen as a means of displaying maternal love, and "we heard several reports of open ruptures developing over the tomato sauce" (Johnson, 1985, p. 167). In spite of these types of irritants, it is reported that 40% of the families have adjusted well to live-in parents.

In general, dutiful daughters are depended upon for support and day-to-day assistance by elderly parents. Johnson (1985) suggests that this preference for daughters over sons results from "the close ties between mothers and daughters . . . in domestic roles" (p. 174) whereas in today's economic conditions sons and fathers seldom share occupational roles or interests. Much of the attention given to parents (frequent phone calls and drop-in visits) appears to be associated with a preoccupation with the possible impending death of parents, and offspring often believe that every contact with parents might be the last, and therefore special attention must be given to birthdays (perhaps their last) and parents must be hugged and kissed on parting as if it were a final farewell.

Complete dependency of elderly parents is a matter of great concern among these people, for nursing homes are considered out of the question. A comparison with Protestant non-Italians in Easton revealed that five times as many Italians totally reject the nursing home care option, consenting only if required for medical care that cannot be given in the home by the family.

And the family insists on continuing its caretaker role in the home even up to the time of death of a parent. Johnson (1985) writes: "One child, usually the daughter, uses her home, often converting a dining room into a hospital room. Her brothers and sisters, and frequently their spouses, take turns being there to sit with the dying parent" (p. 178).

SUMMARY

Anthropology was at one time primarily interested in foreign and often exotic cultures, but considerable work is now being done at home. The United States is a pluralistic society, and the many ethnic subcultures represent highly divergent social and cultural environments within which the elderly function. The nature and effects of marginality, discrimination, and generational conflict are important issues that are only beginning to be understood. Cultural gerontologists are seeking to gain greater knowledge of the many adaptive strategies and familial structures that affect the status and maintenance of the old person of ethnic identity. Of particular interest to researchers in recent years has been the "roots" phenomenon and the effect it has had in establishing prestigious roles for elders as repositories of cultural heritages.

African Americans, by virtue of their West African cultural origins, their devastating history of American slavery, Emancipation, and Reconstruction, and modern racial discrimination, see the world, the family, and their aged in a very different light than do representatives of white America. Elderly African Americans differ from white counterparts in regard to self-concept; they are more comfortable with old age, they remain more a part of the family structure, and generally they are more highly respected.

Native Americans, on the other hand, are more difficult to characterize as a group. They are products of a great variety of cultural heritages, but some general similarities have been noted. These include high value placed on individuality and freedom, a respect for family and clan, and a reverence for all living things, especially the land. Native Americans also have a history of oppression and discrimination and today face the worst deprivation of any ethnic group in America. Many elderly still remain on reservations, which are described as being the home of the "very young and very old." Reservations are less desirable environments for the elderly than urban areas in that they offer fewer services for the elderly, are more isolated, and provide the old with less freedom to make choices regarding their own welfare. The Navajo reservation in the American Southwest, for example, is the residence of some 5,000 elderly out of a total population of 128,338. Here 50% of families have incomes below the poverty level, but the elderly are highly respected and families take great pride in caring for their own aged to the best of their ability. Intergenerational reciprocity—grandparents caring for grandchildren and vice versa—is the traditional pattern, and nursing homes are looked upon with disfavor. A slightly better situation prevails for elderly in urban settings, where they often live in three- and four-generation extended-family situations, and the matrifocal family—often headed by a grandmother with some government income—manages to hold the family together. Many of the problems of the reservation—ill health, alcoholism, lack of education and employable skills—characterize the urban family as well and this can make for a stressful and precarious situation for the older generation.

The Mexican American tradition, of course, has its cultural roots in rural Mexico and has been carried by migrants into the agricultural areas of the Southwest and into the city barrios of a variety of midwestern, West Coast, and southwestern states. This cultural heritage is one that stresses familism, age hierarchy, male leadership, and mutual aid. Ideally, the Mexican American family is devoted to its senior members, but the problems of urban living and the intrusion of dominant American norms often mean that there sometimes is an inability to relate to and care for the elderly in the traditional way, although there is a strong sense of filial obligation to care for elderly family members and a sense of shame if such family responsibilities are not properly undertaken.

The people of Asia—China, Japan, Korea, and Vietnam, for example—have come to the United States to seek economic opportunity or to escape political oppression. Although the cultural traditions of all of these peoples vary a great deal, these groups also have some things in common—values like respect for family, filial piety, mutual obligations and privileges across generations, and a sense of cultural distinctness that has often resulted in their isolation. In America these people from the Far East have often encountered discrimination and oppression, even imprisonment (the Japanese in World War II) merely because of their cultural identity. Chinese and Japanese migrants began arriving in the United States as early as 1850 and 1880, respectively, and it is not surprising that there are a considerable number of elderly American-born Asians in many of our West Coast cities. As is the case with many other immigrant groups, a clash of ideas between the various generations has created a dilemma for Asian aged. The most notable example of this involves the different attitudes and lifestyles of Issei, Nisei, and Sansei Japanese.

Italian Americans conceptualize the role of the family in regard to the elderly much as Mexican Americans. If parents do not live with offspring, they will live in close proximity and relate frequently. No elder in this community is without social interaction with his or her family. Family social occasions are seen as vital to the well-being of elders, and elders are invariably included in birthday celebrations, weddings, and holiday get-togethers. These social occasions are of special importance because elderly Italian Americans tend to shun clubs, lodges, and community senior citizen activities. Daughters are the traditional caregivers for parents, but because Italian mothers often try to dominate the kitchen, this arrangement occasionally has its conflicts. Ailing old people are cared for at home and even dying elders tend to be attended in the house of one of the offspring, who will be assisted by a variety of family members who feel it their duty to participate in the death bed vigil.

8

▣ Applying Anthropology

Culture, Health, and Aging

A nthropology, like every other scientific discipline, has its pure (theoretical) and its applied (practical) interests. Just as medicine has its practitioners and its laboratory research people, anthropology has its scholars researching issues to seek knowledge of humankind for its own sake; other anthropology scholars use anthropological knowledge to solve social, medical, economic, educational, and political problems. The work of these applied anthropologists has proven to be of great value in dealing with a variety of problems in other countries and in the United States when ethnic populations are involved, and in providing answers to difficult problems when services to the aged are concerned. In this chapter we focus on the importance of understanding culture and cultural differences in provision of health care and in institutions providing long-term care for the aged. Several examples from medical settings and a discussion of African American concepts of illness illustrate variant perceptions of health and disease, reactions to treatment regimes, and, above all, the potential for misunderstanding between patient and health professional due to cultural differences. In the field of gerontology there has been a significant emphasis in recent years on the caregivers of aged persons suffering from illness causing dementia. Here we consider ethnic-specific support groups as one response to the needs of some of these caregivers. Although long-term care includes more than just institutional care, nursing homes are the most familiar component of the long-term care continuum. We conclude the chapter with a consideration of nursing homes in our own country and in other cultures.

Cultural Perspectives in Health Care

One of the pioneers in the anthropology of aging, Margaret Clark has long had interests in the application of anthropological principles in the study of health. The book *Culture and Aging*, written by Clark and Anderson (1967), is a classic study of the influence of culture on the process of adjusting to old age, specifically the factors involved in healthy adaptation or experience of mental illness in late life. The participants were 435 elderly (age 60 or over) residents of the city of San Francisco—264 "normal" people from the community, 81 inpatients of the psychiatric ward at San Francisco General Hospital, and 90 former patients of that ward who were now living at home. To assess adjustment, the variables studied were self-evaluation, morale, status, and level of social interaction. Postulating that the major threats to the mental health and well-being of the aged are weak kinship ties, rapid technological change, relative and absolute increases in the number of aged, and the sacred cows of American culture—independence and productivity—Clark and Anderson suggested avenues of survival that might, in opposition to disengagement theory, be labeled *relaxation*. The researchers concluded that, if aging Americans are to achieve positive self-image and morale, they must learn to accept their physical and mental changes, be willing to relinquish certain roles and activities, substitute alternative sources of need gratification for those unavailable to them, modify their basis for self-judgment, and, in general, find a new place for themselves in the larger scheme of things.

Although the mentally ill seemed to have difficulty distinguishing between circumstances that could be changed and those that could not, the mentally healthy elderly seemed to be "able to meet unpleasant but alterable circumstances with action, and unalterable ones with flexibility and forbearance" (Clark & Anderson, 1967, p. 61). There were distinct differences in the level of aspiration of mentally well and mentally ill aged. The former had more modest expectations in life, while the latter seemed to "feel that they must ever strive for perfection. They seem to believe seriously in the Cinderella legend—for them, the life story should have a happy ending, ambition should triumph, and all dreams come true" (p. 61). Clark and Anderson conclude from their study of healthy and unhealthy adjustment in old age that people must learn how their culture defines not only the proper way to grow up but also the proper way to grow old.

Margaret Clark's (1983) interests have also included the kinds of problems that arise in health care delivery when there are disparities in the cultural backgrounds of patients and medical practitioners. These barriers can be grouped into five categories: (a) language use and non-verbal communication patterns, (b) medical roles and responsibilities, (c) explanatory models of medicine, (d) contextual factors, and (e) emotional impact and stigma.

Clark writes that, "without language, the work of a physician and that of a veterinarian would be nearly identical" (p. 807). Unless there is some way for physicians to question patients concerning pain and other symptoms and come to a common understanding about the nature of the complaint, little can be accomplished. Lipson and Meleis (1983) say that for people from Middle Eastern cultures, for example, unless a trusting relationship has developed, discussion of illness with a physician is likely to be hampered by a reluctance to reveal details of a personal nature. Their view of a physician as a respected authority figure may result in "answers designed to please the interviewer, to save face, and to absolve the family from responsibility for an illness" (p. 858). Use of a "culture broker," a bicultural person who can negotiate cultural differences between health care providers and patients, is recommended to alleviate such problems (Lipson & Meleis, 1983).

Cross-cultural misunderstanding is exemplified in the case of an elderly Mexican American woman admitted to the hospital in a coma (Kim, 1983). Extensive tests seemed to indicate she had suffered a stroke. After a week it was determined that she met all criteria for brain death and her family was informed that life support measures would be discontinued. The reaction of the woman's family was dramatic and in opposition to the staff decision. They did not accept or comprehend the concept of brain death. "To them the patient appeared to be asleep, her body still warm, heart still beating, lungs still breathing and a leg or arm twitching every so often; how could she possibly be dead?" (Kim, 1983, p. 887). After several days, life support was withdrawn and the woman "pronounced dead," with no real resolution of the conflict between medical staff and family of the patient.

Kim (1983) describes this situation as one with "woeful breakdown in communication" (p. 887). Misunderstanding was based on very different views about the content of the doctor-patient relationship and the role of family in care of the sick, language differences, and, finally, profoundly divergent ideas about the brain in relation to "being and personhood." For clinicians, "the brain contains the essence of who we are," while Mexican Americans have a "belief that mind and body are inseparable. The soul of a person dwells nevertheless in one who sleeps, or appears to be asleep" (Kim, 1983, p. 887). Kim suggests that a more satisfactory outcome might have resulted for all concerned with this case if "a more courteous, empathic medical team" (p. 887) had sought to establish better communication with the assistance of bilingual persons.

In regard to medical roles and responsibilities, it is of great importance that the family of an ethnic patient be willing to give full control of the patient to medical practitioners. It must be realized that family members often want to be close to the patient as much as possible and to monitor the medical treatment. Lipson and Meleis (1983) note that, if a patient is from the Middle East, "family and friends are expected to show exorbitant concern, never to leave a patient alone and to constantly shower care and attention" (p. 858). Such behavior may be at odds with hospital policies and require tactful negotiations to achieve a satisfactory outcome.

The issue of nursing home placement can create a dilemma concerning control and responsibility. Kim (1983) describes the case of a 78-year-old Filipino cancer patient who was hospitalized for diagnosis of new symptoms. It was found that the cancer had spread but further surgery was considered too great a risk to the patient. The man's daughters had just dealt with the terminal care of their mother, and were overwhelmed at the prospect of providing such care again so soon. In discussions with the hospital social worker, the daughters seemed agreeable to placement of their father in a nursing home but repeatedly failed to inform their father. In the social worker's view, it was the daughters' responsibility to "be honest" with the father about their desire for him to go to the nursing home. The physician intervened in this situation after the resignation of the frustrated social worker from the case. The daughters wanted the doctor to tell their father that "the hospital wants him to go to the nursing home" (Kim, 1983, p. 890). The physician reacted negatively because this contradicted his "cultural values of honesty and disclosure to patients" (p. 891). The daughters, on the other hand, were struggling with Filipino values, which required children to care for elders. To do otherwise would be viewed by family and community as shameful. Ultimately, the physician agreed to their request, which allowed the daughters to save face while ensuring their father received the care he needed. The physician, however, felt his integrity had been compromised (Kim, 1983). Failure to establish meaningful communication or to recognize such significant cultural differences can lead to such feelings of dissatisfaction.

Explanations of the origin and nature of disease provide fertile ground for cross-cultural misunderstandings. People without a germ theory of medicine or with beliefs that evil spirits or the malevolence of witches cause illness can present major roadblocks for the physicians operating in strictly scientific terms. Such beliefs may be viewed by health professionals as mere superstition. Henderson and Gutierrez-Mayka (1992) note that "clinicians perceive their professionally derived knowledge as 'fact' when actually it is an evolving belief system. When a professional belief system is acknowledged, then the structural dynamics of the clinician-patient encounters are more balanced" (p. 61). One need only consider the constantly changing recommendations about normal cholesterol level and how to control it as evidence of the evolving nature of our health beliefs. The way people define illness and the causes of it can have a great effect on what a patient thinks about sickness or health, and how he or she responds to treatment.

It is also recommended that, when dealing with an ethnic patient, health care professionals need to ascertain the status of the patient in terms of acculturation. Whether a person is still strongly entrenched in the views of the culture of origin, is bicultural, or is largely assimilated into the "mainstream culture" will influence the relationship with the health system.

Of particular note are the bicultural and assimilated positions, because these can be mistakenly ignored by clinicians because they don't appear "ethnic enough" to warrant specific attention. In reality, such people have *not* lost their ethnic minority heritage, they have simply added to it a great facility for using the cultural system of the majority population. (Henderson & Gutierrez-Mayka, 1992, p. 62)

It is a relatively safe assumption that elderly members of many ethnic groups are more likely to have a strong commitment to the traditional approaches to health and illness.

Clark (1983) indicates that "laboratory results may have little meaning in the absence of pain, fever, malaise or other symptoms" (p. 808). In other words, what is acceptable as a diagnostic procedure or as a sign of illness may vary considerably from one culture to another. Mitchell (1983) reports an instance in which a Jamaican woman with a diagnosis of diabetes was being treated for a foot problem. The woman also sought treatment from a "bush doctor," who prescribed an herbal tea for the diabetes. On a return visit to the physician, the results of her urinalysis were pronounced "OK." This was erroneously interpreted by the patient as meaning "her diabetes was cured" (p. 845).

In Jamaica, and among Jamaican immigrants in the United States, illness is attributed to six causal categories, each associated with specific locations in the body, specific symptoms, and treatments.

Etiological explanations involving heat, cold, bile and gas/wind are applied mainly to symptoms in which there is a feeling of pain, heat or chill or there is a discharge; those involving imbalances of the blood are applied to internal conditions and changes in the skin; those involving germs are applied primarily, but not exclusively to venereal diseases. (Mitchell, 1983, p. 843)

Only occasionally are germs considered a causative agent, and even then primarily "by middle class, more highly educated Jamaicans" (p. 844).

It is considered essential that there must be "fit" between drugs used in treatment and the illness. Specific characteristics—bitter taste, dark color, or laxative effect, for example—are associated with appropriate medicines. The degree of "fit" in a prescribed medication will determine "how, or whether it is used" (Mitchell, 1983, p. 844). Lack of fit or inability to note any change as the result of taking a prescription may lead to the patient arbitrarily discontinuing use, changing dosage, or adding other remedies of his or her own choosing. Over-the-counter drugs have proven popular with Jamaicans, who can make choices to meet their criteria based on appearance or descriptive claims on labels. The risks inherent in this approach include adverse interactions between prescribed and self-selected over-the-counter drugs, and dangerous long-term effects of certain products (Mitchell, 1983).

African American Concepts of Illness

The problem of cross-cultural misunderstanding about the nature and cause of illness is discussed by Snow (1983) in regard to southern, lower income African Americans. The data represent a warning to medical practitioners that "failure to elicit a patient's understanding of an illness, its cause and how he or she believes it is properly treated can result in anger, frustration and noncompliance" (p. 827).

Particularly characteristic of elderly low-income blacks with minimal education are a series of ideas about illness and its cause that are so bizarre from the medical standpoint that practitioners may not even be aware that they exist. For example, there are the concepts of "natural illness," being the result of sinful or overindulgent behavior, and "unnatural illness," which is seen as resulting from the work of the devil or of malevolent persons with special powers.

Cold as a source of acute or chronic illness is a widely held belief. It involves the idea that temperature influences the thickening or thinning of the blood as well as the possibility that cold and dampness can "settle" in the body and result in arthritis or clotted blood backing up and causing headaches, strokes, or high blood pressure. Dirt is also seen as a cause of illness. The body can become "defiled" by failure to bathe or by gastrointestinal blockages of "bad blood," which must be cleaned out with laxatives.

Physicians need also to be aware that a diagnosis of high blood pressure by them may be understood and interpreted as a diagnosis of "high blood." To these black patients high blood means that the body has too much blood or that blood suddenly rushes to the head producing headaches, dizziness, spots before the eyes, or blacking out. "Low blood," on the other hand, has nothing to do with scientific understanding of blood count or low blood pressure but refers to a condition not unlike anemia with symptoms of weakness, lassitude, fatigue, and blacking out (Snow, 1983, p. 825).

Least compatible with modern medical concepts is the idea that illness can be caused by magic. Snow (1983) explains: "The use of magic for manipulating life events is common where the environment is seen as hostile and dangerous and ungiving, and where people have little control over what happens in their lives" (p. 826). These illnesses may be the result of charms and spells or may involve poisoning a victim's food or drink. A common belief is that "snakes, frogs or lizards may be introduced into the body in the form of eggs or powder," which hatch and live in the victim's blood, stomach, or head. Magical illness may take a variety of forms. It may involve loss of appetite, weight loss, nausea and vomiting, or even mental illness.

The medical practitioner attempting to deal with this belief system should also be aware that "there is no lack of alternative healing sources for a black patient who is alienated from the orthodox medical system, or whose problem will not or cannot respond to orthodox care" (Snow, 1983, p. 827). Where traditional beliefs about an illness and the appropriate remedy are in conflict with those of the physician, there is a real probability that the physician's prescribed treatment may be modified, ignored, or even blamed for a subsequent ailment.

Food Preferences

Clark (1983) explains that contextual factors in health care concern larger issues such as the overall lifestyle of the individual, which would include such factors as "cultural patterns of diet, socialization of children, sexual behavior, exercise, the balance of work and rest, ritual observances and many other everyday activities" (p. 808).

Whether the focus is on nursing home nutrition or agency-operated nutrition programs for aged persons living in an integrated community, the matter of cultural differences in food preferences is one that must be understood by both administrators and staff. Howell and Loeb (1969) warn that

> although culture and ethnicity in the United States is not as precise a variable to define as in other parts of the world, certain characteristics

of the dietary behavior of older persons can properly be considered "culture bound." It should be possible through strategic interviewing, group discussion, and observation, to identify quite specific dietary attitudes and habits of a cultural nature among sub-groups of aged within the United States. (p. 36)

Believing that field research on food preferences, aversion, and food-related health beliefs is needed, Howell and Loeb describe the range of nutritional problems that can be associated with differences in ethnicity, regional or urban-rural cultures, socioeconomic class, and age grades. They remind us that even the frequency of meals is more a matter of custom than physiological need, and that food in some cultures has a kind of prestige value seldom found in the majority culture in America. Food can be regarded as currency and as a means of fulfilling social and kinship obligations, and its preparation may be a means of acquiring creative satisfaction. Eating is often a pleasurable recreational activity, and some foods are looked upon as medicine or as even as commodities of supernatural significance. Freimer, Echenberg, and Kretchmer (1983) comment on the therapeutic benefits and liabilities of particular foods stressing that they may be "assigned opposing qualities such as hot and cold, tonic and nontonic. Foods in each category are considered hazardous or beneficial depending on the setting" (p. 929).

It has been noted that middle-aged and elderly acculturated individuals of Pacific island and Native American groups are prone to obesity and non-insulin dependent diabetes because of their conversion to Western food habits, which involve increased total caloric consumption, increased fat and protein consumption, plus decreased consumption of complex carbohydrates. The failure of health professionals to link dietary patterns to cultural identities and recognize the negative effects of introducing Western dietary practices may indeed be responsible for any number of serious diseases such as diabetes, coronary disease, and serious dental problems.

Dementia

Emotional impact and stigma are related to how patients react to the knowledge of their having a particular disease such as cancer, AIDS, or mental illness. All are greatly feared and will produce ongoing emotional states that may be a vital concern in treatment (Clark, 1983). Henderson and Gutierrez-Mayka (1992) explain that

> Alzheimer's disease carries with it symptoms which the general public would interpret as characteristic of someone who is "crazy." The stigma attached to mental disorders is well known within this culture and many others. . . . The issue of a family member being "crazy" has been a common one in the Latin Alzheimer's support groups meetings. Members may launch a personal crusade to be sure that friends and family understand that Alzheimer's disease is an organic disease and therefore, not under the control of the individual, thus relieving the patient and family of social stigma liability. (p. 67)

Eric Pfeiffer (1977) has estimated that approximately 15% of Americans 60 and over suffer from some mental health disorder. It may be depression, which can be cured, or some form of dementia, which, with very few exceptions, cannot. Alzheimer's disease is the most common form of dementia, accounting for about half of all cases. This disease, which affects as many as 20%-25% of people by the time they reach age 80-85, has been labeled "the number one health problem of the next century" (Henderson, 1987, p. 360). Other forms of dementia include multi-infarct dementia, which results from brain cell loss due to numerous "strokes," combinations of Alzheimer's disease and multi-infarct dementia, and rare varieties such as Pick's disease, Huntington's chorea, and Benswanger's disease.

The term *Alzheimer's disease*, which is currently very much in the public eye because of considerable attention by the media, is often applied to all forms of dementia, but in terms of the response and attitudes of the medical profession and the impact on families, all forms of dementia have much the same effect. To begin with, Henderson points out that "the medical model . . . perpetuates an acute care orientation emphasizing treatment with rapid cessation of symptoms" (p. 366). Not only does the medical culture not deal well with chronic incurable disease, but practitioners often are oriented to inpatient care and have very little experience in geriatrics. Nor is the American family structure prepared to take on the tragedy of Alzheimer's disease or other forms of dementia. Our norm of nuclear families, where a spouse or, in rare cases, another family member must assume the day-to-day nightmare of care-giving, is not adequate for the job. Caregiving burdens have to be spread over a broad network of kinsmen, a requirement better realized in extended-family-oriented societies. Nor does the American pattern of division of labor prepare the spouse for assuming the total caregiving responsibilities for the broad spectrum of domestic duties.

Ethnic/Minority Support Groups

One of the few solutions for dealing with dementia, aside from institutionalization of the patient, a step that many caregivers are not psychologically or financially prepared to take, is the mutual aid society better known as the "support group." Henderson (1987), who has inti-mate knowledge of the value of such groups in a variety of American subcultures, writes:

> Alzheimer's disease support groups function socially as fictive kinship groups. They arise in a culture in which fragmented kinship networks are typical and serve to supplement the immediate, face-to-face interac-tion and assistance that could occur were it not for kindred dispersion. Support groups also function to fill gaps created by the acute care medical system in the long-term management of the disease. (p. 368)

While support groups of many types have become popular, they rarely attract individuals from ethnic minorities. In attempting to under-stand the lack of interest of minority families, medical anthropologist Neil Henderson of the Suncoast Gerontology Center undertook a study among black and Latin families in Jacksonville and Tampa, Florida. In attempting to develop rapport with the target populations, Henderson (1992) developed the following procedures:

(1) *Leave the desk.* That is, get out into the community and attempt to develop "personal qualities such as resourcefulness, initiative, flexibil-ity, and open-mindedness" (p. 25) rather than spending time in the li-brary reading the literature on minorities.

(2) *Discover the key members of the community who might be "willing to serve as liaisons or coaches for the support group project"* (p. 25). These leaders will

be very useful in introducing the "project staff to the significant branches of the community" (p. 25).

(3) "Test out the intervention models" (p. 25). That is, try to discover who are the leaders or institutions that can help you facilitate change. Here Henderson found that the African American churches first had to be enlisted in the effort if the project was to succeed. He therefore scheduled the support group meetings in one of the churches in the black neighborhood.

This was a step in the right direction but not the final key to success. For three weeks running, only three African American individuals showed up for the support group meeting. Henderson (1992) had "overlooked a significant aspect of church 'etiquette:' the loyalty of members to their own church created boundaries between churches that were too strong for members to cross" (p. 25). The members of the several churches in the community felt that they would be disloyal to their own pastor if they attended support group meetings in the church of another.

A similar problem occurred in dealing with the Latino community. Here the meetings were scheduled for a hospital in the center of the Latino community, but because the hospital had been founded by people from northwestern Spain, immigrants with roots in north-central Spain felt that they would not be welcome and none attempted to attend the meeting.

In both cases the researchers then decided upon a neutral site, but one located close to the ethnic community targeted. The African American support group was scheduled in a public library in the black neighborhood, and the Latino group used a privately owned medical clinic in their part of town. Both support groups were successful in attracting caregivers for Alzheimer patients. Actually three successful Alzheimer support groups were formed with attendance running as high as 20 people; each had its own cultural flavor and format, and each led to valuable sharing of problems and feelings.

Black and Hispanic Caregivers

Cox and Monk (1993) have investigated the plight of black and Hispanic caregivers when dementia is involved. Because both of these groups are notable for their strong feelings of filial obligations to their senior family members, the investigators were particularly interested in the emotional and practical consequences of the commitment. Initially, Cox and Monk did not believe that black and Hispanic caregivers feel the same sense of isolation as do Anglo caregivers. This is because the blacks, only slightly more than the Hispanics, have broad and supportive networks of confidants who visit them daily and with whom they discuss their frustrations and dilemmas. Of those studied, 34% of the blacks and 43% of the Hispanics also had someone who could assume the caregiver role on a temporary basis, therefore giving some respite. While the blacks and Hispanics received emotional support from a wide circle of friends and relatives, and claimed that they derived great spiritual support from their religion, the actual burden of care nevertheless rested on the shoulders of a single person, usually a middle-aged female.

Cox and Monk found that, although both blacks and Hispanics knew about formal services and were willing to use them, the Hispanics were more prone to use this kind of assistance as the patient's physical condition worsened. Both black and Hispanic families were willing to make use of Medicaid programs, but such use was negatively related to income. Families whose income exceeded the level allowed for Medicaid recipients were also least likely to be able to afford private caregiving services. Other formal assistance such as day care or respite care were often not used because none existed in their area or there were long waiting lists.

Long-Term Care Institutions

A critical area where applied researchers have brought their anthropological knowledge to bear is that of the nursing home. One of the first to study the philosophy and operation of such residences was the late Jules Henry. In his discussion of the institutionalization of our elderly in *Culture Against Man*, Henry (1963) makes the point that

society has been established primarily for the purpose of guaranteeing food and protection. And from this primitive necessity has emerged the central problem of the human species, the fact that inner needs have scarcely been considered. . . . Although culture is "for" man, it is also "against" him. (pp. 11-12)

In his analysis of how culture is "against" human beings, Henry describes three nursing homes: Muni San (an institution supported by public funds) and two private, profit-making institutions—Rosemont (for paupers) and Tower Nursing Home (for the middle class). According to Henry (1963), "Tower is comfortable and humane, Rosemont is inhumane, and Muni San is somewhere in between" (p. 391) Although the public institution, Muni San, is described as providing adequate if not inspired care, and the residents receive proper medical attention and sufficient food, they suffer from a sense of being obsolete and abandoned, inferior to the least qualified employee, and nuisances to everyone.

Rosemont, on the other hand, is labeled *hell's vestibule,* and it epitomizes America's lack of concern for the aged, particularly the aged poor. Henry's description of the "national character" of the inmates and staff suggests that the institution sees the residents as "child-animals" and treats them accordingly. This is made possible because "in our culture personality exists to the extent of ability to pay, and in terms of performance of the culturally necessary tasks of production, reproduction, and consumption" (p. 440). The fact that the inmates are paupers (who have Social Security income only) has been impressed on them to the extent that they expect to have no rights. They are both economically and intellectually poor. Their education level plus the cultural environment in which they have spent their lives provided them with no inner resources for making their lives more bearable. Henry described life for the residents of Muni San as one of "apathy, preoccupation with food and excreta, the adoption of the role of child-animal . . . and preoccupation with reminiscence" (pp. 440-441).

Even Tower Nursing Home, functioning as it does within the American value system, failed to meet the inner needs of its middle-class residents. Although the staff is solicitous and kind, it "seems to maintain an attitude of indulgent superiority with the patients whom they consider disoriented children" (Henry, 1963, p. 474). The staff is oriented toward bodily needs, not mental ones, but this perhaps is because they do not understand the mental characteristics of the elderly. Because of staff insensibility, patients' lives are marked by anxiety and silent reminiscing punctuated by outbursts of bad temper. Social life is minimal and, although there is a desire for communication, there is an inability to achieve it. Henry maintains that the fault does not necessarily lie with the nursing home director or the staff but with the values of the culture.

Through the use of cross-cultural comparison, Henry (1963) brings the characteristics of American culture into sharp focus:

> In many primitive societies the soul is imagined to leave the body at death or just prior to it; here, on the other hand, society drives out the remnants of the soul of the institutionalized old person while it struggles to keep his body alive. Routinization, inattention, carelessness, and deprivation of communication—the chance to talk, to respond, to read, to see pictures on the wall, to be called by one's name rather than "You" or no name at all—are ways in which millions of once useful but now obsolete human beings are detached from their selves long before they are lowered into the grave. (p. 393)

Maria Vesperi (1983) provides further documentation of the influence of American values on the treatment of the aged in her paper "The Reluctant Consumer: Nursing Home Residents in the Post-Bergman Era." Vesperi believes that the quality of life in American nursing homes and the administrative policy that characterizes most of these homes is a direct reflection of how old age is perceived in our culture. That perception can be characterized as a time of dependence requiring a paternalistic management of the residents' lives. Patients are thought to be incapable of making decisions about their own situations, having to have their food selected for them and decisions made concerning their movement from one place to another. Passivity, dependence, and compliance with staff-imposed decisions are considered appropriate responses, and contrary behavior invites retaliation in the form of sedation or physical restraints. And Colleen Johnson (1987) believes that American values of independence, optimism, and self-determination can be maintained only by overlooking the plight of the frail elderly and those suffering with dementia as well as the failure of biomedicine to prevail over chronic, incurable diseases afflicting many nursing home patients.

A decade after Jules Henry's study of nursing homes, Gubrium (1975) focused on the organizational structure of the nursing home in *Living and Dying at Murray Manor*. Approaching Murray Manor as a special community with all the complexities that might be found in any other, Gubrium focused on the dynamics of patient-staff interaction in this 360-bed, sectarian, nonprofit facility. Here he found that the staff measured the quality of their operation by whether or not patients and their families registered complaints. But when problems developed, the operational structure of the home was not blamed; rather, the patients and their families were accused of being "too individualistic" and as a result were not cooperating in regard to the goals of the institution.

Administrative decisions seldom took into account the social complexities of nursing home life from a patient's point of view. Patients were not only not involved in administrative planning and decision making, but there was almost no interaction between management and those who were managed. Nurse aides exercised a great deal of responsibility in care delivery and functioned as intermediaries between administrative staff and patients.

A unique aspect of the Murray Manor study had to do with patients' perceptions of "passing time" and patients' evaluation of the importance of the various activities. Gubrium examines the meaning of such time passing events as sitting around, keeping track of time, eating, walking, sleeping, watching, talking, and time spent in therapy and ceremonials. For example, he notes that people who spend a great deal of time in bed sleeping during the daytime are looked upon negatively and described as "not knowing what to do with themselves," while those who fall asleep sitting in the lobby or the lounges are "merely dozing off."

Also concerned with interaction between nursing home personnel and patients was the study of Pecan Grove Nursing Home by Henderson (1981). Seeking to ascertain actual staff performance characteristics regardless of job title and work description, Henderson found nurse aides providing basic bed and body care while housekeepers served as psychotherapists in their informal but more frequent contact with patients. Housekeepers, who wear street clothes, are middle aged, and have often worked as nurse aides, spend at least 20 minutes a day with patients, providing much appreciated social contact. While the administrative staff was not even aware of this very positive role played by the housekeeper, patients were quick to point out that "while nurses tend to the body, housekeepers tend to the mind" (Henderson, 1981, p. 303). Quoting one of the housekeepers, Henderson (1981) records: "Like Miss Thompson, for instance, before she left [for cancer radiation therapy] she was, you know, just very depressed, and I came in and just sat down on a stool and talked a little while and had her laughing before I went out" (p. 303).

Ethnicity and Institutionalization

Ethnicity has been shown to be an important consideration in nursing home operation and in the interaction between residents and staff. Wilbur Watson and Robert Maxwell (1977) compared a home for blacks (174 patients) with one for Jewish elderly (328 patients) in regard to similarities and differences in health care and social interactions between patients and staff. Both homes had predominantly black staffs in the wards. In the home for blacks there was a joking relationship between staff and residents about institutional and other matters. No such relationship between patients and ward attendants was observed in the home for Jewish elderly; any joking that took place in this home was restricted to white staff members.

Apparently in America people carry the "color line" even into nursing homes, because in the Jewish home black licensed practical nurses (LPNs) reported that they were often the target of racially based hostility, while in the home for blacks none of the staff reported abuse or feelings of alienation with patients. On the basis of their findings, Watson and Maxwell conclude that positive interaction is more likely in nursing homes where caretakers and elderly share a common class and/or ethnic background.

While observing the operations of a home for Jewish elderly, Maxwell, Bader, and Watson (1972) turned their attention to spatial behavior, staff-patient interaction in terms of physical and psychological limitations of patients, and protective measures of staff members to promote their own self-interests. The study revealed that the most highly trained members of the nursing staff were the least involved in providing direct care and they limited their attentions to the least disabled of the patients. The mentally and physically disabled were consequently left to the care of the lower ranking, less educated, and often less experienced staff members.

While considering ethnic identity of caregivers in nursing homes, it should be noted that Samoans have been singled out as being outstanding employees in long-term care facilities. Ablon (1970) explains:

From early childhood, the Samoan learns to respect and care for the very young, the infirm, and especially the old, whose needs are given very careful attention. . . . They are conscientious and patient in their work with the sick and the aged, and resourceful and exceptionally witty in their dealings with difficult patients. (p. 33)

Samoan culture instills respect for authority, for wisdom, and for age, thus making these people amenable to the requirements of both employers and patients. The first school of nursing (for practical nurses) was established by the U.S. Navy at the hospital in Pago Pago, American Samoa, in 1914, and nursing has been a respected profession for women ever since. Therefore there is a tendency, even for women who have not attended nursing school, to favor this profession when they migrate to the United States. Describing Samoan nursing aides as having a reputation for "kindness, gentleness, efficiency and thoroughness" and with a special talent for working in long-term care institutions because of their calm demeanor, it is not surprising that Ablon reports that these Pacific Islanders make up upward of 50% of many San Francisco Bay area nursing home staffs.

While Watson and Maxwell (1977) reported that residents of a home for Jewish elderly had problems relating to black employees, Ablon writes: "The San Francisco Jewish Home for the Aged employs some 25 Samoan women as graduate practical nurses and nursing aides. These women comprise almost one half of the nursing staff and are highly respected employees" (Ablon, 1970, p. 33).

Knowledge of cultural differences is particularly important in explaining whether or not Mexican Americans use nursing home facilities. A study conducted in Arizona revealed a great underuse of nursing care facilities by this population. Although other ethnic groups have a tendency to place their elderly in nursing homes as their income and standard of living rise, just the opposite is true of Mexican Americans. Eribes and Bradley-Rawls (1978) write:

Institutional residency rises with poverty rather than increased income. . . . The nursing home is a culturally defined alternative of last resort. As family income increases, families tend to provide alternatives to institutionalization, either within an existing family or through support toward independent living. (p. 370)

While Lacayo (1993) generally confirms the pattern of Hispanics priding themselves on caring for their own elders, he writes: "The onslaught of urbanization and industrialization has caused an erosion of what would be considered the 'traditional Hispanic family' " (p. 227). The number of women (the traditional primary caregivers) active in the labor force will grow to 2½ million (69%) by the year 2000, which means that fewer will be available to provide long-term care to the elderly.

The importance of cultural factors in meeting the needs of nursing home patients of different ethnic groups was the subject of a research project by Peter Chee and Robert Kane (1983). A comparison of a 99-bed nursing home for blacks with a 95% black staff was made with a home of the same size for Japanese Americans with a 90% Japanese staff. Both institutions were in Los Angeles, but the Japanese American residents represented a somewhat higher economic status than the blacks. Both homes were located in areas of the city inhabited by people of the same ethnic identity as the patients. The location of the nursing homes within these enclaves made it possible for a rather high rate of visitation by family members. Members of families of both ethnic groups visited their relatives in the respective homes slightly more than four times per week.

When family members and patients were queried concerning their feelings about the importance of ethnic foods, similarity of ethnicity of staff and patients and their families, similarity of ethnicity of fellow patients, and the importance of ethnic community involvement in the operation of the homes, it was found that the Japanese Americans were much more concerned with ethnic differences than were the African American patients and their families. For example, on a scale of 1 to 5 (1 equaling "not very important" and 5 equaling "very important"), black patients felt that ethnic foods were only relatively important (3.9), while Japanese Americans thought them of utmost importance (5.0). As a result of this attitude, the Japanese American nursing home had a policy of always serving a Japanese-style lunch and serving larger than usual quantities of rice with other meals. The African American nursing home, on the other hand, did try to cater to patient's tastes but only to the extent of serving more beans and cornbread.

While black family members scored a modest 2.2 and black patients scored 2.7 on the importance of having a staff of the same ethnic identity as the patients, the Japanese Americans felt this was very important, with family members scoring 4.9 and patients scoring 4.5. The same appeared to be true concerning the question of whether they wanted to live with fellow patients of the same ethnic identity, and Chee and Kane (1983) explain this as follows:

Some of the Japanese-American patients interviewed were still mistrustful of other ethnic groups, largely because of their experiences in World War II internment camps and the resultant losses of homes, property, and jobs. For many, the humiliation they experienced still strongly influences their attitudes toward non-Japanese. (p. 110)

Ethnic community involvement was seen as relatively important to African Americans and very important to Japanese Americans. The Japanese American community is described as having a strong community involvement in its home "in the form of monetary donations, gifts, and volunteer services from various organizations and groups" (p. 111), while the black community's support of its home was mainly through the visitation of church members with residents of the home.

Nursing Homes in Other Cultures

Cross-cultural comparisons of nursing homes also have been made by anthropologists although such facilities have only recently been established in many foreign countries. Beginning with comparisons of nursing homes in Western countries, we might cite the study of a 96-bed, government-owned, continuing-care institution in Scotland with a similar 85-bed, for-profit nursing home in an urban setting on the West Coast of the United States carried out by Jeanie Kayser-Jones (1981). To begin with, the investigator found two very different overall health care systems in operation in Scotland and the United States. The Scots definitely have greater access to medical and nursing care because of their national health care system; residents have more choice, freedom, and independence; and residents' lives are more like others in the greater society. Kayser-Jones reports also that the Scottish home had a much more dedicated staff. Nurses who work in geriatric institutions in Scotland are paid a salary equivalent to nurses in hospitals, plus bonuses.

American elderly, who Kayser-Jones describes as having fewer resources and being more dependent on the system, have inferior health care and often a less qualified staff, because American nursing home proprietors were prone to cut services to increase profits. American nurses who work in nursing homes receive approximately 25% less than hospital nurses. Kayser-Jones also found an imbalance in social power because patients in America were more dependent on the staff. Moreover, she confirms what Jules Henry perceived, that American societal attitudes concerning old age are very negative. Kayser-Jones (1981) writes: "In a youth-oriented society, the aged are characterized as useless, dependent, physically and mentally weak, poor, and non-contributing; in short, they are a burden" (p. 249). While the investigator found the elderly nursing home residents in Scotland being treated with dignity and respect, their American counterparts were "infantilized, depersonalized, dehumanized and sometimes victimized by the staff" (p. 240). They often had personal property stolen from them, there was a tendency to address them either by their first names or by such terms as "Mother," "Honey," or "Baby," and little or no attention was paid to their modesty during bath time.

The authors have studied the first home for the aged in western Polynesia (Holmes & Holmes, 1987; Rhoads & Holmes, 1981). This home could most logically be categorized as a combined assisted-living and nursing facility. Mapuifagalele (haven of peace) opened in 1975 a few miles away from the port town of Apia, Western Samoa, and is operated by the Little Sisters of the Poor. Cardinal Pio, who was instrumental in its development, envisioned it as a home for retired Catholic catechists, but soon realized that there were others who could benefit from living there. Although Samoa is a place where people vehemently insist that families should and do take good care of their own elderly, in 1976 this home was at capacity with 83 Samoans in residence and a waiting list.

The nuns in charge were a multinational group, all of whom spoke Samoan. Residents had individual rooms except for the few married couples, who had slightly larger quarters. With the exception of the latter group, men and women occupied separate wings, each with an infirmary section for those who needed nursing care (about 25%). There was no charge to the residents to live at Mapuifagalele. The majority of the residents were ambulatory, and those who wished could assist with work around the home. Activities included card games, occasional movies, some television viewing, visiting, and a lot of religious observances. Not all the residents were Catholic, but even the Protestants attended Mass. Because the cardinal's home was on the grounds of Mapuifagalele, many special ceremonies were held in the large chapel.

Native foods were routinely served in the dining room, and sharing of food brought by family members was a Sunday evening ritual. Much family visiting occurred, with residents going back to their villages for

Residents of Mapuifagalele, Samoa's first long-term care home for the aged. (Photos by Lowell D. Holmes.)

extended visits on occasion. The nuns were very amenable to continuation of local cultural patterns by the residents; residents met as a group with a leader of their choice to deal with inappropriate behavior by residents or to plan special activities; a resident "bush doctor" was allowed to treat any resident who made such a request; and they took those who wished to the beach down the hill so they could swim in the sea. Although rooms were furnished with beds, some of the old people preferred the traditional pattern of sleeping on a mat on the floor, which was also allowed.

We found these aged Samoans satisfied with this living situation, which none of them could have anticipated as a possible option in their old age. They were admitted for a variety of reasons, but an overriding issue seems to be changing economic and social conditions. We concluded:

> The economic picture in Western Samoa, along with shifting value emphases, appears to be a major factor associated with the development of the institution. There is very little industry and wages are generally low. Education has become increasingly important to Western Samoans, but it is not free. It is the opinion of some informants that the emphasis on education and the concomitant cost of tuition for families with several school-age children has resulted in a shift in priority from the aged to the young. (Rhoads & Holmes, 1981, pp. 132-133)

We would not have predicted the degree of acceptance and contentment with institutional residence among aged Samoans. Two factors seem to explain this outcome: (a) the success of the nuns in adapting the institutional setting to Samoan cultural patterns and (b) the congruence between the role of religion in Samoan society and sponsorship of the home. "Samoans maintain that old age is a time when one thinks about God and prepares to meet Him, and where better might this be done than in a place like Mapuifagalele" (Holmes & Holmes, 1987, pp. 372-373).

SUMMARY

Anthropology, like most scholarly disciplines, has both theoretical and applied interests. Applied anthropologists draw on the facts and findings of their science and apply this knowledge in the solution of practical social, economic, political, or medical problems. In applying this knowledge it is necessary to emphasize the importance of cultural traditions on a people's behavior and why it is necessary to work within the cultural system in seeking solutions to problems. Margaret Clark and Barbara Anderson have assessed the philosophical and psychological climate in which the elderly in America must function and have suggested ways of improving senior participation, thus safeguarding the mental health and well-being of the elderly.

Cultural gerontologists have done considerable research in regard to health care delivery and the problems that arise from cross-cultural misunderstandings. These may be based on linguistic differences in verbalizing medical problems or differences in how members of different ethnic groups conceptualize disease and beliefs about how the human body functions.

Food preferences are another topic where anthropologists, by virtue of their cross-cultural knowledge, can make a contribution to food programs serving the elderly. Various ethnic groups view food and eating in very different ways. There are matters of prestige, sociability, religious significance, and health beliefs relating to foods that must be understood by those who attempt to provide food programs to people of different cultural backgrounds.

Caregiving, as it is provided by family members of different cultural identities, has been investigated with the goal of improving the effectiveness of patterns of care for both the recipient and the caregiver. It has been found that members of some groups are so conscientious in personally attending a loved one that they will not avail themselves of day-care facilities and often do not make use of such help as can be provided by support groups or formal service programs.

One of the most characteristic types of applied research carried on by anthropological gerontologists has to do with the philosophy and operational characteristics of long-term care institutions. Jules Henry's pioneer study *Culture Against Man*, carried out over 30 years ago, drew a depressing picture of how culture is against residents in three nursing homes, and he documented how our culture views long-term care patients—as obsolete human beings awaiting death. Vesperi, Gubrium, Henderson, Kayser-Jones, and others also discuss how American values influence the way patients are perceived and treated in nursing homes.

They are often treated as incapable of making their own decisions and as if withdrawal is a normal and desirable response to aging, and administrative planning and decisions rarely seek patient input. Studies have been made of how patients "pass time," how various levels of nursing home personnel interact with patients, and how problems between patients and staff arise from racial and cultural differences.

9

◉ The Aged and Cultural Change

The study of social and cultural change has always been an important interest of anthropologists, and it is therefore understandable that it has been a primary focus of investigation for anthropologists concerned with cultural gerontology. This chapter will emphasize change associated with the influences of modernization and the many ways in which societies, and more specifically the aged, are affected by such change. Following discussion of several components and theoretical aspects of modernization, we conclude with a case study of Japan, a highly modernized nation with historical traditions requiring honorific treatment for the aged.

Change, which can influence the status and treatment of the aged, may come from within the culture or from outside. Internally generated change may be caused by "technical inventions, individual struggles for land and power, reformulations of ideas by specially gifted inquiring minds, . . . pressure of population on the means of subsistence, and perhaps climatic changes" (Firth, 1958, p. 148). All these factors can conceivably affect the care, status, and opportunity for participation enjoyed by the aged in our own as well as other cultures. This chapter singles out one internal factor in particular for special scrutiny: population composition. For many years America has been characterized as a youth-dominated and youth-oriented society, but recent developments in health technology and in attitudes toward family size have resulted in an altered population age profile that is characterized by an ever-increasing percentage of middle-aged and elderly citizens and a progressively rising average age. This change in age composition is called by some writers "the graying of America." As we saw in Chapter 2, many other countries are already experiencing or face the prospect of such a demographic shift in the future.

Cultural systems are also affected by external change. Change that comes from outside the society involves borrowing ideas, and it has been estimated that few societies in the world have themselves invented more than about 10% of their cultural content. When borrowing results from ongoing contact between representatives of societies with different cultures, the situation is referred to as one of *acculturation*. Examples of this are white frontier settlers and American Indians or southern white masters and their African slaves. In such situations, borrowing seems to be two way, regardless of whether or not one society is more technologically advanced than the other. Sometimes change takes place as the result of ideas or traits of one culture being borrowed by another but without day-to-day interaction of peoples. An example of this is the introduction of noodles and gunpowder into Italy in the thirteenth century, when Marco Polo returned with these items on one of his trading trips to China. This kind of spread of ideas from one society to another is called *diffusion*.

Regardless of the source or variety of change, it must be recognized that change is constantly taking place in all societies whether folk or modern, Western or non-Western, provincial or cosmopolitan. Some societies, however, welcome change more than others, and therefore change is more rapid and pervasive. Arensberg and Niehoff (1964) maintain that change is ever present for the "single reason that people of different cultures are always in competition with one another. . . . This competition between peoples of different cultures is the basis of the drive toward modernization by the underdeveloped countries" (pp. 57-58).

This particular kind of change, *modernization*, has dominated the interest of anthropologists in recent years, particularly those who are interested in what happens to old people when societies become subject to rapid and profound transformation of their lifestyle through contact with the West. It characteristically involves changes in culture in the direction of urbanization, industrialization, scientific development, and the establishment of mass education and higher levels of communication through mass media exposure.

Contacts between Western countries and hunting, herding, and agricultural societies have in some cases only added a few new ideas to these preindustrial cultures, which by and large retain their traditional form. In other cases, however, lifestyles have been revolutionized and there has been a wholesale imposition of new legal, economic, political, and religious values and behavior. Modernizing influences have often shattered customs and institutions that preindustrial peoples have built up with painstaking effort over long periods of time. In these situations modernization represents a form of external change, because the source of the transforming culture items is outside the culture. It is, however, possible to talk about modernization as an internal force for change as we look at the history of technological development, industrialization, and urbanization in America.

In 1972 Donald O. Cowgill and Lowell D. Holmes investigated the influence of modernization on the status of the aged in 14 societies, each representing different positions along a continuum running from preliterate (sometimes called "primitive" or "preindustrial"), to peasant (agricultural and herding), to modern industrial societies. Based on evidence from an earlier cross-cultural work by Simmons (1945a) and a variety of reports by other cultural gerontologists, the two investigators hypothesized that *as societies become increasingly modern there is a concomitant drop in status of the elderly.* Although the study was cross cultural rather than longitudinal (with different societies representing the various gradations of modernization), the study demonstrated a general fall in status accompanying increased modernization, with only two exceptions, and these the authors believe could be explained and should have been predicted in terms of unique cultural circumstances. The study, however, was admittedly not methodologically perfect, and the researchers recognized that variations in values and social structure among the societies could greatly influence how each of them reacted to the forces of modernization. For example, Holmes (1972) cautioned:

How a society develops under the impact of modernizing forces depends to a great extent upon the values it held previously. A society whose major religion is Buddhism may be quite differently affected by industrialization and urbanization than one operating under a Judeo-Christian tradition. The same is true for traditional differences in political or economic philosophy. . . . There are many examples in the anthropological literature to support the idea that traditional values are of great importance in shaping the attitudes toward the aged in societies undergoing technological and economic change. (p. 87)

Various theorists have hypothesized that the way the aged are treated in a society and the way they feel about their own status is related to such things as rate of change, family structure (extended or nuclear), nature of the economy, amount of physical mobility, or percentage of aged in the population. However, long-term value orientations can conceivably overshadow any or all of these variables. An analysis of 13 preindustrial societies described by Margaret Mead (1937) in *Cooperation and Competition Among Primitive Peoples* revealed a strong correlation between low valuation of the aged and a value orientation marked by emphasis on personal achievement, private property, and security based on individual activity. On the other hand, she observed that societies that accord the aged high status and ensure their physical welfare are those that tend to submerge the individual in the group and provide people of all ages with an unthreatened sense of security. While sedentary agriculturalists generally are deferential to elders, variations in value orientations seem to explain why for some people in Mead's sample (the Zuni, for example) status increases with age, whereas among the Ifugao (also sedentary agriculturalists) the aged experience a decline of status with advancing age.

The value system of the United States is one that, like many of the societies in Mead's sample, stresses individual achievement and a low degree of security. Francis Hsu (1961) sees the American core value as "self-reliance," and he singles out dependency as the cardinal American sin. He believes that these ideas are rooted as deep as the Reformation and have therefore prevailed for more than 400 years in spite of modifications in technology, economics, family structure, and other factors that might affect the status and treatment of the aged. Philip Slater (1970) maintains that in the American ideological environment everything . . . rests upon the assumption that the world does not contain the wherewithal to satisfy the needs of its human inhabitants. From this it follows that people must compete with one another for these scarce resources. . . . The key flaw is, of course, the fact that the scarcity is spurious—man-made in the case of bodily gratifications and man-allowed and man-maintained in the case of material goods. (p. 103)

What clearly is needed to understand the effects of modernization on a society's elderly population without the complications of having to deal with value variables is a longitudinal study in a society that has been transformed from a hunting or peasant culture to an industrial one. Longitudinal research has been done in American Samoa (Holmes, 1972; Holmes & Holmes, 1992; Rhoads, 1981, 1984) and with Samoan migrants in California (Holmes, 1978; Holmes & Holmes, 1992; Rhoads, 1981, 1984). Rhoads studied communities with varying amounts of modernization and then assessed what effects their varying conditions had on the elderly residents. She compared Ta'ū village in the conservative and isolated Manu'a Group, Fagatogo (the port city and capital of American Samoa), and the Samoan migrant community of the San Francisco Bay area. She also compared her data with a 1962 study of Samoan aged made by Holmes (1972). The 1962 study was, however, somewhat general, and specific data comparisons were not always possible. Nonetheless, general impressions derived from a comparative analysis were valuable because a great deal of modernization was forced upon American Samoa between the years 1963 and 1976.

Using observation, information gleaned from government documents, and extended interviews with elderly and with younger family members (approximately 50 of each in each community), Rhoads (1981) found that, although the level of community modernization varied from "low" in Ta'ū to "medium" in Fagatogo to "high" in San Francisco, there was not a clear-cut or consistent decline in the status of the elderly in the more modern localities. She maintains that the status of the elderly in all three communities is relatively high, and suggests

several factors which I believe explain why the Samoan aged have retained a great deal of the high status characteristic of traditional

Samoa. These factors—the family, reciprocal obligations, and for migrant Samoans in San Francisco, an emphasis on ethnicity—actually constitute a complex of ideas and values which are interrelated and seem to reinforce each other. At the same time that they maintain support for the status of the aged, these values seem to have mitigated against development of some of the more negative effects of modernization. (Rhoads, 1981, p. 145)

This is not to suggest that modernization was without impact on the aged in Samoa; Rhoads felt that there were implications in the data that the future could bring erosion of the status of Samoan elders, especially with the ever-increasing rate of emigration. And in the migrant community of San Francisco, there was concern as to "what directions the lives of future generations of the Samoans in the U.S. will take, when the majority are American-born, second- or third-generation members of these communities" (Rhoads, 1981, p. 146).

Of the research in San Francisco in 1977, Rhoads (1981) wrote:

I was surprised to find that the migrants still seem as much Samoan as the people living in their homeland. The Bay area Samoans in the sample are still undeniably operating according to *fa'asamoa*. . . . Their ethnic identity seems to be a significant unifying principle. As other ethnic groups have sometimes done in the face of foreign influences, Samoans in San Francisco "compartmentalize" their lives to a great extent. They deal with the larger society at work or in other situations when they have to, but the larger part of their world is very much Samoan. (pp. 140-141)

Part of this emphasis on "Samoanness" is a reaffirmation of traditions that place great value on old age and great emphasis on more than adequate concern for satisfaction of elders' social and material needs.

The authors returned to San Francisco in 1992 to again assess the status of the elderly in the Samoan migrant community after an additional period of 15 years of exposure to modern influences. All of the aged Samoans that we interviewed have lived in the United States about 20 years or more with the exception of one couple who had only been in San Francisco for 3 years. In the latter case the husband's health had prompted them to move both to be with children and for access to better health care. In almost every case the motivation for coming to or remaining in California was the presence of children in the area and a strong desire to be with family. All were living in extended-family households, a situation unchanged in this community since our initial research in 1977. The elderly still say that their children seek their advice and that the family acts in accordance with their wishes, although there was sometimes a hint of amusement as they said, "They better do what I say!"

There are serious problems for Samoans in the United States, especially in the area of economics. The National Office of Samoan Affairs, with offices in San Francisco, the Los Angeles area, and San Diego in California does an excellent job of trying to assist their people acquire the education and skills necessary for survival in this modern environment. They try to reinforce the strengths of the cultural system and, at the same time, counteract points of conflict with the dominant culture. The family and the church remain the focal points of social activity and support for all Samoans, especially the aged, but a generation gap is becoming increasingly apparent as the younger generation struggles with being, in the words of one Samoan leader, "neither completely Samoan nor completely American." Some aged Samoans now say that their grandchildren do not like the *fa'aSamoa* (the Samoan way), and many of these American-born children cannot speak Samoan.

Although much more research is needed to acquire a complete understanding of the relationship between modernization and the status and support of the aged, some generalizations can be made based on what has been observed in a variety of Third and Fourth World countries and in the United States. These generalizations, borrowed in many cases from Cowgill and Holmes's (1972) *Aging and Modernization*, are as follows:

(1) The concept of old age itself appears to be relative to the degree of modernization. Even the definition of old age varies according to the degree of societal modernization. In preindustrial societies, where life spans tend to be shorter, people are inclined to perceive that old age comes earlier than in more modern societies; perhaps it does if life is hard and the life cycle has been characterized by strenuous labor, repeated periods of famine, and little effective medical care.

When Holmes (1972) investigated the chronological age at which people in Samoa began to be referred to as *matuaali'i* (old man) and *lo'omatua* (old woman) in 1962—when the society was still very traditional—he was told it was at age 50, whereas in 1976, after a decade and a half of intensive Western change, the Samoans responded that they thought of old age as beginning between the ages of 60 and 65 (Rhoads, 1981). The Igbo of West Africa see the onset of old age as occurring between 40 and 50, and the Sidamo of Ethiopia (also a preindustrial society) consider a person old when he or she reaches 55. All modern Western nations, on the other hand, maintain that the threshold of old age is between 65 and 70. Not only is there a decided tendency for the perception of when old age begins to be altered by modernization, there is a pronounced change in how old age is conceptualized. Most preindustrial societies hold a functional view of aging—that is, one is old when no longer able to perform normal adult duties. Modern societies have a chronological view, selecting an arbitrary year (65 or 70) as the threshold.

(2) Longevity is directly and significantly related to the degree of modernization. Cowgill (1972a) believes that "longevity may well be the best index of modernization" (p. 8), given that average age of life has steadily increased as societies have modernized. Neanderthals, who lived as hunters and gatherers 100,000 years ago, had a life expectancy of less than 20 years; Egyptians (based on mummy evidence) averaged 22.5 years of life, and Greeks in 400 B.C. could expect to live about 30 years on average. In North America, Late Woodland (c. 1500 A.D.) Indian populations in Maryland were averaging 23 years. Philadelphians in the 1780s had an average life span of 25 years, and Americans as a whole in 1900-1902 had a life expectancy of 48.2 years. By 1990 this figure had risen to 75.6. Although life expectancy has fluctuated in various places and at various times, the index has tended to accelerate rapidly as societies move toward modernization, urbanization, and industrialization.

(3) Modernized societies have a relatively high proportion of old people in their populations. This phenomenon results from two interrelated factors—the reduction of birthrates and an increase in life span resulting from advances in medical technology—that tend to be associated with modern urban and industrial life. The proportion of children (0 to 17) in the United States has declined from 40% in 1900 to 28% in 1980, while the group 65 years and over increased from 4% to 11% in the same time period. By the year 2030 the two groups will be approximately equal in size (21% children and 22% aged) (U.S. Senate Committee on Aging et al.,

1991). In 1977 the median age in America was 29.4; by 2030 the average age of Americans will be 41. In part this is due to a "baby bust" that has driven birthrates downward since the 1960s and to a dramatic reduction in heart disease deaths that has boosted life expectancy nearly five years since 1970.

Modern societies also have higher proportions of older women and subsequently higher proportions of widows. In some developing countries, however—Cuba, Guatemala, Malaysia, and India, for example—the ratio of elderly men per 100 women is nearly equal to or even exceeds 100. It is expected that in many developing areas the proportion of older women in populations will be increasing as life expectancy improves (Kinsella & Taeuber, 1992). In America the 1880 census recorded that for people 65 and older there were 101 men per 100 women; by the 1990 census the differential was to 68.7 men per 100 women. By 2025 the number of men per women will increase to 83 due to an anticipated "faster decline in mortality rates for men than for women" (Kinsella & Taeuber, 1992, p. 47).

(4) The aged are the recipients of greater respect in societies where they constitute a low proportion of the total population. Diamonds, gold nuggets, and first editions of books are valued because there are so few of them. Perhaps the same applies to people. Some societies believe that very old people have special value because they are favored by the gods or because they have some superior innate quality that has allowed them to survive. This was true in Colonial America (Fischer, 1978). Some very old men in American Indian and Eskimo societies were believed to be alive because of special supernatural power, and therefore they were the most appropriate people to serve as religious or medical practitioners.

Preindustrial societies seldom have more than 3% of the population over the age of 65; modern societies have between 12% and 18%. The authors propose that there may be a phenomenon that might be labeled *societal carrying power*, and suggest that when a society reaches a point where dependent members cannot be supported comfortably the status and concern for these recipients decline. Some evidence indicates that this is what is occurring in America in regard to Social Security financing. When a few elderly were supported by the contributions of a large number of productive workers, little in the way of resentment was expressed, but when the percentage of recipients relative to contributors increased, there were indications of both anxiety and resentment on the part of those members of the workforce who were financially responsible for the continuation of the program. It is, however, difficult to establish cause-and-effect relations in areas such as this. Actual numbers may have little to do with status considerations. Perhaps both the increase in number of elders and a decline in the status of old people are merely correlated with modernization and its many pervasive social, economic, and political manifestations.

(5) *Societies that are in the process of modernizing tend to favor the young, while the aged are at an advantage in more stable, sedentary societies.* In the article "Aging in Modern Society," Simmons (1959) observed that "there is a pattern of participation for the aged that becomes relatively fixed in stable societies but suffers disruption with rapid social change" (p. 7). Press and McKool (1972) note that modernization causes breaks in the continuity of roles and results in reduced prestige for the elderly. They maintain that the principal factors associated with reduced senior status are economic interests, minimization of number and importance of ascriptive roles, nuclear family independence, economic activity outside of the household, and early turnover of family resources from father to son.

In conservative, preindustrial societies, the aged, because they are custodians of both family property and cultural tradition, become entrenched in positions of power and authority, and their roles and status are guaranteed by seniority rights. Roles and statuses are well defined and well understood. Tradition provides security, and that security is in part based on the fact that prediction is possible. There are few surprises. The events of the past are repeated, and the elders who have been through these situations many times before can easily attend to them. The elders appear to be decisive, wise, and confident, and they are objects of admiration.

In situations of rapid change, social conditions become unstable and the old solutions to problems are not always adequate. Because the aged under these conditions cannot always continue to exhibit their wisdom and control, they become vulnerable and subject to replacement by younger people who are more flexible, less prone to call upon old solutions, more daring, and more willing to experiment and learn new solutions. Maxwell and Silverman (1977) further clarify the ramifications of modernization:

Because of culture contact with a more dominant complex society, the information controlled by the aged becomes rapidly obsolete. This high rate of informational obsolescence is reflected in a decline in the social participation of the elderly. The low incidence of social participation in turn contributes to their loss of status. (pp. 379-380)

Maria Cattell's (1989) work with the Samia of Kenya provides an example of the impact of change on the value of old people's knowledge. She discusses the concept of *amakesi*, which has connotations of knowledge and wisdom and "refers to different qualities, depending on the individual's life course stage" (p. 228). It is the old who have wisdom and are therefore best qualified to be advisers, a role that provides "high status and power in families and communities" (p. 228). With modernization has come an emphasis on the value of education as the means to success, but the desired education is less and less concerned with the knowledge controlled by the elderly. As Cattell (1989) explains: "Old people's *amakesi* has been devalued, displaced, replaced, and a significant basis of their respect has been eroded" (p. 236).

(6) Respect for the aged tends to be greater in societies in which the extended family is prevalent, particularly if it functions as the household unit. Rosow (1965) maintains that the position of aged in a society is relatively higher when the extended family is central to the social structure because "a clan can and will act much more effectively to meet crises and dependency of its members than a small family. Mutual obligations between blood relatives—specifically including the aged—are institutionalized as formal rights, not generous benefactions" (p. 22).

The literature provides us with abundant examples of the supportive nature of the extended family. Munsell (1972) observed that, among the Pima Indians, recent developments that have brought the nuclear family into prominence at the expense of the extended form have to a large extent deprived the elderly of decision-making functions and therefore resulted in loss of elders' status and authority. Press and McKool (1972) found in Chinaulta, Guatemala, that

loss of extended family viability goes hand in hand with low, dependent status of the aged. . . . Where the economic unit is largely coterminous with the extended family, the elder members *de facto* remain economically active and may exert considerable control over the behavior of others. (p. 303)

Frances M. Adams (1972), on the other hand, stresses the importance of the extended family as a socialization influence that provides family members with a positive attitude toward growing old. She writes:

Changes in behavior expectations as a person gets older . . . are understood in advance through close association with older people who have already made the transitions. For example, a person knows how to be an old person because he has observed first his grandfather and then his father in this role. The emotional security developed in childhood in the context of the extended family is not lost in old age. (p. 110)

Shelton (1972) stresses still another aspect of extended-family organization in West African Igbo society that contributes to respect for the aged. This is the emphasis this society puts on the cyclic flow of family members and spiritual forces. He notes:

The dead are not buried and forgotten, but are "returners" who reappear in the patriline. The aged persons in the family, accordingly, are not simply individuals who have served their brief span on earth and are soon due to disappear forever, but indeed are getting closer to the apogee of their cycle—they are soon to be ancestral spirits, in that most powerful condition in the endless cycle of existence. (p. 35)

Although extended-family household organization is somewhat rare in modern societies, McKain reported in 1972 that in the Soviet Union at least a modified form was being preserved and that it was a key ingredient in the economic security of both young and old. He wrote:

Not many older persons in the Soviet Union live alone. For the most part unattached older persons live with their children, with older relatives or with an unrelated family. . . . The presence of grandparents in the house may also be prevalent for other more materialistic reasons. Since aged persons receive a pension, the added income is a very welcome supplement to the household budget. (p. 156)

More recently, an investigation by Sternheimer (1985) of the *babushka* (grandmother) role in Russia and other areas of the former Soviet Union indicates increasing numbers of nuclear families and more older women living alone. Some of these women are no longer interested in assuming the traditional role of *babushka*, focused on child-care and housekeeping responsibilities, and prefer a more leisure-oriented life after retirement. Others lack the opportunity to follow tradition due to changes in family structure, often associated with relocation of children to urban areas. Russian sociologist Natalya Rimashevskaya comments that "the social crisis is working to break up the family, and positive values—like taking care of your parents—are being lost" (cited in Elliott, 1994, p. 37). Where elderly parents live with married offspring in crowded city apartments, the former are often abused "out of sheer frustration" (p. 37).

Sheehan (1976) points out, however, that when a community turns away from an extended-family emphasis and kinship loyalties are replaced by structures that emphasize peer allegiance and other-directed individualism, there is, in effect, a return to the less binding ties associated with nomadic life. In nomadic societies, he maintains, "social and geographic mobility become goals; individual autonomy emerges as a value" (p. 437). This is not unlike what happens with increased modernization. "As urban-industrial society increasingly technologizes, seniors ever more lose their family ties along with accompanying status, decision-making power and security" (Sheehan, 1976, p. 437).

(7) In nonindustrial societies the family is the basic social group providing economic security for dependent aged, but in industrial ones the responsibility tends to be partially or totally that of the state. Although nonindustrial societies often provide for elderly through certain kinds of food sharing practices and through certain food taboos, it is nearly impossible to find any traditional tribal society where support of the elderly is the primary responsibility of the greater society rather than the family or clan. There is one historical exception—Inca society. Although this group has usually been called a civilization, it certainly was not a modern industrial society. The Inca, whose government at one time controlled most of the Pacific coastal region of South America, divided the land under their control into sections to be worked communally by their subjects. These lands, under the administration of appointed government officials, were designated as being (a) those to be cultivated for the support of the Inca

(king) and his government officials, including a hierarchy of priests, (b) those that could be used for support of the workers themselves and their families, and (c) those to be cultivated for the support of "soldiers, invalids, the aged and orphans" (Flornoy, 1958, p. 111). Widows were to be taken care of by their brothers-in-law although war widows received special help. Because national policy reserved the produce from some public lands for support of the elderly and other dependent individuals, the Inca represent a case of state-sponsored welfare within an indigenous Indian culture.

But turning to the twentieth century, we find that a few Third World countries have established programs that offer meager pensions to retired government employees and limited governmental assistance to the elderly based on need, but such countries rarely have government-operated residences for the aged. Martin (1988) maintains that "in most countries of Asia, only the urban elite receive pensions, and for the vast majority of Asians, pensions are not available" (p. S106). Most developing countries do not have the governmental capacity to collect and disperse benefits like modern industrial nations, because such systems require an effective means of obtaining funds from employees and employers. Furthermore, developing countries do not have a large enough population of full-time workers to support such a system. Singapore and Sri Lanka have pension funds that cover a small proportion of workers, but these involve lump sum retirement payments. In China a pension program is available for workers in state-owned industries, for government workers, and for career soldiers but only about half of these are actually covered. All in all, only about 10% of the total Chinese workforce can rely on retiring with a pension.

Tracy (1991) writes that in these extended-family-oriented societies "the dilemma . . . is how to offer support through federal and state programs without destroying the traditional responsibility of families to care for their elderly members" (p. 5). And Martin (1988) makes the point that in many developing countries institutionalization of the elderly lags far behind the industrial world because it is seen as undesirable and as a last resort, necessary only when families cannot meet their filial obligations. In 1982, Singapore had nursing homes for only 2.5% of the elderly population, China institutionalized a mere 0.33%, and Hong Kong (the most modern of all) housed but 1% of its elderly population in nursing homes. In Japan (a world leader in industrialization and primarily an urban society), we find elaborate government pension, insurance, and assistance programs. Palmore (1975) writes that with the end of World War II and with increased industrialization has come the "belief that pensions or social security, rather than the children, should be primarily responsible for the support of older persons" (p. 90).

The most modernized societies are also those with the most extensive developments in programs and services for their elderly. And many of these programs are government sponsored. In the United States, for example, although the Social Security Act was passed in the 1930s, it is primarily in the years since 1965 that services have proliferated. At that time both Medicare and the Older Americans Act were passed, and there are now a variety of employment, housing, nutrition, adult day-care, homemaker and home health care, respite care, educational, socialization, and volunteer programs/services, most of them at least partially funded by government sources and available to persons age 60 and over.

In spite of the many programs, there is also an emphasis on social and financial independence, and there is definitely not a pattern of family support of elderly in the United States. In fact, says Cowgill (1972b), "as far as financial assistance is concerned, the flow is definitely from parents to children, although of course this varies with social classes" (p. 254). In the 1990s, as the population of frail elderly increases, the trend in service provision (government funded) is toward keeping the aged in their own homes, or at least out of institutions, perhaps maintaining the facade of independence. Not unlike the situation in China, it is the very poor and the wealthy who have easiest access to services.

(8) The proportion of aged who retain leadership roles in modern societies is lower than in preindustrial ones. In modern societies, few people manage to retain leadership roles into old age. A few judges, owners of industrial or commercial businesses, and a handful of lawyers and physicians often manage to maintain their positions of authority and continue to command the respect of younger colleagues well into old age, but most elderly are subject to a great amount of prejudice and pressure to turn over leadership roles, even if they are not subject to mandatory retirement regulations. Citing McConnell, Noreen Hale (1990) writes that

age discrimination, originally subscribed to by pockets of industry, spread to the larger society after 1915. . . . The older worker, believed to be in inevitable decline, was a handy target in an era of rapid technological advance and a new emphasis on speed, efficiency, and adaptability. By then, the mature employee was considered ineffectual and expendable. In the late 1920s, approximately 20 percent of companies used physical exams to screen workers. These exams often were not directly related to job performance but were used instead to eliminate "outmoded" employees, who tended to be older. (pp. 5-6)

Such prejudice continues today as evidenced by the fact that in 1987 some 20,000 cases of age discrimination were filed with the Equal Employment Opportunity Commission (Hoopes, 1989).

On the other hand, among the Dusun of Borneo, headmen are drawn from among the elderly and can never be removed or recalled; they remain in authority until they die or voluntarily retire (Williams, 1965). Charles Fuller (1972) maintains that the control of social organization in Bantu society has consistently been in the hands of elders. Old men have traditionally occupied positions with varying amounts of authority from lineage heads to tribal chiefs, but they have also held positions of leadership as judges, priests, teachers, and historians. Fuller (1972) writes: "The most significant roles . . . are roles attained only at the more advanced years. . . . Almost every elder in most Bantu tribes . . . has a respected role as a wise counsellor" (p. 67).

The Hutterites, a North American subculture famous for its rejection of modernization, place great importance on age as a criterion for leadership. The oldest men occupy executive posts and serve as members of the village council. The elderly also hold leadership positions such as department heads for their various economic enterprises, and there is a general pattern of progress to higher and higher status positions as one grows older (Hostetler & Huntington, 1967).

(9) Religious leadership is more likely to be a continuing role of the aged in preindustrial than in modern societies. Gerontologists disagree on whether or not people turn more to religion as they reach the end of their lives, but they do seem to agree that elders in preindustrial societies have a greater tendency to function in religious leadership roles than in modern societies. Ethnographers tell us that the majority of shamans among the Eskimo are old and that elderly West Africans are believed to have great

The Fijian kava *(yanggona)* ceremony is a sacred ritual directed by village elders on sociopolitical occasions. (Photo by Lowell D. Holmes.)

power in dealing with spirits because they are "almost ancestors," but there is little evidence that it is appropriate for elders in America to play any kind of significant role in religious leadership. In fact, the first professional group to have mandatory retirement imposed upon them in America was New England ministers. Although many Protestant churches have a group of congregation officers called "elders," such positions are rarely occupied by people over 40 or 50 years of age. Church congregations are more concerned with recruiting youth than recruiting the elderly, and youth ministries and youthful ministers abound.

A comparison of two religious groups with common doctrinal origins illustrates the point: The Amish maintain a leadership largely of elderly men and are renowned for their deliberate rejection of modernization. The Mennonites of America (Roth, 1981), on the other hand, have developed a youthful leadership and have openly and unashamedly adopted modernization.

There is no retirement on Paros Island. This 93-year-old fisherman goes out three or four times a week. (Photo courtesy of Jeff Beaubier; used by permission.)

Where ceremonialism and ritual are important, it is not uncommon for the elderly to be caretakers of procedure and protocol, but religion in modern societies has in many cases dispensed with ceremonialism and ritual, leaving little opportunity for participation or leadership by elders.

(10) Retirement is a modern invention found only in modernized, high-productivity societies. Preindustrial societies have less need for modifying and

abandoning roles in old age than modern society, where retirement from economically productive roles has become expected. Advanced age in traditional societies often necessitates a shift from one kind of productive role to another—for example, from the role of hunter to religious practitioner or from warrior to counselor—but the role shift usually involves an increase in prestige and authority rather than a reduction in status. The role shifts in tribal societies are also more easily accomplished because there is often a traditional pattern of role shifts as in the case of formal age-grading systems.

In modern societies there "are no automatic roles awaiting many members of the society who must build new lives through their own efforts" (Lopata, 1972, p. 276). Role shifts must be worked out by the individual with no help from the society. There are no rules and very little precedent for extending productivity after the age of formal retirement. Although traditional societies make provision for shifts to less strenuous but not necessarily less important or less honorific roles, modern society offers elders no role at all. Even when elders in traditional societies perform the same roles relegated to old people in modern society, we find that they are valued in very different ways. Such menial tasks as housekeeping or baby-sitting are often viewed in preindustrial societies as vital social functions and activities that bring honor and respect. The role adjustment problem particularly affects men in modern societies who must make the transition from respected work activities to purposeless inactivity, while women, particularly housewives, continue domestic roles well into old age.

In developing societies such as Samoa or Thailand, there is today the concept of retiring at age 60 or 65 because a few people are now employed in civil service occupations and in modern commercial and industrial firms. However, in the rural areas of these societies where traditional occupations and subsistence economic activities prevail,

> retirement as a formal process is not common; instead there is only a gradual process of withdrawal from an occupation. Life in old age tends to be a continuation of living within a family context. . . . There are always useful things to do and old people are certainly not inactive. One of the types of activities that actually increases in the later years is religious activities. For the most part, the transition from middle age to old age is smooth and graceful, and older

persons in this society usually are supported by a respectful and helpful circle of relatives and friends, stimulated and enlivened by continuing useful social roles, and comforted and encouraged by a religion which promises continuity of life. (Cowgill, 1972c, pp. 100-101)

Salient Aspects of Modernization

Having established in *Aging and Modernization* (1972) that there is a tendency for the status of the aged to decline when a society's degree of modernization increases, Cowgill (1974) next began an inquiry into the factors that cause such a phenomenon. His theory is that certain aspects of modernization are more important than others in creating a sociological environment that places the elderly at a disadvantage. These aspects are (a) the development of modern health technology, (b) modern economic technology, (c) urbanization, and (d) education. The situation, which Cowgill has carefully outlined, can be described as follows.

Modernization invariably brings improvements in health and economic technology. Improvements in sanitation, medical diagnostic skills, and preventive and therapeutic medicine profoundly change the vital statistics of a population. Medical advances most noticeably affect infant and child mortality, but they also prolong life for everyone. Therefore life expectancy figures increase and life spans are generally lengthened. Mead (1967) suggests, however, that these life-extending medical advances may be a mixed blessing for the elderly, because before the advent of Western medicine the elderly were revered for their own resources for surviving while today they may be perceived as being kept alive by modern medicine. The smallness of their numbers in traditional societies automatically seemed to render them objects of admiration. Mead believes that in modern society "we are now developing a generation which is over-burdened with the care of old people who no longer have any relationship to the rest of the world, who are using up family funds, hospital beds, and social resources" (p. 36). She points out that old people in preindustrial societies are vigorous, active, and interesting people and, because of this, children in these societies have a positive attitude toward the elderly. Children in modern societies, on the other hand, often have very different experiences. Many of the aged they have observed have been reduced almost to a vegetable state, kept alive by drugs and nursing homes. Understandably then, children in modern societies perceive old age as a horror to be put out of their minds as long as possible.

Medical technology has not only brought more effective ways of curing disease and prolonging life, it also has developed contraceptive devices that have made family planning possible. In time, a combination of longer life spans and a reduction in the birthrate will result in a "graying" effect in the population with the consequence that a considerable proportion of individuals will be in the productive work period of their lives. With greater numbers of working-age individuals in the society, fewer openings in the labor force will result, and there will be greater and greater competition between the older workers who hold the jobs and the younger workers who would like to take them over. Because medical science increases life expectancy, there will be social pressure from aggressive young people to open up the job market by substituting *retirement* for death.

Modern economic technology also changes the work situation. New technical processes result in the creation of new jobs and changes in old ones. The younger workers with their technologically-oriented educations tend to be attracted to the new occupations, while older workers make minimal adjustments to cope with the new technology or attempt to carry on in the more traditional roles as long as possible. The steady reduction of traditional roles, however, represents still another pressure for retirement.

As the new technology makes industrial expansion possible, there will be an increase in profits. The young pioneers in the new technology are well rewarded materially and psychologically for their productive efforts. The modernizing society reveres efficiency and evolves a work ethic that values work as the chief role in life and an important end in itself. In the case of America's modern development, this ethic has taken on the complexion of the Protestant ethic, which links Christianity and capitalism and interprets the material wealth of captains of modern industry as evidence of God's reward for diligent work. These ideas intensify the conflict and competition between generations and greatly affect attitudes toward retired workers. At retirement the sudden and drastic reduction in material, psychological, and spiritual rewards is demoralizing. Given that modern work ethic societies commonly equate unemployment with sloth and failure, the retirement forced by competition for jobs is accompanied by a sense of dissatisfaction and depression.

There is therefore a loss of both income and prestige and a dilemma concerning what one's role should consist of after one's work life is completed.

Attracted by the promise of high pay and prestigious positions that the new technology and economics produce, young people in modernizing societies flock to the cities. The young migrants come singly or as nuclear families, and the emigration has a decided effect on the social structure of the communities they leave. Extended-family units are weakened in the rural areas while in the city the emphasis is increasingly toward independent biological families. The rural areas have always been strongholds of traditional culture, with elders not only in control of property but of knowledge and prestige as well. In the city the young escape the control of the elders and begin to question their authority and priorities. Rowe (1961) relates that in India when young men return home from the cities where they have been employed they are impatient with the slow pace of life and outmoded procedures. The wealth they bring back disturbs the traditional association of affluence and old age. Similarly, Arth (1972) reports that among the Ibo of Nigeria young men can now acquire independent wealth from wage work in the cities and no longer have to depend on their fathers for bride price. All of this results in an inversion of status, which puts the young in roles of authority and leadership. As the young Ibos increase their participation in and the domination of the lifestyle of the city even the older urban residents will come to understand that old ideas are of less value than new ideas, old jobs are less lucrative than new, and old roles are less prestigious than new.

The elderly in the city do not have the same emotional support as the elderly in more traditional areas, as the cross-generational kin networks are replaced by peer groups. In general, "cities are settled by young refugees liberated from the stifling control exercised in the small community by old men, religious leaders and omni-present extended family" (Gutmann, 1977, p. 320).

Traditional societies have a much greater proportion of illiterates than modern ones, for traditional skills—hunting, herding, and horticulture—can be passed on from generation to generation by word of mouth and through informal teaching by example. Furthermore, the wisdom and practical know-how of preindustrial societies has tended to remain valid for hundreds of years with minimal modification. In such societies

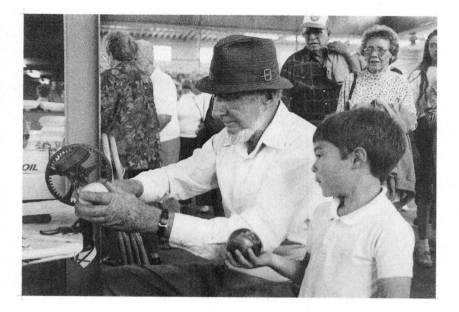

Amish youngster learning the traditional skill of apple peeling for fritters from an elder at a religious festival. (Photo by Lowell D. Holmes.)

the people who exercise the greatest control and enjoy the greatest respect are those who have lived the longest and have experienced the most. Because conditions have remained much the same over long periods of time, these people are most effective in advising, legislating, and administering.

Modernization renders experience in traditional lifeways of little importance, as it changes the rules, challenges values, and alters the direction in which the society moves. Oral tradition and learning by imitation are inadequate in communicating the knowledge that people must have to function in a world of rapid change, urban life, and complex technology. No longer can individual heads carry the information requisite for a modern society. Modernization demands literacy, libraries, and formal education. Not only is more technical knowledge needed to function in a modernizing society but it is needed in a hurry and in large amounts. Thus education in such societies is mass education—formal, impersonal, and designed to cultivate skills that will be called into play at some future time. Practical education is valued over general education, and education is primarily directed at the young. As it is they who are attracted to the new jobs and new challenges of a technologically complex world, and as it is they who will carry the burden of modernization progress, education as an avenue to success is viewed as indispensable for young people. Parents strive to provide their children with better educations than they themselves were able to acquire.

In Western Samoa, a Third World country new to independence and modernizing influences, Rhoads and Holmes (1981) found that the establishment of a home for the aged in this society where families had always taken extreme pride in being able to care for their aged was related to increased emphasis on education. In this relatively poor country where most families have many children and all must pay tuition for schooling, there often simply is not enough money for the needs of both the elderly and schoolage children. Although families want to continue their generous support of their aged, medical bills and other special expenses involved in their care are often beyond family means, and therefore they have reluctantly been forced to allow their elderly to enter the retirement home.

Because mass formal education is prerequisite to industrialization, it takes on a special value in modernizing societies. In old Samoa, chiefs were elected to titles by their extended families based on the candidates' knowledge of ceremonial protocol and traditional lore, family service, and age (one had to be at least 40 to qualify), but in modern Samoa, many chief titles are held by young men who have good educations and consequently important jobs in government or industry. Harlan (1964) also found that in traditional Indian villages education and urban work experience were more important factors in village leadership than age.

In modern societies the young are, as a group, better educated than the old. Because the value system is tipped in favor of the better educated, and because better education is required for the more lucrative and prestigious jobs, the young are in a position to question old procedures and old symbols of respect and authority. A generation gap is created and tends to widen progressively as a "youth culture" and work ethic emerge. Conflict is introduced, and because the young in these new societies command the bulk of the resources for coping with modernization, they are the inevitable winners, monetarily, psychologically, and in terms of elevated prestige.

In Samoa old age is a prerequisite for family and political leadership roles.
(Photos by Lowell D. Holmes.)

Criticism of Aging and Modernization Theory

The aging and modernization theory has generated a great deal of research effort, having been tested in many societies. These studies have revealed support in many cases but have also raised questions. The theory has its share of critics as well. Perhaps the most common criticism is that the theory assumes a "golden age" for the aged earlier in history, sometimes stated as a "world we have lost" (Fischer, 1978; Laslett, 1972, 1976). They argue that the life and status of the aged is not now, and was not always, better before modernization. Quadagno (1982) agrees with this view but goes further to state that extended-family living was not necessarily characteristic of traditional societies, nor does she believe retirement is a modern development. She emphasizes "industrialization" in her critique, a process that Cowgill (1986) says differs from modernization, with "modernization being a much broader concept and commanding a longer historical sweep than the more limited technological change identified as industrialization" (p. 192).

A primary concern of Laslett (1976) is his belief that the theory is predicated on the existence of the extended family in traditional societies, a point on which he disagrees. Dowd (1980), who has presented one of the more balanced critiques of aging and modernization theory, points out that "a hypothesis of an extended family era never played a central role in the modernization theory" (p. 68). And Cowgill (1986), in discussing this problem, emphasizes that "the issue here is: Of those few people who do survive to old age, what proportions live in multiple-generation households? When the question is posed in this way, even Laslett's data point toward extended family arrangements" (p. 93).

It is often pointed out that linking decline in status of the aged to the advent of modernization overlooks the point that frail or decrepit elders—those who become physically or mentally incompetent—may never have fared very well. Barbara Logue (1990) echoes this view but also suggests that

processes associated with modernization, especially in the health care sector, have exacerbated their plight as potential victims by expanding their numbers, enhancing their vulnerability, increasing the duration of their dependence, and making solutions more problematic. (p. 347)

Logue suggests that under these circumstances death-hastening may occur, but prolonged dying is increasingly common.

Numerous factors appear to influence the changing status of elders. Such things as political ideology (Cherry & Magnuson-Martinson, 1981), religious ideology (Roth, 1981), and cultural values (Rhoads, 1984) are but a few of the variables suggested. Other researchers have suggested that we need better definitions of the concept of status (Goldstein & Beall, 1981). In research using data from some 31 societies, Palmore and Manton (1974) have found evidence of status decline being of limited duration with improvement occurring once modernization is well established. They discovered that the relationship between old age status and modernization was a "J-shaped" pattern. That is, they found that status of the aged fell during the early stages of modernization but bottomed out and began to climb in the advanced stages. They suggest that "longitudinal analysis of changes in status of the aged within modernizing countries is needed to test the applicability of these theories to specific countries" (p. 210).

Case Study in Modernization: Japan

When the aging and modernization theory was put forward by Cowgill and Holmes in 1972 in the book *Aging and Modernization*, the Japanese were described as being somewhat ambivalent in their attitudes toward the aged, and in spite of traditional culture tenets that accorded high status and respect to the elderly, a number of factors tended to indicate that in this society old age was not always to be considered the "best time of life."

While David Plath's (1972) chapter in *Aging and Modernization* on Japanese aging is described as picturing the "darker side of aging in Japan" (p. 150), he maintains that this is necessary to "combat the tenacious western habit of romanticizing life in 'lotus land' " (p. 150). Equally cognizant of this tendency is Joseph Tobin (1987), who writes that "Americans hold on to a highly idealized picture of Japanese old age" (p. 53). Much like the yearning for a Shangri-la (as in James Hilton's 1933 *Lost Horizon*, where people never die) our elderly would like to believe that

if even in Japan, the land of robotics, early retirement, and postindustrial industry, the elderly are not just tolerated but venerated, appreciated, and indulged as they were in pre-modern times, then Americans can believe that the future need not look so bleak to them. (Tobin, 1987, p. 57)

Tobin holds that this view is also frequently encountered in the writings of American social scientists. He particularly cites Erdman Palmore's publications (1975; Palmore & Maeda, 1985) as the best example of such idealization. An equally "golden vision," however, was presented by Ruth Benedict in her book *The Chrysanthemum and the Sword* (1946).

Citing such benevolence as reserved "silver seats" on public transportation, honorific salutations, bowing, priority in serving, bathing, and going through doors, a tradition of respect supported by the religious doctrine of filial piety, and numerous government programs and holidays especially for the aged, Palmore asserts that Japan should be a role model for America and that it can be cited as an exception to the modernization theory. He believes that (a) in Japan the status of the aged has not been inversely proportional to the rate of social change, (b) the status of the aged is not higher in agricultural societies than in this urban one, and (c) in Japan the proportion of aged who have been able to maintain leadership roles has not declined with modernization. However, Tobin argues that Palmore's own writing cites statistics that show that there has been a steady decline in the elderly living with their children in the last 50 years, and that respect for the aged is more characteristic of rural than urban areas and more typical of the middle aged than the young. In regard to Palmore's (1975) *The Honorable Elders*, Tobin (1987) writes: "Much of the data Palmore presented in both editions of the book suggest a general and continued decline in the status of the elderly since the beginning a century or so ago of intense modernization and Westernization" (p. 55).

Tobin, Plath, and a host of other cross-cultural gerontologists believe Japan has an abundance of serious problems and that Japanese elderly are not completely satisfied with their present status and are very insecure about their future.

Tobin (1987) cites the plethora of problems that affect elderly Japanese. They are

(a) stress associated with the impact of rapid social change,
(b) nuclearization of the family coupled with the decline of the extended household,

(c) ambivalence of the young about responsibilities for parent care,
(d) "racial and caste inequities" (p. 53),
(e) "rigidity of the retirement system" (p. 53),
(f) demographic change resulting in migration of children to urban areas,
(g) inadequacies in geriatric services, and
(h) threat of population growth overwhelming limited public services for the aged.

Plath (1988a) maintains that "Japanese today see a need to redefine the place of older people in just about every public setting" (p. 507). And several observers report that Japanese elderly feel they have not had an equal share of the power that economic prosperity has conferred upon this progressive industrial nation.

It is true, however, that there are a number of positive supports for the status and welfare of the elderly, the most important being an age-graded kinship system based on the patrilineal clan or "*ie*," which involves a hierarchy of interrelated household units. This system has long featured authority based upon seniority, primogeniture, and male dominance. Add to this the influence of Confucianism (borrowed from China in the fifth century), which admonishes the young to respect, obey, and support their parents. Describing this kinship system, Elliot and Campbell (1993) write:

> The elderly have traditionally depended on the "*ie*" successor [usually eldest son] and especially his wife . . . for physical care, financial security, emotional support, and integration into a social group. Dependency on others is valued and encouraged in the family system. (p. 121)

There is also the Japanese norm that Kiefer refers to as the "corporate emphasis," that is, the subordination of individuals to the welfare of the group. All and all, this is a support system that should represent a substantial bulwark against any derogatory effects of modernization, but Plath (1988a), quoting Morris, records that "people had been complaining for years, but the traditional family system still lingered on, with all its inefficiency, hypocrisy, sentimentality and injustice" (pp. 509-510). And Koyano (1989) writes that studies investigating Japanese attitudes toward the elderly have revealed the presence of strongly negative feelings (p. 342). S. C. Taylor (1993) quotes a 56-year-old Tokyo housewife, Sumiko Yoshida, who states concerning the "silver seats": "I can see already on the train that young children are happy to sit while old people remain standing" (p. 36).

Without question, attitudes concerning family cohesion are changing. While it is still expected that families should be responsible for the care for their aged, and about 70% of them are, only 21.5% of Japanese surveyed in 1988 by the Ministry of Health said that elderly should live with their children. In a 1963 survey conducted by the Mainichi newspapers, women under the age of 50 responded that caring for elderly was either a "good custom" (39%) or a "natural duty" (41%) while only 3% felt that it was "not a good custom." By 1990, however, attitudes had changed to the extent that only 20% thought it a "good custom" while 30% believed it a "natural duty"; 12% responded that it was "not a good custom." The biggest change over this 27-year period, however, was in their own expectations of care. In 1963, 35% expected care from children in old age but by 1990 only 18% expected it (Ogawa & Retherford, 1993). Between 1960 and 1990 the percentage of senior citizens living with offspring declined from 87% to 50%.

Another problem is that in the future there will be fewer offspring available to take parents in. Between the years 1947 and 1992 the number of children per female fell from 4.5 to 1.5 (Aita, 1994). Salaried young people working for large corporations find it difficult to care for the elderly in small but expensive apartments in urban areas. Such individuals are also required to relocate whenever the corporation demands. There has also been a great change in the roles and status of women. Women have always been the primary caregivers, but in this growing economy more and more of them are now working and therefore not at home to provide the needed care. In 1963 only 13% of women worked outside the home, but that proportion had grown to 42% by 1990. On the other hand, more and more Japanese seniors are interested in remaining self-reliant and living on their own as long as they are able. But, of course, they would like the assurance that a child will take them into his or her home when it is absolutely necessary (Ogawa & Retherford, 1993).

Ogawa and Retherford (1993) write that in this industrial society "the burden of caring for elderly parents tends to shift from adult children to the state, to businesses, unions, and other private sector organizations, and to the elderly themselves" (p. 586). This eventuality is entirely consistent with the tenet of the modernization theory that holds that in industrial societies responsibility for elderly care "is increasingly shifted to the larger community, chiefly the state" (Cowgill & Holmes, 1972, p. 11).

Because of the traditional expectation of family support for the elderly, there is a great shortage of alternative housing. There are now only a little more than a dozen retirement communities, and in spite of a distaste for the idea of nursing homes, Japan is now experiencing a boom in construction of such facilities. Actually only 1.7% of those 65 and older are in nursing homes at present, with 90% of the physically and mentally ill seniors being cared for by their families. Of the 600,000 bedridden Japanese aged, over 40% receive home care (Harris & Long, 1993, p. 101).

Much of the dilemma in modern Japan is related to the extraordinary population expansion. The total population of Japan has grown from 30 million in 1860 to 46 million in 1900 to 120 million today. With Japan's life expectancy being the highest of any country in the world—75.23 for men and 80.93 for women—Japan also leads the world in population growth of the elderly. Harris and Long (1993) point out that "the demographic transition from a population of about 7 percent elderly to that of 14 percent elderly took 75 years in the United States, but is occurring in only 26 years in Japan" (p. 98). By 2010 it is estimated that the elderly will constitute 20% of the population and will stabilize at 23.6% in 2020 (Elliot & Campbell, 1993).

In the year 2022 more than one Japanese out of every five will be over 65, but people of working age who will have to support the benefits of the elderly will be half their present number. Consequently, Aita (1994, p. 7) sees a somewhat dismal future wherein the elderly will no doubt enervate society and create considerable hardship for the young. Currently Japan spends 15% of its income on public services for the elderly, but by 2020 that percentage will have to be doubled, and Japan is no longer the affluent nation that it once was.

National health care insurance in Japan is such that Americans would love to call it their own. It covers nearly all costs of treatment of illnesses (including catastrophic ones) and even provides for free annual medical examinations for those over 70 years of age. The somewhat perplexing reality, however, is that almost no attention is paid to rehabilitation therapy for such things as strokes, fractures, or sensory degeneration. While this might be puzzling to Americans, it is believed that it is compatible with Japanese behavioral patterns in that rehabilitation "requires the care-taker to cause the patient discomfort or stress or to be firm in overcoming the patient's resistance" (Kiefer, 1990, p. 193).

While the elderly of Japan are the recipients of many programs American senior citizens wish they had, Japan actually spends less than most industrial nations. Critics of Japan's present program of elder care are demanding expanded rehabilitation services, doctors who will make house calls, and a comprehensive home care program, because such a high percentage of elderly are cared for within the home.

The growing proportion of aged presents yet another problem that must be dealt with in the foreseeable future. With the high cost of living that is characteristic of industrial Japan, and with the elderly no longer entirely certain that they can depend upon family economic support, many older Japanese feel that they must continue working as long as they are physically and mentally able. There is, of course, medical insurance and old age benefits similar to America's Social Security, but unless one has worked for a major corporation with private pensions and retirement bonuses, retirement income is inadequate. Even those with private pensions but little in the way of savings may be in trouble, as Japan's pensions are well below American levels.

McConatha, McConatha, and Cinelli (1991) tell us that "many retirees are being 'forced' to return to work to keep up with the demands of higher and higher costs" (p. 231). It is not a particularly satisfactory situation even if the corporation agrees to rehire the retired worker, because jobs open to retirees pay only about half the regular salary. Even if retirees are financially comfortable, retirement in Japan is described as far from rewarding. Plath (1988b) writes that retired corporate officials are stereotypically referred to as *soodaigomi*, "a big heap of trash." They are no longer welcome at the office, and their wives complain that they are underfoot at home.

If the realities of life are less than idyllic for seniors in Japan, how, might we ask, do we reconcile the above problems with Palmore's characterization of Japan as a serene, bountiful environment where old people are respected, cherished, and well cared for? Koyano (1989) provides a reasonable answer. This Japanese scholar calls attention to the difference between *tatemae* (norms) and *honne* (actually feelings). In every culture that has thus far been studied, anthropologists have been able to differentiate between the "ideal" and the "real," and according to Koyano, Japan is no exception. Quoting Makizono, Koyano (1989) records:

> We Japanese feel ashamed at reading Palmore's indication, because we know that people's behavior and regime, which might be taken as manifestations of respect for the elderly, are mostly courtesy custom without substance, and that Japanese respect for the elderly is merely *tatemae*. (p. 343)

It must be remembered, however, that to a large extent Palmore's impressions of Japanese life are derived from statistical data provided by government agencies. He criticizes Plath's characterization of Japan as less than a paradise for the elderly, because "he apparently had access to little of the statistical data we have presented" (Palmore & Maeda, 1985, p. 114), and "the survey method is the most accurate and feasible approach to estimate the prevalence of various subjective attitudes and motivations" (p. xvii). On the other hand, it should be pointed out that Plath's descriptions of Japanese life are based on intimate and long-term association with numerous Japanese households and with information derived from participant observation and interview by an investigator fluent in the language. Respect, self-esteem, and feelings of well-being and emotional security are abstract and very personal concepts, and their investigation requires extremely sensitive research procedures. They cannot be discovered through government survey procedures.

Modernization has brought many problems and innovations to Japan, and the future promises more. Plath (1972) writes:

> Modern society, in Japan, as in many nations has bestowed longevity. It has turned old people loose into new lifespan territory. But it has equipped them only with medieval maps, full of freaks and monsters and imaginary harbors. The aged are among the true pioneers of our time, and pioneer life is notoriously brutal. (p. 150)

SUMMARY

The study of change has always been an important aspect of anthropology, and this emphasis continues among those who concern themselves with the elderly in this and other cultures. It is well documented that change can greatly influence societal attitudes toward senior status and role assignment and can alter traditional practices in regard to care and treatment. This is particularly true where there have been contacts between preindustrial and modern societies. Newly acquired values and institutional procedures often undermine age-old support systems for the elderly. The effects of modernization have been studied by Cowgill and Holmes (1972) in 14 preindustrial and industrial societies, and they contend that there is an inverse relationship between the degree of modernization and the status of the aged. Status declines are particularly noticeable where there is emphasis on personal achievement, independence, private property, and security based on individual activity.

Even the definition of old age can vary according to the degree of modernization. In more modern societies, old age is seen as beginning later in life, and because modernization has the effect of increasing the average length of life in a society, longevity has been cited as an excellent index of modernization. Modern societies have greater proportions of old people than traditional societies, but the tendency is to favor the young and the mobile. This has, in turn, led to the demise of the extended family, always a refuge for the aged. The more flexible and mobile nuclear family is compatible with an urban industrial lifestyle, but it represents a movement away from kin reliance. Consequently, in modern societies there is a shift away from family responsibility for the welfare of the aged to community or state responsibility. Cowgill (1974) has also postulated that some aspects of modernization have a more detrimental effect on the elderly than others, and he specifically cites modern technology (both in industry and in medicine), urbanization, and education. A combination of these factors results in a generation gap, the development of a youth culture, obsolescence of traditional knowledge and skills, and a decline in authority and leadership of older members of the society. Modernization also introduces entirely new cultural concepts, such as retirement and deculturation, which tend to deprive senior people of any meaningful productive role.

The modern industrial nation of Japan serves as a case study of what the impact of modernization can be. Japan has long been held up by some scholars as a modern society where the elderly enjoy a high status evidenced by "silver seats" on public transportation and the use of honorific salutations and respectful actions in dealings with them. More recently, however, students of Japanese culture have been questioning this characterization as idealistic and cite numerous problems being faced by Japanese aged, the most serious of which are the nuclearization of the family, ambivalence of the young about caring for aged parents, inadequacies in gerontological and geriatric services, and unprecedented growth of the elderly population associated with the pronounced lengthening of the average life span.

10

⊡ The Future of Aging in America

The *graying of America* is a phrase used by gerontologists to refer to changes in the age composition that have already begun and will continue well into the future. As noted earlier in Chapter 2, the elderly population of the United States is expanding at an alarming rate; 12½% of the population is 65 years old or older and by 2030 that figure will reach 20%. Then senior citizens will outnumber teenagers by a factor of two to one (Doka, 1992). This development is primarily a matter of internal change brought about by triumphs in medical technology (lengthening the life span) and by concomitant ideas about proper standards of living, which have resulted in adjustments to the size and composition of the American family. With more people living longer and fewer babies being born, the median age of American citizens progressively creeps upward. By the year 2030 it will be 41. This will have a number of obvious effects. There will be, in time, less need for classrooms and schoolteachers and less interest in supporting education. There will also be continuing problems with Social Security financing, because relatively fewer young people will be entering the labor force and larger percentages of recipients will be eligible. While there are approximately

3.4 workers per retiree contributing to Social Security today, by the year 2035 less than two workers per recipient will be supporting this retirement system (Longman, 1986).

The graying phenomenon will, however, have much more widespread influences. First, all kinds of senior services will be in much greater demand. The needs of the elderly will become a major item in federal, state, and local government budgets, and there no doubt will be greater investment on the part of the private sector in businesses dealing in drugs, corrective devices, home health care, respite care, retirement residences, and nursing homes. Other businesses will prosper, catering to the special educational and recreational needs of old people. Attempts to trim or do away with government benefits for the aged will run into more and more opposition as the percentage of citizens nearing 65 increases. The elderly are notoriously faithful voters, and they are organized. The American Association of Retired Persons (AARP) has a membership of over 32 million (which is only slightly less than the population of Argentina). This group has 20 full-time lobbyists at the federal level and 20 volunteer lobbyist/advisers at the state level, and the AARP can rely on 350,000+ active volunteers. In addition to the AARP there are 20,000 senior citizens in the Older Women's League, 74,000 Gray Panthers in chapters in 30 states, 2.2 million in the National Alliance of Senior Citizens, and 4.5 million in some 4,000 local chapters of the National Council of Senior Citizens, an organization founded by the AFL-CIO to fight for Medicare (Dychtwald & Flower, 1989).

The future will also bring new ideas about the appropriate age of retirement. Pension plans will be modified to enable people to voluntarily retire at age 55, but on the other hand, there will be a successful movement to do away with the few remaining mandatory age limits for retirement in some professions. With the lengthening of the average life span, Willard (1989) suggests that "retirement may be a thing of the past, as seniors remain in jobs at all levels in the workplace. Many people will return to work after a sabbatical, acting as consultants or becoming senior apprentices as they learn new skills for a second or third career" (p. 39).

Postretirement employment may very well appeal to many workers who dread the inactivity of retirement. It will also reduce the problems associated with financing Social Security. However, Atchley (1994) remarks that much of the rhetoric about the employment of older people in the future is based on the assumption that large numbers of retirees are eager to get back to employment and that only the opportunity for employment, any kind of useful employment, is required to mobilize this potential. Having studied retirement over 25 years, I believe that these assumptions drastically overestimate the proportion of retirees who wish to have ongoing job responsibilities. . . . Even the assumption that older people will be needed in the labor market is debatable. (p. 531)

Some social scientists (Henderson, 1988; Longman, 1986, 1988) see a potential for conflict in the society of tomorrow as the emphasis on youth gives way to emphasis on maturity. Phillip Longman (1986) has written "Age Wars: The Coming Battle Between Young and Old," and Henderson (1988) maintains that "by the year 2000 'age' warfare will pit workers against retirees on issues such as Social Security taxes, educational goals, and community projects" (p. 39). Mann (1977) quotes Philip M. House:

Now that the high expectations of . . . rising generations are starting to collide with reality the stage is set for a lot of social strife. The frustration is going to be especially acute among the fast-growing minority groups such as Hispanic and blacks. (p. 5)

The change in population profile will have some positive aspects, however. For example, there should be a great reduction in traffic accidents and crime, given that young people are principal causes of both. The peak age for auto theft and burglary is 18 and violent crime and murder are committed primarily by young people between the ages of 18 and 20 (Henderson, 1988). DUI and speeding violations are likewise follies of youth.

The birthrate in the United States fell from 3.5 per female in 1957 to 1.8 in 1986, and demographers do not anticipate a reversal in this trend. In fact, a 7% decline in the percentage of children in our population is expected in the next 40 years. This definitely should have an impact on welfare costs for dependent children as well as educational expenditures. Some youth-directed funds may, in the future, be reallocated to benefits for the aged—perhaps even for elder-generation education for retraining for second careers or for postretirement personal fulfillment.

With declining numbers of young people in the society, the nation's emphasis on youth will also decline. Advertising will begin to be directed more and more toward the more affluent middle-aged and elderly market. Dychtwald and Flower (1989) point out that Americans 50 and over purchase 48% of all luxury cars and 80% of all luxury travel, eat out an average of three times a week, spend more per capita in grocery stores than any other age group, and own 80% of all the money in American savings and loan institutions.

In regard to elderly recreational needs, Dychtwald and Flower (1989) write:

> In the decades ahead, the range and scope of adult-focused recreational opportunities will blossom. Imagine all the new hobby-craft centers, mind expanding amusement parks, longevity training centers, adult sports camps, sophisticated computer games, adventure and travel clubs, theme focused retirement communities, worldwide time-share lifestyle complexes, and recreation counseling centers that will proliferate in the years ahead. These and other futuristic options will be the outgrowth of what today's retirees make of their new-found time off. (pp. 121-122)

Just as the Woolworth and Kresge "5 and 10 cent" stores became a thing of the past in the 1980s and 1990s, eclipsed by discount department stores, perhaps the popularity of fast food and junk food establishments will be replaced by sit-down restaurants with menus featuring more than hamburgers, hot dogs, and multiple-topping pizzas. And Roseanne, Madonna, the Simpsons, and Beavis and Butt-head may very well give way to Masterpiece Theater and the Hallmark Hall of Fame. The choice of leisure time activities will in part be affected by the rapidly rising educational level. A generation ago, less than one senior citizen in five had a high school diploma, but by 1990, 50% held that credential.

The elderly will also have a new attitude toward leisure. A large share of the people who are over 65 today were raised in a world where a 50-hour workweek was not unusual, where vacations were rare and never longer than two weeks, where unemployment was looked upon as a personal failure, and where idleness was a sin (because "idle hands do devil's work"). Investing time and money in leisure activities is foreign to their thinking and their value system. At the turn of the century, Americans were working 24% of their lives while today that figure is 14%. The elderly of the year 2000—now employed for only 40 hours or less a week, accustomed to three- and four-week vacations and numerous three-day weekends—will be more interested in and more comfortable with leisure. America will probably never be able to shake off its deep-seated puritanical prejudice against idleness, but there is good indication that in addition to honoring the work ethic we are also beginning to honor an activity ethic, particularly if it is seen in the light of therapeutic recreation to restore an individual's mental acuity, physical health, and energy level. Dychtwald and Flower (1989) tell us that YMCA and YWCA exercise programs enroll more than 1,200,000 seniors annually, that there are over a quarter of a million bowlers over 55, that 3,200,000 Americans over 60 play golf regularly, and more than 50,000 people compete in regional "Senior Olympics," which are held in 50 cities in the United States.

While the middle and upper classes have been the main participants in leisure activities in the past, the future will open up participation to the masses. The shift may be gradual, however, with leisure activities tending to resemble work (through interest in home workshops, do-it-yourself home projects, practical craft skills like sewing or knitting, and volunteerism in community charities and projects).

Although the retired of the future may want to spend their leisure becoming better educated, the national forecasts for the future of public education in the United States are not encouraging. With the decrease in the percentage of young people in the population and with funding in state-supported secondary and higher educational institutions to a large extent based on numbers of students served, we can expect a considerable decline in the availability and quality of educational opportunities for people of all ages. Mann (1977) writes: "Increasingly, these institutions, long the symbols of America's vitality as a young and growing nation, are being hit by budget cuts, layoffs of younger workers, aging staffs, flagging promotions and sagging morale" (p. 56).

The next century will see the rise of a unique age grade that has been labeled the "young-old." These will be people between the ages of 65 and 74. At the present time this group represents about 58% of the elderly population but it will steadily grow in size and influence as the baby-boomers age. As Neugarten (1975) describes this age category:

As a group, they are already markedly different from the out-moded stereotypes of old age. They are relatively free from tradi-tional social responsibilities of work and family, they are relatively healthy, relatively well off, and they are politically active. . . . With regard to work, some will opt for early retirement; some will want to continue to work beyond 65; some will want to undertake new work careers at one or more times after age 40. (p. 8)

Another characteristic of these "young-old," often overlooked by gerontologists, is that in the year 2000 these will be the people who were between the ages of 20 and 25 during the traumatic 1960s and early 1970s. They are the people who generated and sustained the civil rights, con-sumer, antipollution, women's, antiwar, and ecology movements, and while these people have not been heard from for some time, the idealism can no doubt be revived along with the protest skills. Political admini-strations will need to pay attention to them.

Even though the future is expected to see the growth of a highly motivated and involved "young-old" group, a concomitant increase in the "old-old" will result in greater demands for health care and support services. Some of them will continue to live independently, but many will need services such as elder-oriented public transportation, home health service and nutrition programs, drug and grocery delivery serv-ices, and special modification of their surroundings (for example, home elevators, high-volume phone receivers, better lighted streets) to com-pensate for their disabilities. There will also have to be special commu-nity-sponsored programs to provide the security that will allow old people to walk city streets in safety. The elderly will have a growing desire for independence, and based on present interest in aging pro-grams, society will probably provide the means to make this possible. Home services will allow a large percentage of even the old-old to remain at home or forestall institutionalization, but by the year 2000 nearly a million people 85 and older will require such facilities. Gerontologists predict an institutional population of 3 million by 2050 (Atchley, 1994, p. 520). But Atchley (1994) also believes that long-term care facilities in the future will be very different than nursing homes today. He postulates: "They may look more like independent apartments with service facilities attached and residents may have more independent decision making and receive a less standardized array of services compared to today's long term care population" (p. 520).

The future of aging in America will involve a variety of changes in both type and locations of residence. During the last 15 to 20 years we have seen a great increase in migration of senior citizens to "sun-belt" states such as Florida and Arizona, where the population of elderly has increased approximately 45% since 1970. However, a number of gerontologists believe that this trend may not continue into the future. Kevin McCarty of the Rand Corporation (cited in Dychtwald & Flower, 1989) is reported as maintaining that if one wishes to forecast where the elderly of the twenty-first century will locate one should not look to the elderly of today, and Dychtwald and Flower (1989) suggest that

> tomorrow's seniors might prefer a different spectrum of offerings beyond lifecare [that is, full service—housing, health, and recreation—retirement maintenance], old fashion villages, and mobile towns. To anticipate the future needs of retirement living, the best place to look is in the lifestyle preferences of today's middle-aged men and women. (p. 142)

They believe that these individuals are increasingly being drawn to the spots they have enjoyed while on vacation—places such as "Ashland, Oregon; Green Bay and Rice Lake, Wisconsin; the Ozarks; Alpena and Huron counties in Michigan; Cape Cod; and the New Jersey shoreline" (p. 143).

But whether or not seniors migrate to such retirement areas depends greatly on economic and educational factors. Bultena and Wood (1969) have shown that elderly migrants to Florida and Arizona came, to a large extent, from the upper social and economic strata of American society. The same will be true of those who settle in resort areas. The majority of aged, however, are the least likely segment of the population to migrate. In fact, they are the ones most likely to be left behind when emigration occurs. At first they were overrepresented in the older rural areas when the young people moved to the cities. Then they were the ones who were left behind in the inner city when the young and middle aged moved to the suburbs. Now it is believed that in the future they will be overrepresented in the city suburbs as the young move back into renovated inner-city areas where residence involves less commuting time and less expenditure for gasoline or mass-transit fares.

Numerous aspects of our value system appear to devalue and oppress the aged, but there is also an indication that the future will produce a more secure and satisfying old age for citizens of the United States in spite of any spiraling inflation. In a study of the effect of modernization (mainly Western and Third World societies), Palmore and Manton (1974) discovered that when peasant societies first begin to move toward urbanization and industrialization, and when the level of literacy and education begins to rise, the status of the elderly tends to decline. However, once the society is well into modernization, its valuation and support of old people increases. This involves increases in retirement benefits, inauguration of more social and health services, a rise in adult education opportunity, and a reversal of policies that had formerly discriminated against the old.

Considerable evidence indicates that the United States is well into this stage of modernization and that the future will bring even greater growth of industries and cities. Such developments should be accompanied by a trend toward fewer discrepancies between the young and the old in regard to educational level, technology, and life experience. As a result, there will be a basis for greater understanding and greater empathy between generations and greater insight into the problems and needs associated with old age. The last two decades in America have been ones of urban and industrial growth, and they have been ones that have seen significant growth in services for the aged. A science of gerontology has emerged during this period; new agencies to aid the elderly have come into being; the specialty of geriatrics has begun to expand and attract young physicians; and politicians have become acutely conscious of the senior segment of the population and their needs. There is, however, some question as to whether or not our society will choose to support the strides that have been made researching the needs of our elderly. Atchley (1994) is somewhat pessimistic, stating:

> Unfortunately, federal support for education in gerontology has all but disappeared. As a result, many financially troubled universities have found it difficult to sustain their relatively new gerontology programs when resources are scarce and the existence of even traditional disciplines seems threatened. (p. 536)

No utopia is predicted for America's elderly, but the "graying of America" combined with an educational effort to communicate what the elderly want and need, plus an aggressive senior citizen population pressing for their own rights—to respect and a comfortable lifestyle—should result in a future with promise for everyone.

SUMMARY

Cultural gerontologists have speculated on the probable trends in America's future development and how they will affect tomorrow's aged. Predictions are that (a) we can expect a "graying of America," that is, an increase in the percentage of aged in the population (20% by 2030), and consequently, (b) there will be a greater demand for services for senior citizens, such as medical care, drugs, home care services, retirement residences, and nursing homes; (c) there will be the possibility of intergenerational conflict over financing of education, care for dependent children, Social Security, Medicare, and Medicaid. In regard to government-funded programs, the elderly will wield considerable political clout as they are growing increasingly more organized and more likely to vote than the general population. (d) There will be a change in leisure activities more in line with the abilities and interests of elderly as well as changes in the nature of television programming, movie fare, and reading material. (e) There will be a growth in the science of gerontology, which will meet the educational requirements of people wishing to diagnose and attend the needs of the elderly. (f) There will be new ideas about retirement—early retirement for some; no retirement for some; and second careers for others. But, above all, there will be a greater demand for independence and choice in regard to lifestyles, leisure activities, choice of residence, and use of services.

▣ References

Ablon, J. (1964). Relocated American Indians in the San Francisco Bay area: Social interaction and Indian identity. *Human Organization, 23,* 296-304.

Ablon, J. (1970). Samoans in stateside nursing. *Nursing Outlook, 18*(12), 32-33.

Abrams, A. (1951). Trends in old age homes and housing for the aged in various parts of the world. In *No time to grow old* (Legislative Document No. 12, pp. 250-258). Albany: New York State Joint Legislative Committee on the Problems of Aging.

Acsadi, G., & Nemeskeri, J. (1970). *History of human life span and mortality.* Budapest: Akademiai Kiado.

Adams, F. M. (1972). The role of old people in Santo Tomás Mazaltepec. In D. Cowgill & L. Holmes (Eds.), *Aging and modernization* (pp. 103-126). New York: Appleton-Century-Crofts.

Agar, M. H. (1980). *The professional stranger: An informal introduction to ethnography.* New York: Academic Press.

Aiken, L. (1978). *Later life.* Philadelphia: W. B. Saunders.

Aita, K. (1994, January 24-30). Aging of society is expected to give birth to new challenges. *Japan Times Weekly International Edition,* p. 7.

American Association of Retired Persons & Administration on Aging. (1993). *A profile of older Americans: 1993.* Washington, DC: AARP.

Amoss, P. (1981). Coast Salish elders. In P. T. Amoss & S. Harrell (Eds.), *Other ways of growing old: Anthropological perspectives* (pp. 227-247). Stanford, CA: Stanford University Press.

Anderson, B. G. (1972). Deculturation among the aged. *Anthropological Quarterly, 45,* 209-216.

Anderson, E. N. (1972). Some Chinese methods of dealing with crowding. *Urban Anthropology, 1,* 41-50.

Arensberg, C., & Kimball, S. (1968). *Family and community in Ireland.* Cambridge, MA: Harvard University Press.

Arensberg, C., & Niehoff, A. (1964). *Introducing social change.* Chicago: Aldine.

Arth, M. (1972). Aging: A cross-cultural perspective. In D. P. Kent, R. Kastenbaum, & S. Sherwood (Eds.), *Research planning and action for the elderly: The power and potential of social science* (pp. 352-364). New York: Behavioral Publications.

Atchley, R. C. (1994). *Social forces and aging* (7th ed.). Belmont, CA: Wadsworth.

Bailey, T. (1857). *Records of longevity.* London: Darton.

Barbato, C. A., & Feezel, J. D. (1987). The language of aging in different age groups. *The Gerontologist, 27*(4), 527-531.

Barker, J. (1990). Between humans and ghosts. In J. Sokolovsky (Ed.), *The cultural context of aging* (pp. 295-313). New York: Bergin and Garvey.

Barnes, J. A. (1972). *Social networks* (Module in Anthropology, 26). Reading, MA: Addison-Wesley.

Barone, M., & Ujifusa, G. (1991). *The Almanac of American politics, 1992.* Washington, DC: National Journal.

Bateson, G. (1950). Cultural ideas about aging. In H. E. Jones (Ed.), *Research on aging* (Proceedings of a conference held in August 7-10, 1950, at the University of California, Berkeley, pp. 49-54). New York: Pacific Coast Committee on Old Age Research, Social Science Research Council.

Beall, C. M., Goldstein, M. C., & Feldman, E. S. (1985). The physical fitness of elderly Nepalese farmers residing in rugged mountain terrain and flat terrain. *Journal of Gerontology, 40,* 529-535.

Beall, C. M., & Weitz, C. A. (1989). The human population biology of aging. In M. A. Little & J. D. Hass (Eds.), *Human population biology: A transdisciplinary science* (pp. 189-200). New York: Oxford University Press.

Beaubier, J. (1976). *High life expectancy on the island of Paros, Greece.* New York: Philosophical Library.

Beaubier, J. (1980). Biological factors in aging. In C. L. Fry (Ed.), *Aging in culture and society: Comparative viewpoints and strategies* (pp. 21-41). New York: J. F. Bergin.

Becker, E. (1973). *The denial of death.* New York: Free Press.

Benedict, R. (1934). *Patterns of culture.* Boston: Houghton Mifflin.

Benedict, R. (1946). *The chrysanthemum and the sword.* New York: Houghton Mifflin.

Benet, S. (1974). *Abkhasians: The long-living people of the Caucasus.* New York: Holt, Rinehart & Winston.

Benet, S. (1976). *How to live to be 100: The life-style of the people of the Caucasus.* New York: Dial.

Bennett, N. G., & Garson, L. K. (1983). The centenarian question and old-age mortality in the Soviet Union, 1959-1970. *Demography, 20,* 587-606.

Bennett, N. G., & Garson, L. K. (1986). Extraordinary longevity in the Soviet Union: Fact or artifact? *The Gerontologist, 26,* 358-361.

Berdyshev, G. D. (1968). *Ecologic and genetic factors of aging and longevity.* Leningrad: Nauka.

Biesele, M., & Howell, N. (1981). The old people give you life: Aging among !Kung hunter-gatherers. In P. Amoss & S. Harrell (Eds.), *Other ways of growing old: Anthropological perspectives* (pp. 77-98). Stanford, CA: Stanford University Press.

Billingsley, A. (1968). *Black families in white America.* Englewood Cliffs, NJ: Prentice Hall.

Block, M. (1979). Exiled Americans: The plight of Indian aged in the United States. In D. Gelfand & A. Kutzik (Eds.), *Ethnicity and aging* (pp. 184-192). New York: Springer.

Borthwick, E. M. (1977). *Aging and social change on Lukunor Atoll, Micronesia.* Unpublished doctoral dissertation, University of Iowa.

Boyer, E. (1980). Health perception in the elderly: Its cultural and social aspects. In C. L. Fry (Ed.), *Aging in culture and society: Comparative viewpoints and strategies* (pp. 198-216). New York: J. F. Bergin.

Broeg, B. (1989). *Baseball's Barnum.* Wichita, KS: Wichita State University, Center for Entrepreneurship.

Brown, M. S. (1978). A cross-cultural look at aging. *Health Values, 2*(2), 96-100.

Brown, R. E., & Barnes-Nacoste, R. W. (1993). Group consciousness and political behavior. In J. S. Jackson, L. M. Chatters, & R. J. Taylor (Eds.), *Aging in black America* (pp. 217-232). Newbury Park, CA: Sage.

Bultena, G., & Wood, V. (1969). The American retirement community: Bane or blessing? *Journal of Gerontology, 24,* 209-217.

Burch, E. S., Jr. (1975). *Eskimo kinsmen* (AES Monograph). St. Paul, MN: West.

Caen, H. (1993, May 10). Matters of age. *San Francisco Chronicle,* p. B1.

Cahn, E. (Ed.). (1969). *Our brother's keeper: The Indian in white America.* New York: New Community Press.

Cantor, M. (1975). Life space and the social support system of the inner city elderly of New York. *The Gerontologist, 15,* 23-27.

Cattell, M. G. (1989). Knowledge and social change in Samia, Western Kenya. *Journal of Cross-Cultural Gerontology, 4,* 225-244.

Chazanov, M. (1987, June 15). Bulgaria: Land of the centenarian. *Los Angeles Times,* pp. 1, 10.

Chee, P., & Kane, R. (1983). Cultural factors affecting nursing home care for minorities: A study of black American and Japanese-American groups. *Journal of the American Geriatrics Society, 31*(2), 109-112.

Cheng, E. (1978). *The elder Chinese.* San Diego, CA: Campanile.

Cherry, R. L., & Magnuson-Martinson, S. (1981). Modernization and the status of the aged in China: Decline or equalization? *Sociological Quarterly, 22,* 253-261.

Clark, M. M. (1967). The anthropology of aging: A new area for studies of culture and personality. *The Gerontologist, 7,* 55-64.

Clark, M. M. (1972). An anthropological view of retirement. In F. Carp (Ed.), *Retirement* (pp. 117-156). New York: Human Sciences Press.

Clark, M. M. (1983). Cultural context of medical practice. *Western Journal of Medicine, 139,* 806-810.

Clark, M. M., & Anderson, B. G. (1967). *Culture and aging.* Springfield, IL: Charles C Thomas.

Coleman, L. M. (1993). The black Americans who keep working. In J. S. Jackson, L. M. Chatters, & R. J. Taylor (Eds.), *Aging in black America* (pp. 253-276). Newbury Park, CA: Sage.

Committee on the Family. (1970, March). *The case history method in the study of family process* (Vol. 2, Report No. 76). New York: Group for the Advancement of Psychiatry.

Condon, R. G. (1987). *Inuit youth: Growth and change in the Canadian Arctic.* New Brunswick, NJ: Rutgers University Press.

Connelly, J. R. (1980). An expanded outline and resource for teaching a course on the Native American. In G. A. Sherman (Ed.), *Curriculum guidelines in minority aging* (Vol. 6, pp. 1-66). Washington, DC: National Center on Black Aged, Inc.

Cook, C. D. (1990). American Indian elderly and public policy issues. In *Minority aging: Essential curricula content for selected health and allied health professions* (pp. 137-143). Washington, DC: U.S. Department of Health and Human Services.

Cool, L. E. (1980). Ethnicity and aging: Continuity through change for elderly Corsicans. In C. L. Fry (Ed.), *Aging in culture and society* (pp. 149-169). New York: J. F. Bergin.

Cool, L. E. (1981). Ethnic identity: A source of community esteem for the elderly. *Anthropological Quarterly, 54,* 179-189.

Cool, L. E. (1987). The effects of social class and ethnicity on the aging process. In P. Silverman (Ed.), *The elderly as modern pioneers* (pp. 263-282). Bloomington: Indiana University Press.

Connell, B. (1981, June 4). Ill couple threatened by eviction—by son. *Wichita Eagle-Beacon,* pp. 1A, 13A.

Counts, D. A., & Counts, D. R. (Eds.). (1985a). *Aging and its transformations: Moving toward death in Pacific societies.* Lanham, MD: University Press of America.

Counts, D. A., & Counts, D. R. (1985b). I'm not dead yet! Aging and death: Process and experience in Kaliai. In D. A. Counts & D. R. Counts (Eds.), *Aging and its transformations: Moving toward death in Pacific societies* (pp. 131-155). Lanham, MD: University Press of America.

Counts, D. A., & Counts, D. R. (1992). They're my family now: The creation of community among RVers. *Anthropologica, 34,* 153-182.

Covey, H. C. (1988). Historical terminology used to represent older people. *The Gerontologist, 28*(3), 291-297.

Cowgill, D. O. (1972a). A theory of aging in cross-cultural perspective. In D. O. Cowgill & L. D. Holmes (Eds.), *Aging and modernization* (pp. 1-13). New York: Appleton-Century-Crofts.

Cowgill, D. O. (1972b). Aging in American society. In D. O. Cowgill & L. D. Holmes (Eds.), *Aging and modernization* (pp. 243-261). New York: Appleton-Century-Crofts.

Cowgill, D. O. (1972c). The role and status of the aged in Thailand. In D. O. Cowgill & L. D. Holmes (Eds.), *Aging and modernization* (pp. 91-100). New York: Appleton-Century-Crofts.

Cowgill, D. O. (1974). Aging and modernization: A revision of the theory. In J. F. Gubrium (Ed.), *Late life: Communities and environmental policy* (pp. 123-146). Springfield, IL: Charles C Thomas.

Cowgill, D. O. (1986). *Aging around the world*. Belmont, CA: Wadsworth.

Cowgill, D. O., & Holmes, L. D. (1972). *Aging and modernization*. New York: Appleton-Century-Crofts.

Cox, C., & Monk, A. (1993). Black and Hispanic caregivers of dementia victims: Their needs and implications for services. In C. M. Barresi & D. E. Stull (Eds.), *Ethnic elderly and long-term care* (pp. 57-67). New York: Springer.

Crane, J. G., & Angrosino, M. V. (1992). *Field projects in anthropology* (3rd ed.). Prospect Heights, IL: Waveland.

Crawford, M. H., & Oberdieck, L. (1978). Aging, longevity and genetics. *Dialogue, 4*, 37-40.

Cuellar, J. B. (1978). El Senior Citizens Club. In B. Myerhoff & A. Simic (Eds.), *Life's career—aging: Cultural variations on growing old* (pp. 207-229). Beverly Hills, CA: Sage.

Cumming, E., & Henry, W. E. (1961). *Growing old: The process of disengagement*. New York: Basic Books.

Cutler, R. G. (1975). Evolution of human longevity and the genetic complexity governing aging rate. *Proceedings of the National Academy of Science, U.S.A., 2*, 4664-4668.

Cutler, R. G. (1978). Evolutionary biology of senescence. In J. Behnke, C. Finch, & G. Moment (Eds.), *The biology of aging* (pp. 311-360). New York: Plenum.

Cutler, R. G. (1981). Life-span extension. In J. L. McGaugh & S. B. Kiesler (Eds.), *Aging: Biology and behavior* (pp. 31-76). New York: Academic Press.

Dacey, J. S. (1989). Peak periods of creative growth across the lifespan. *Journal of Creative Behavior, 23*(4), 224-247.

de Beauvoir, S. (1972a). *Coming of age*. New York: Putnam.

de Beauvoir, S. (1972b). The harsh arithmetic of old age in America. *Saturday Review of Society, 8*, 262-264.

Delaney, W. (1981). Is Uncle Sen insane? *International Journal of Aging and Human Development, 13*, 137-150.

de Tocqueville, A. (1899). *Democracy in America* (2 vols.). New York: Knopf.

Directory of nursing homes 1991-1992. (1991). (5th ed.). Phoenix: Oryx.

Doka, K. (1992, July/August). When gray is golden. *The Futurist*, pp. 16-20.

Donner, W. W. (1987). Compassion, kinship and fosterage: Contexts for the care of childless elderly in a Polynesian community. *Journal of Cross-Cultural Gerontology, 2*(1), 43-60.

Douglass, F. (1855). *My bondage and my freedom*. New York: Miller, Orton & Mulligan.

Dowd, J. J. (1980). *Stratification among the aged*. Monterey, CA: Brooks/Cole.

Driver, J. (1969). *Indians of North America* (2nd ed.). Chicago: University of Chicago Press.

Dychtwald, K., & Flower, J. (1989). *Age wave: The challenges and opportunities of an aging America*. Los Angeles: Jeremy P. Tarcher.

Eckert, J. K. (1980). *The unseen elderly: A study of marginally subsistent hotel dwellers*. San Diego, CA: Campanile.

Eckert, J. K. (1983). Dislocation and relocation of the urban elderly: Social networks as mediators of relocation stress. *Human Organization, 42*(1), 39-45.

Eisenstadt, S. N. (1956). *From generation to generation*. Glencoe, IL: Free Press.

Elliot, K., & Campbell, R. (1993). Changing ideas about family care for the elderly in Japan. *Journal of Cross-Cultural Gerontology, 8*(2), 119-136.

Elliott, D. (1994, March 28). No market for grannies: Babushkas have lost their traditional roles. *Newsweek,* p. 37.

Ellis, A. B. (1887). *The Tshi-speaking peoples of the Gold Coast of West Africa.* London: Chapman and Hall.

Ellis, G. W. (1914). *Negro culture in West Africa.* New York: Neale.

The encyclopedia of Japan. (1983). Old age and retirement (pp. 98-100). Tokyo: Kodansha, Ltd.

Eribes, R. A., & Bradley-Rawls, M. (1978). The underutilization of nursing home facilities by Mexican-American elderly in the Southwest. *The Gerontologist, 18,* 363-371.

Erickson, R., & Eckert, K. (1977). The elderly poor in downtown San Diego hotels. *The Gerontologist, 17*(5), 440-446.

Eshleman, J. R. (1988). *The family: An introduction* (5th ed.). Boston: Allyn & Bacon.

Firth, R. (1958). *Human types.* New York: Mentor.

Fischer, D. H. (1978). *Growing old in America.* New York: Oxford University Press.

Fitzgerald, M. H., & Howard, A. (1990). Aspects of social organization in three Samoan communities. *Pacific Studies, 14*(1), 31-54.

Flornoy, B. (1958). *The world of the Inca.* Garden City, NY: Doubleday/Anchor.

Foner, N. (1984). *Ages in conflict: A cross-cultural perspective on inequality between old and young.* New York: Columbia University Press.

Frazier, E. F. (1939). *The Negro family in the United States.* Chicago: University of Chicago Press.

Frazier, E. F. (1959). The Negro family in America. In R. N. Anshen (Ed.), *The family: Its function and destiny* (pp. 65-84). New York: Harper & Row.

Freimer, N., Echenberg, D., & Kretchmer, N. (1983). Cultural variation: Nutritional and clinical implications. *Western Journal of Medicine, 139*(6), 928-933.

Freuchen, P. (1961). *Book of Eskimos.* Greenwich, CT: Fawcett Crest.

Fries, J. F., & Crapo, L. M. (1981). *Vitality and aging: Implications of the rectangular curve.* San Francisco: Freeman.

Fromm, E. (1962). Alienation under capitalism. In E. Josephson & M. Josephson (Eds.), *Man alone* (pp. 56-73). New York: Dell.

Fry, C. L. (1980). Cultural dimensions of age: A multidimensional scaling analysis. In C. L. Fry & J. Keith (Eds.), *Aging in culture and society: Comparative viewpoints and strategies* (pp. 42-64). New York: J. F. Bergin.

Fuller, C. (1972). Aging among Southern African Bantu. In D. O. Cowgill & L. D. Holmes (Eds.), *Aging and modernization* (pp. 51-72). New York: Appleton-Century-Crofts.

Ganschow, T. W. (1978). The aged in a revolutionary milieu: China. In S. Spicker, K. Woodward, & D. Van Tassel (Eds.), *Aging and the elderly: Humanistic perspectives in gerontology* (pp. 305-320). Atlantic Highlands, NJ: Humanities Press.

Garcia, C. (1993). What do we mean by extended family? A closer look at Hispanic multigenerational families. *Journal of Cross-Cultural Gerontology, 8,* 137-146.

George, L. K. (1988). Social participation in later life: Black-white differences. In J. S. Jackson (Ed.), *The black American elderly* (pp. 99-126). New York: Springer.

Gide, A. (1931). *The counterfeiters.* New York: Modern Library.

Glascock, A. P. (1990). By any other name, it is still killing: A comparison of the treatment of the elderly in America and other societies. In J. Sokolovsky (Ed.), *The cultural context of aging* (pp. 43-56). New York: Bergin and Garvey.

Glascock, A. P., & Feinman, S. L. (1981). Social asset or social burden: Treatment of the aged in non-industrial societies. In C. L. Fry (Ed.), *Aging, culture, and health: Comparative viewpoints and strategies* (pp. 13-31). Brooklyn: J. F. Bergin.

Glazer, N., & Moynihan, D. P. (1963). *Beyond the melting pot.* Cambridge: MIT Press and Harvard University Press.

Goldstein, M. C., & Beall, C. M. (1981). Modernization and aging in the Third and Fourth World: Views from the rural hinterland in Nepal. *Human Organization, 40,* 48-55.

Goody, J. (1976). Aging in non-industrial societies. In R. H. Binstock & E. Shanas (Eds.), *Handbook of aging and the social sciences* (pp. 117-129). New York: Van Nostrand Reinhold.

Gorer, G. (1967). The pornography of death. In G. Gorer, *Death, grief, and mourning* (pp. 169-175). New York: Doubleday.

Graburn, N. H. H. (1969). *Eskimos without igloos.* Boston: Little, Brown.

Grattan, F. J. H. (1948). *An introduction to Samoan custom.* Apia, Samoa: Samoa Printing and Publishing Company.

Groger, L. (1992). Tied to each other through ties to the Lord: Informal support of black elders in a southern U.S. community. *Journal of Cross-Cultural Gerontology, 7,* 205-220.

Gubrium, J. F. (1975). *Living and dying at Murray Manor.* New York: St. Martin.

Guemple, L. (1974). The dilemma of the aging Eskimo. In C. Beattie & S. Crysdale (Eds.), *Sociology Canada: Readings* (pp. 203-214). Toronto: Butterworth.

Guralnik, J. M., Land, K. C., Blazer, D., Fillenbaum, G. C., & Branch, L. G. (1993). Educational status and active life expectancy among older blacks and whites. *New England Journal of Medicine, 329*(2), 110-116.

Gutmann, D. (1976). Alternatives to disengagement: The old men of the Highland Druze. In J. Gubrium (Ed.), *Time, roles, and self in old age* (pp. 232-245). New York: Human Science Press.

Gutmann, D. (1977). The cross-cultural perspective. In J. E. Birren & K. W. Schaie (Eds.), *Handbook of the psychology of aging* (pp. 302-326). New York: Van Nostrand Reinhold.

Gutmann, D. (1987). *Reclaimed powers: Toward a new psychology of men and women in later life.* New York: Basic Books.

Guttmann, D. (1986). Perspective on Euro-American elderly. In C. L. Hayes, R. A. Kalish, & D. Guttmann (Eds.), *European-American elderly: A guide for practice* (pp. 3-15). New York: Springer.

Hale, N. (1990). *The older worker.* San Francisco: Jossey-Bass.

Hamer, J. (1972). Aging in a gerontocratic society: The Sidamo of southwest Ethiopia. In D. O. Cowgill & L. D. Holmes (Eds.), *Aging and modernization* (pp. 15-30). New York: Appleton-Century-Crofts.

Harlan, W. H. (1964). Social status of the aged in three Indian villages. *Vita Humane, 7,* 239-252.

Harrell, S. (1981). Growing old in rural Taiwan. In P. Amoss & S. Harrell (Eds.), *Other ways of growing old: Anthropological perspectives* (pp. 193-210). Stanford, CA: Stanford University Press.

Harris, P. B., & Long, S. O. (1993). Daughter-in-law's burden: An exploratory study of caregiving in Japan. *Journal of Cross-Cultural Gerontology, 8,* 97-118.

Hayflick, L. (1988). Why do we live so long? *Geriatrics, 43*(10), 77-79, 82, 87.

Hearth, A. H. (1993, October). Bessie and Sadie: The Delaney sisters relive a century. *Smithsonian, 24*(7), 144-164.

Henderson, C. (1988, March/April). Old Glory. *The Futurist,* pp. 36-40.

Henderson, J. N. (1981). Nursing home housekeepers: Indigenous agents of psychosocial support. *Human Organization, 40*(4), 300-305.

Henderson, J. N. (1987). Mental disorders among the elderly: Dementia and its socio-cultural correlates. In P. Silverman (Ed.), *The elderly as modern pioneers* (pp. 357-374). Bloomington: Indiana University Press.

Henderson, J. N. (1992). The power of support. *Aging Magazine,* No. 363-364, pp. 24-28.

Henderson, J. N., & Gutierrez-Mayka, M. (1992). Ethnocultural themes in caregiving to Alzheimer's disease patients in Hispanic families. In T. L. Brink (Ed.), *Hispanic aged mental*

health. *Clinical Gerontologist, 11*(3-4), 59-74.

Henry, J. (1963). *Culture against man.* New York: Vintage.

Hentoff, N. (1966). The other side of the blues. In H. Hill (Ed.), *Anger and beyond: The Negro writer in the United States* (pp. 76-85). New York: Harper & Row.

Herskovits, M. J. (1938). *Dahomey* (Vol. 1). New York: J. J. Augustin.

Herskovits, M. J. (1941). *Myth of the Negro past.* New York: Harper.

Herskovits, M. J. (1949). *Man and his works.* New York: Knopf.

Herskovits, M. J. (1967). *The backgrounds of African art.* New York: Biblo and Tennen.

Hilton, J. (1933). *Lost horizon.* New York: Morrow.

Hochschild, A. R. (1973). *The unexpected community.* Berkeley: University of California Press.

Hollis, A. C. (1909). *The Nandi.* Oxford: Clarendon.

Holmes, E. R., & Holmes, L. D. (1987). Western Polynesia's home for the aged: Are concept and culture compatible? *Journal of Cross-Cultural Gerontology, 2*(4), 359-376.

Holmes, L. D. (1972). The role and status of the aged in a changing Samoa. In D. O. Cowgill & L. D. Holmes (Eds.), *Aging and modernization* (pp. 73-89). New York: Appleton-Century-Crofts.

Holmes, L. D. (1978). Aging and modernization: The Samoan aged of San Francisco. In C. Macpherson, B. Shore, & R. Franco (Eds.), *New neighbors: Islanders in adaptation* (pp. 205-213). Santa Cruz: University of California, Center for South Pacific Studies.

Holmes, L. D., & Holmes, E. R. (1992). *Samoan village then and now* (2nd ed.). Fort Worth, TX: Harcourt Brace Jovanovich.

Holmes, L. D., & Schneider, K. (1987). *Anthropology: An introduction* (4th ed.). Prospect Heights, IL: Waveland.

Holmes, L. D., & Thomson, J. W. (1986). *Jazz greats getting better with age*. New York: Holmes and Meier.

Hoopes, R. (1989, April/May). Working late: The case of the myopic watchdog. *Modern Maturity*, pp. 36-43.

Hostetler, J. A., & Huntington, G. E. (1967). *The Hutterites in North America*. New York: Holt, Rinehart & Winston.

Howell, S. C., & Loeb, M. B. (1969). Culture, myths, and food preferences among aged. *The Gerontologist*, 9, 31-37.

Hsu, F. (1969). *The study of literate civilizations*. New York: Holt, Rinehart & Winston.

Hsu, F. (1961). American core values and national character. In F. Hsu (Ed.), *Psychological anthropology* (pp. 209-230). Cambridge, MA: Schenkman.

Hsu, F. (1971, Spring). Filial piety in Japan and China: Borrowing, variation and significance. *Journal of Comparative Family Studies*, pp. 67-74.

Hsu, F. (1981). *Americans and Chinese: Passage to difference* (3rd ed.). Honolulu: University of Hawaii Press.

Hughes, C. C. (1960). *An Eskimo village in the modern world*. Ithaca, NY: Cornell University Press.

Hunt, M. (1988). The naturally occurring retirement community. In G. M. Gutman & N. K. Blackie (Eds.), *Housing the very old* (pp. 161-172). Burnaby, British Columbia: Simon Fraser University, Gerontology Research Centre.

Huntingford, G. W. B. (1960). Nandi age-sets. In S. Ottenberg & P. Ottenberg (Eds.), *Cultures and societies of Africa* (pp. 214-226). New York: Random House.

Hurtado, A. D., Hayes-Bautista, D., Valdez, R. B., & Hernandez, A. C. (1992). *Redefining California: Latino social engagement in a multicultural society*. Los Angeles: University of California, Chicano Studies Research Center.

Ikels, C. (1975). Old age in Hong Kong. *The Gerontologist*, 15, 230-235.

Ikels, C. (1980). The coming of age in Chinese society: Traditional patterns and contemporary Hong Kong. In C. L. Fry (Ed.), *Aging in culture and society* (pp. 80-100). New York: J. F. Bergin.

Ikels, C. (1983). *Aging and adaptation: Chinese in Hong Kong and the United States*. Hamden, CT: Archon.

Ikels, C., Keith, J., Dickerson-Putnam, J., Draper, P., Fry, C. L., Glascock, A., & Harpending, H. (1992). Perceptions of the adult life course: A cross-cultural analysis. *Ageing and Society*, 12, 49-84.

Jackson, J. J. (1982). Death rates of aged blacks and whites: United States, 1964-1978. *Black Scholar*, 13, 21-35.

Jacobs, J. (1974a). An ethnographic study of a retirement setting. *The Gerontologist*, 14, 483-487.

Jacobs, J. (1974b). *Fun City*. New York: Holt, Rinehart & Winston.

Jacobs, J. (1975). *Old persons and retirement communities*. Springfield, IL: Charles C Thomas.

Japan Ministry of Health and Welfare. (1988). *Health and welfare in Japan.* Tokyo: Japan International Corporation of Welfare Services.

Jayakody, R. (1993). Neighborhoods and neighbor relations. In J. S. Jackson, L. M. Chatters, & R. J. Taylor (Eds.), *Aging in black America* (pp. 21-37). Newbury Park, CA: Sage.

Jeffers, F. C., & Verwoerdt, R. (977). How the old face death. In E. Busse & E. Pfeiffer (Eds.), *Behavior and adaptation in late life* (pp. 163-181). Boston: Little, Brown.

Johnson, C. L. (1983). Interdependence and aging in Italian families. In J. Sokolovsky (Ed.), *Growing old in different societies: Cross-cultural perspectives* (pp. 92-103). Belmont, CA: Wadsworth.

Johnson, C. L. (1985). *Growing up and growing old in Italian-American families.* New Brunswick, NJ: Rutgers University Press.

Johnson, C. (1987). The institutional segregation of the aged. In P. Silverman (Ed.), *The elderly as modern pioneers* (pp. 375-388). Bloomington: Indiana University Press.

Jonas, K., & Wellin, E. (1980). Dependence and reciprocity: Home health aid in an elderly population. In C. L. Fry (Ed.), *Aging in culture and society: Comparative viewpoints and strategies* (pp. 217-238). New York: J. F. Bergin.

Jorgensen, J. G. (1990). *Oil age Eskimos.* Berkeley: University of California Press.

Josephson, E., & Josephson, M. (1962). *Man alone.* New York: Dell.

Kagan, D. (1980). Activity and aging in a Colombian peasant village. In C. L. Fry (Eds.), *Aging in culture and society: Comparative viewpoints and strategies.* New York: J. F. Bergin.

Kalish, R. (1986). The meanings of ethnicity. In C. L. Hayes, R. A. Kalish, & D. Gutmann (Eds.), *European-American elderly: A guide for practice* (pp. 16-34). New York: Springer.

Kastenbaum, R., & Aisenberg, R. (1972). *The psychology of death.* New York: Springer.

Kayser-Jones, J. S. (1981). Quality of care for the institutionalized aged: A Scottish-American comparison. In C. L. Fry (Ed.), *Dimensions: Aging, culture, and health* (pp. 233-254). Brooklyn, NY: J. F. Bergin.

Keesing, F. (1953). *Cultural dynamics and administrative proceedings.* Auckland, New Zealand: Seventh Pacific Science Congress.

Keesing, R. M. (1975). *Kin groups and social structure.* New York: Holt, Rinehart & Winston.

Keith, J. (Vol. Ed.). (1979). The ethnography of old age [Special issue]. *Anthropological Quarterly, 52*(1).

Keith, J., Fry, C. L., & Ikels, C. (1990). Community as context for successful living. In J. Sokolovsky (Ed.), *The cultural context of aging: World perspectives* (pp. 245-262). New York: Bergin and Garvey.

Kerns, V. (1980). Aging and mutual support relations among the Black Carib. In C. L. Fry (Ed.), *Aging in culture and society: Comparative viewpoints and strategies* (pp. 112-125). New York: J. F. Bergin.

Kiefer, C. W. (1974). *Changing cultures, changing lives.* San Francisco: Jossey-Bass.

Kiefer, C. W. (1990). The elderly in modern Japan: Elite, victims, or plural *players*? In J. Sokolovsky (Ed.), *The cultural context of aging: World perspectives* (pp. 181-195). New York: Bergin and Garvey.

Kim, S. S. (1983). Ethnic elders and American health care: A physician's perspective. *Western Journal of Medicine, 139,* 885-891.

Kimball, S. T. (1946). Review of Leo Simmon's *The role of the aged in primitive society. American Journal of Sociology, 52,* 287.

Kinoshita, Y., & Kiefer, C. W. (1992). *Refuge of the honored: Social organization in a Japanese retirement community.* Berkeley: University of California Press.

Kinsella, K. (1988). *Aging in the Third World* (U.S. Bureau of the Census, International Population Reports, Series P-95, No. 79). Washington, DC: Government Printing Office.

Kinsella, K., & Taeuber, C. M. (1992). *An aging world II* (U.S. Bureau of the Census, International Population Reports, P-25, 92-3). Washington, DC: Government Printing Office.

Kinzer, N. S. (1974). The beauty cult. *The Center Magazine, 7,* 2-9.

Kitano, H. L. (1969). *Japanese Americans: The evolution of a subculture.* Englewood Cliffs, NJ: Prentice Hall.

Kluckhohn, C. (1949). *Mirror for man.* New York: McGraw-Hill.

Kneller, G. F. (1965). *Educational anthropology.* New York: Wiley.

Knight-Ridder Tribune News Service. (1993, November 24). French woman said to be nearly 119. *Wichita Eagle-Beacon,* p. 5A.

Kogan, N. (1973). Creativity and cognitive style: A life-span perspective. In P. B. Baltes & K. W. Schaie (Eds.), *Lifespan developmental psychology: Personality and socialization* (pp. 145-178). New York: Academic Press.

Koty, J. (1933). *Die Behandlung der Alten und Kranken bei den Naturvolkern.* Stuttgart: W. Kohlhammer.

Koyano, W. (1989). Japanese attitudes toward the elderly: A review of research findings. *Journal of Cross-Cultural Gerontology, 4*(4), 335-346.

Kroeber, A. L. (1948). *Anthropology.* New York: Harcourt, Brace.

Kunitz, S. J., & Levy, J. E. (1991). *Navajo aging: The transition from family to institutional support.* Tucson: University of Arizona Press.

Lacayo, C. G. (1993). Hispanic elderly: Policy issues in long-term care. In C. M. Barresi & D. E. Stull (Eds.), *Ethnic elderly and long-term care* (pp. 223-234). New York: Springer.

Landor, A. H. (1893). *Alone with the Hairy Ainu.* London: J. Murray.

Laslett, P. (1972). Introduction: The history of the family. In P. Laslett (Ed.), *Household and family in past time* (pp. 1-89). Cambridge, UK: Cambridge University Press.

Laslett, P. (1976). Societal development and aging. In R. Binstock & E. Shanas (Eds.), *Handbook of aging and social sciences* (pp. 87-116). New York: Van Nostrand & Reinhold.

Leaf, A. (1973a). Every day is a gift when you are over 100. *National Geographic, 143,* 93-119.

Leaf, A. (1973b, September). Getting old. *Scientific American,* pp. 291-299.

Leaf, A. (1975). *Youth in old age.* New York: McGraw-Hill.

Lebon, J. H. G. (1969). *An introduction to human geography* (6th ed.). London: Hutchinson University Library.

Lee, R. (1992). Work, sexuality, and aging among !Kung women. In V. Kerns & J. K. Brown (Eds.), *In her prime: New views of middle-aged* *women* (2nd ed., pp. 23-35). Urbana: University of Illinois Press.

Legesse, A. (1979). Age sets and retirement communities. In J. Keith (Ed.), The ethnography of old age [Special issue]. *Anthropological Quarterly, 52*(1), 61-69.

Lehman, H. C. (1953). *Age and achievement.* Princeton, NJ: Princeton University Press.

Lehman, H. C. (1962). The creative production rates of present versus past generations of scientists. *Journal of Gerontology, 17,* 409-417.

Lehman, H. C. (1966). The psychologist's most creative years. *Psychology, 21,* 363-369.

Leonard, O. E. (1967). The older rural Spanish-speaking people of the Southwest. In E. G. Youmans (Ed.), *Older rural Americans: A sociological perspective* (pp. 239-261). Lexington: University of Kentucky Press.

Lepowsky, M. (1985). Gender, aging, and dying in an egalitarian society. In D. A. Counts & D. R. Counts (Eds.), *Aging and its transformations: Moving toward death in Pacific societies* (pp. 157-178). New York: University Press of America.

Levy, J. E. (1967). The older American Indian. In E. G. Youmans (Ed.), *Older rural Americans: A sociological perspective* (pp. 221-238). Lexington: University of Kentucky Press.

Levy, R. (1973). *The Tahitians: Mind and experience in the Society Islands.* Chicago: University of Chicago Press.

Lipson, J. G., & Meleis, A. I. (1983). Issues in health care of Middle Eastern patients. *Western Journal of Medicine, 139,* 854-861.

Litwak, E. (1965). Extended kin relations in an industrial democratic society. In E. Shanas & G. Strieb (Eds.), *Social structure and the family generational relations* (pp. 290-323). Englewood Cliffs, NJ: Prentice Hall.

Logue, B. J. (1990). Modernization and the status of the frail elderly: Perspectives on continuity and change. *Journal of Cross-Cultural Gerontology, 5,* 345-374.

Longman, P. (1986, January-February). Age wars: The coming battle between young and old. *The Futurist,* pp. 33-37.

Longman, P. (1988, September-October). The challenge of an aging society. *The Futurist,* pp. 33-37.

Lopata, H. Z. (1972). Role changes in widowhood: A world perspective. In D. O. Cowgill & L. D. Holmes (Eds.), *Aging and modernization* (pp. 275-304). New York: Appleton-Century-Crofts.

Lorge, I. (1963). The adult learner. In I. Lorge, H. Y. McClusky, G. E. Jensen, & W. C. Hallenbeck (Eds.), *Psychology of adults* (pp. 1-9). Washington, DC: Adult Education Association of the U.S.A.

Lovejoy, C. O., Meindl, R. S., Pryzbeck, T. R., Barton, T. S., Heiple, K. G., & Kotting, D. (1977). Paleodemography of the Libben Site, Ottawa County, Ohio. *Science, 198,* 291-293.

Lozier, J., & Althouse, R. (1975). Retirement to the porch in rural Appalachia. *International Journal of Aging and Human Development, 6,* 7-16.

Maduro, R. (1974). Artistic creativity and aging in India. *International Journal of Aging and Human Development, 5,* 303-329.

Maldonado, D. (1975, May). The Chicano aged. *Social Work,* pp. 213-216.

Maldonado, D. (1979). Aging in the Chicano context. In D. E. Gelfand & A. J. Kutzik (Eds.), *Ethnicity and aging* (pp. 175-183). New York: Springer.

Mann, A. E. (1968). *The paleodemography of Australopithecus.* Unpublished doctoral dissertation, University of California, Berkeley.

Mann, J. (1977, October 3). End of youth culture. *U.S. News & World Report,* pp. 54-56.

Manton, K. (1982). Differential life expectancy: Possible explanations during the later years. In R. C. Manuel (Ed.), *Minority aging: Sociological and social psychological issues* (pp. 63-70). Westport, CT: Greenwood.

Martin, L. G. (1988). The aging of Asia. *Journal of Gerontology, 43*(4), S99-S113.

Martin, P. (1976). The old men and women of the mountains. *Parade, 4,* 10, 12.

Matula, L. (1969). Testimony. In *Availability and usefulness of federal programs and services to elderly Mexican Americans* (pp. 233-236). Hearings before the Special Committee on Aging, U.S. Senate (Part 3, San Antonio, Texas, held December 19, 1968). Washington, DC: Government Printing Office.

Maxwell, R., Bader, J. E., & Watson, W. (1972). Territory and self in a geriatric setting. *The Gerontologist, 12,* 413-417.

Maxwell, R. J., & Silverman, P. (1970). Information and esteem: Cultural considerations in the treatment of the aged. *International Journal of Aging and Human Development, 1,* 361-392.

Maxwell, R., Silverman, P., & Maxwell, E. (1982). The motive for gerontocide. In J. Sokolovsky (Ed.), Aging and the aged in the Third World. Part 1 [Special issue]. *Studies in Third World Societies, 22,* 67-84.

Mayer, P. J. (1982). Evolutionary advantage of the menopause. *Human Ecology, 10*(4), 477-494.

Mazess, R. B., & Forman, S. H. (1979). Longevity and age exaggeration in Vilcabamba, Ecuador. *Journal of Gerontology, 34*(1), 94-98.

Mazess, R. B., & Mathisen, R. W. (1982). Lack of unusual longevity in Vilcabamba, Ecuador. *Human Biology, 54*(3), 517-524.

McConatha, D., McConatha, J. T., & Cinelli, B. (1991). Japan's coming crisis: Problems for the honorable elders. *Journal of Applied Gerontology, 10,* 224-235.

McKain, W. C. (1972). The aged in the U.S.S.R.. In D. O. Cowgill & L. D. Holmes (Eds.), *Aging and modernization* (pp. 151-166). New York: Appleton-Century-Crofts.

McKellin, W. H. (1985). Passing away and loss of life: Aging and death among the Managalase of Papua New Guinea. In D. A. Counts & D. R. Counts (Eds.), *Aging and its transformations: Moving toward death in Pacific societies* (pp. 181-201). Lanham, MD: University Press of America.

McKinley, K. R. (1971). Survivorship in Gracile and Robust Australopithecines: A demographic comparison and a proposed birth model. *American Journal of Physical Anthropology, 34,* 417-426.

Mead, M. (1928). *Coming of age in Samoa.* New York: William Morrow.

Mead, M. (1937). *Cooperation and competition among primitive peoples.* New York: McGraw-Hill.

Mead, M. (1967). Ethnological aspects of aging. *Psychosomatics, 8,* 33-37.

Medvedev, Z. A. (1974). Caucasus and Altay longevity: A biological or social problem? *The Gerontologist, 14,* 381-387.

Messer, M. (1968). Race differences in selected attitudinal dimensions of the elderly. *The Gerontologist, 8,* 245-249.

Mintz, S. W., & Price, R. (1976). *An anthropological approach to the Afro-American past* (Occasional Paper). Philadelphia: Institute for the Study of Human Issues.

Mitchell, M. F. (1983). Popular medical concepts in Jamaica and their impact on drug use. *Western Journal of Medicine, 139,* 841-847.

Moore, C. D. (1979). The Native American family: The urban way. In *Families today* (National Institute of Mental Health Science Monograph 1, Vol. 1, pp. 441-484). Washington, DC: U.S. Department of Health, Education and Welfare.

Moore, M. (1987). The human life span. In P. Silverman (Ed.), *The elderly as modern pioneers* (pp. 54-72). Bloomington: Indiana University Press.

Munsell, M. (1972). Functions of the aged among the Salt River Pima. In D. O. Cowgill & L. D. Holmes (Eds.), *Aging and modernization* (pp. 127-132). New York: Appleton-Century-Crofts.

Murdock, J. (1887-1888). *Ethnological results of the Point Barrow expedition* (Annual Reports of the Bureau of American Ethnology, Vol. 9). Washington, DC: Bureau of American Ethnology.

Murrillo, N. (1971). The Mexican American family. In N. N. Wagner & M. J. Haug (Eds.), *Chicanos: Social and psychological perspectives* (pp. 97-108). St. Louis: C. V. Mosby.

Mutran, E. (1985). Intergenerational family support among blacks and whites: Response to culture or to socioeconomic differences. *Journal of Gerontology, 40,* 382-389.

Myerhoff, B. (1978). Aging and the aged in other cultures: An anthropological perspective. In E. Bauwens (Ed.), *The anthropology of health* (pp. 151-166). St. Louis: C. V. Mosby.

Myerhoff, B., & Simic, A. (Eds.). (1978). *Life's career—aging: Cultural variations on growing old.* Beverly Hills, CA: Sage.

Nahemow, N., & Adams, B. (1974). Old age among the Baganda: Continuity and change. In J. Gubrium (Ed.), *Late life: Communities and environmental policy* (pp. 147-166). Springfield, IL: Charles C Thomas.

Nanry, C. (1979). *The jazz text.* New York: Van Nostrand.

Nason, J. D. (1981). Respected elderly or old person: Aging in a Micronesian community. In P. Amoss & S. Harrell (Eds.), *Other ways of growing old: Anthropological perspectives* (pp. 155-173). Stanford, CA: Stanford University Press.

National Center for Health Statistics. (1992). *Vital statistics of the United States, 1989* (Vol. 1, sec. 6, life tables). Washington, DC: Public Health Service.

National Indian Conference on Aging. (1978, August). *Final report.* Washington, DC: Author.

Neugarten, B. (1975). Aging in the year 2000: A look at the future. *The Gerontologist, 15*(1), 1-40.

Nyanguru, A. (1987). Residential care for the destitute elder: A comparative study of two institutions in Zimbabwe. *Journal of Cross-Cultural Gerontology, 2,* 345-358.

Ogawa, N., & Retherford, R. D. (1993). Care of the elderly in Japan: Changing norms and expectations. *Journal of Marriage and the Family, 55,* 585-597.

Older parents continue helping out "the kids." (1993, May 18). *San Francisco Chronicle,* p. B5.

O'Leary, T. J., & Levinson, D. (Eds.). (1991). *Encyclopedia of world cultures: Vol. 1. North America.* Boston: G. K. Hall.

Olshansky, S. J. (1993). The human lifespan: Are we reaching the outer limits? *Geriatrics, 48*(3), 85-88.

Olshansky, S. J., Carnes, B. A., & Cassel, C. K. (1993, April). The aging of the human species. *Scientific American,* pp. 46-52.

Osako, M. M. (1979). Aging and family among Japanese Americans: The role of ethnic tradition in the adjustment to old age. *The Gerontologist, 19,* 448-455.

Palmore, E. B. (1975). *The honorable elders: A cross-cultural analysis of aging in Japan.* Durham, NC: Duke University Press.

Palmore, E. B. (1984). Longevity in Abkhazia: A reevaluation. *The Gerontologist, 24,* 95-96.

Palmore, E. B., & Maeda, D. (1985). *The honorable elders revisited.* Durham, NC: Duke University Press.

Palmore, E. B., & Manton, K. (1974). Modernization and status of the aged: International correlations. *Journal of Gerontology, 29,* 205-210.

Pappas, G., Queen, S., Hadden, W., & Fisher, G. (1993). The increasing disparity in mortality between socioeconomic groups in the United States, 1960-1986. *New England Journal of Medicine, 329*(2), 103-109.

Pearson, J. D. (1992). Attitudes and perceptions concerning elderly Samoans in rural Western Samoa, American Samoa, and urban Honolulu. *Journal of Cross-Cultural Gerontology, 7,* 69-88.

Pfeiffer, E. (1977). Psychopathology and social pathology. In J. E. Birren & K. W. Schaie (Eds.), *Handbook of the psychology of aging* (pp. 650-671). New York: Van Nostrand Reinhold.

Plath, D. (1972). Japan: The after years. In D. O. Cowgill & L. Holmes (Eds.), *Aging and modernization* (pp. 133-150). New York: Appleton-Century-Crofts.

Plath, D. (1988a, March). The age of silver. *The World and I,* pp. 505-513.

Plath, D. (1988b, May). The eighty-year system. *The World and I,* pp. 464-471.

Pollard, L. J. (1978). Age and paternalism in a slave society. *Perspective on Aging, 7*(6), 4-8.

Powdermaker, H. (1936). *After freedom.* New York: Viking.

Powdermaker, H. (1966). *Stranger and friend: The ways of an anthropologist.* New York: Norton.

Prescott, J. W. (1975, April). Body pleasure and the origins of violence. *The Futurist,* pp. 64-74.

Press, I., & McKool, M. (1972). Social structure and status of the aged: Toward some valid cross-cultural generalizations. *International Journal of Aging and Human Development, 3,* 297-306.

Purdy, J. K., & Arguello, D. (1992). Hispanic familism in caretaking of old adults: Is it functional? *Journal of Gerontological Social Work, 2,* 29-43.

Quadagno, J. (1982). *Aging in early industrial society.* New York: Academic Press.

Quain, B. (1948). *Fijian village.* Chicago: University of Chicago Press.

Rasmussen, K. (1908). *The people of the polar north.* Philadelphia: J. B. Lippincott.

Rattray, R. S. (1923). *The Ashanti.* Oxford: Clarendon.

Ray, P. H. (1885). Ethnographic sketch of the natives of Point Barrow. In *Report of the international polar expedition to Point Barrow, Alaska, in response to the resolution of the House of Representatives of December 11, 1884* (pp. 35-87). Washington, DC: Government Printing Office.

Redfield, R. (1947). The folk society. *American Journal of Sociology, 52,* 293-308.

Redfield, R. (1960). *The little community and peasant society and culture.* Chicago: University of Chicago Press.

Reichard, G. (1928). *Social life of the Navajo Indians* (Contributions to Anthropology, 7). New York: Columbia University.

Rhoads, E. C. (1981). *Aging and modernization in three Samoan communities.* Unpublished doctoral dissertation, University of Kansas.

Rhoads, E. C. (1984). Reevaluation of the aging and modernization theory: The Samoan evidence. *The Gerontologist, 24*(3), 243-250.

Rhoads, E. C., & Holmes, L. D. (1981). Mapuifagalele, Western Samoa's home for the aged: A cultural enigma. *International Journal of Aging and Human Development, 13,* 121-135.

Roget's II, The new thesaurus (expanded ed.). (1988). Boston: Houghton Mifflin.

Romaniuk, J. G., & Romaniuk, M. (1981). Creativity across the lifespan: A measurement perspective. *Human Development, 24,* 366-381.

Rose, M. R. (1991). *Evolutionary biology of aging.* New York: Oxford University Press.

Rosenwaike, I., & Logue, B. (1985). *The extreme aged in America.* Westport, CT: Greenwood.

Rosenwaike, I., & Preston, S. H. (1984). Age overstatement and Puerto Rican longevity. *Human Biology, 56,* 503-525.

Rosow, I. (1965). And then we were old. *Transaction, 2*(2), 21-26.

Ross, J. K. (1977). *Old people, new lives.* Chicago: University of Chicago Press.

Roth, D. (1981). *Aging and modernization among the Yoder Amish and Hesston Mennonites.* Unpublished master's thesis, Wichita State University, Wichita, KS.

Rowe, W. (1961). The middle and later years in Indian society. In R. Kleemeier (Ed.), *Aging and leisure* (pp. 104-112). New York: Oxford University Press.

Rubinstein, R. L. (1987). Childless elderly: Theoretical perspectives and practical concerns. *Journal of Cross-Cultural Gerontology, 2,* 1-14.

Salamon, S., & Lockhardt, V. (1979, December). *Land ownership and the position of elderly in farm families.* Unpublished paper presented at the annual meeting of the American Anthropological Association, Cincinnati, OH.

Sankar, A. (1981). The conquest of solitude: Singlehood and old age. In C. L. Fry (Ed.), *Dimensions: Aging culture and health* (pp. 65-83). South Hadley, MA: J. F. Bergin.

Scheper-Hughes, N. (1983). Deposed kings: The demise of the rural Irish gerontocracy. In J. Sokolovsky (Ed.), *Growing old in different societies: Cross-cultural perspectives* (pp. 130-146). Belmont, CA: Wadsworth.

Schulz, C. M. (1980). Age, sex, and death anxiety in a middle-class community. In C. L. Fry (Ed.), *Aging in culture and society: Comparative viewpoints and strategies* (pp. 239-252). New York: J. F. Bergin.

Schweitzer, M. (1983). The elders: Cultural dimensions of aging in two American Indian communities. In J. Sokolovsky (Ed.), *Growing old in different societies: Cross-cultural perspectives* (pp. 168-178). Belmont, CA: Wadsworth.

Shahrani, M. N. (1981). Growing in respect: Aging among the Kirghiz of Afghanistan. In P. T. Amoss & S. Harrell (Eds.), *Other ways of growing old: Anthropological perspectives* (pp. 175-191). Stanford, CA: Stanford University Press.

Shakespeare, W. (1957). *As you like it.* In J. Munro (Ed.), *The London Shakespeare.* New York: Simon & Schuster.

Shanas, E. (1979). *National survey of the elderly* (Report to the Administration on Aging). Washington, DC: Department of Health & Human Services.

Sharp, H. S. (1981). Old age among the Chipewyan. In P. Amoss & S. Harrell (Eds.), *Other ways of growing old: Anthropological perspectives* (pp. 99-109). Stanford, CA: Stanford University Press.

Sheehan, T. (1976). Senior esteem as a factor of socioeconomic complexity. *The Gerontologist, 16,* 433-440.

Shelton, A. J. (1965). Aging and eldership: Notes for gerontologists and others. *The Gerontologist, 5,* 20-23.

Shelton, A. J. (1972). The aged and eldership among the Igbo. In D. O. Cowgill & L. D. Holmes (Eds.), *Aging and modernization* (pp. 31-49). New York: Appleton-Century-Crofts.

Shomaker, D. (1990). Health care, cultural expectations and frail elderly Navajo grandmothers. *Journal of Cross-Cultural Gerontology, 5,* 24-31.

Sichinava, G. N. (1965). *On the question of the character and range of work done by the aged people of Abkhasia: Anthology of papers by physicians of Ostroumov Republican Hospital.* Sukhumi, Russia: Alashara.

Silverman, P., & Maxwell, R. J. (1978). How do I respect thee? Let me count the ways: Deference towards elderly men and women. *Behavior Science Research, 13*(2), 91-108.

Silverman, P., & Maxwell, R. J. (1983). The significance of information and power in the comparative study of the aged. In J. Sokolovsky (Ed.), *Growing old in different societies: Cross-cultural perspectives* (pp. 43-55). Belmont, CA: Wadsworth.

Simic, A. (1977). Aging in the United States and Yugoslavia: Contrasting models of intergenerational relationships. *Anthropological Quarterly, 50,* 53-63.

Simic, A. (1978). Winners and losers: Aging Yugoslavs in a changing world. In B. G. Myerhoff & A. Simic (Eds.), *Life's career—aging: Cultural variations on growing old* (pp. 77-106). Beverly Hills, CA: Sage.

Simic, A. (1990). Aging, world view, and intergenerational relations in America and Yugoslavia. In J. Sokolovsky (Ed.), *The cultural context of aging: Worldwide perspectives* (pp. 89-107). New York: Bergin and Garvey.

Simic, A., & Myerhoff, B. G. (1978). Conclusion. In B. G. Myerhoff & A. Simic (Eds.), *Life's career—aging: Cultural variations on growing old* (pp. 231-246). Beverly Hills, CA: Sage.

Simmons, L. (1942). *Sun Chief: The autobiography of a Hopi Indian*. New Haven, CT: Yale University Press.

Simmons, L. (1945a). *The role of the aged in primitive society*. New Haven, CT: Yale University Press.

Simmons, L. (1945b). A prospectus for field-research in the position and treatment of the aged in primitive and other societies. *American Anthropologist, 47*, 433-438.

Simmons, L. (1959). Aging in modern society. In *Toward better understanding of the aging* (Seminar on the Aging, Aspen, Colorado, September 8-13, 1958). New York: Council on Social Work Education.

Simmons, L. (1960). Aging in pre-industrial societies. In C. Tibbits (Ed.), *Handbook of social gerontology* (pp. 62-91). Chicago: University of Chicago Press.

Simmons, L. (1962). Aging in primitive societies: A comparative survey of family life and relationship. *Law and Contemporary Problems, 27*, 36-51.

Slater, P. (1970). *Pursuit of loneliness: American culture at the breaking point*. Boston: Beacon.

Smith, R. (1961). Cultural differences in the life cycle and the concept of time. In R. Kleemeier (Ed.), *Aging and leisure* (pp. 83-86, 95-100). New York: Oxford University Press.

Snow, L. F. (1983). Traditional health beliefs and practices among lower class black Americans. *Western Journal of Medicine, 139*(6), 820-828.

Sokolovsky, J., & Cohen, C. (1978). The cultural meaning of personal networks for the inner-city elderly. *Urban Anthropology, 7*, 323-339.

Sokolovsky, J., & Cohen, C. (1987). Networks as adaptation: The cultural meaning of being a "loner" among the inner-city elderly. In J. Sokolovsky (Ed.), *Growing old in different societies: Cross-cultural perspectives* (pp. 189-201). Action, MA: Copley.

Spencer, R., & Jennings, J. D. (1977). *The Native Americans*. New York: Harper & Row.

Stenning, D. J. (1958). Household viability among the pastoral Fulani. In J. Goody (Ed.), *The developmental cycle in domestic groups* (pp. 94-119). Cambridge, UK: Cambridge University Press.

Stephen, A. M. (1936). *Contributions to anthropology: Vol. 33. Hopi journal of Alex Stephen* (E. C. Parsons, Ed.). New York: Columbia University Press.

Sternheimer, S. (1985). The vanishing babushka: A roleless role for older Soviet women? In Z. S. Blau (Ed.), *Current perspectives on aging and the life cycle* (pp. 315-333). Greenwich, CT: JAI.

Stokes, E. M. (1990). Ethnography of a social border: The case of an American retirement community in Mexico. *Journal of Cross-Cultural Gerontology, 5*(2), 169-182.

Strom, R., Collinsworth, P., Strom, S., & Griswold, D. (1992-1993). Strengths and needs of black grandparents. *International Journal of Aging and Human Development, 36*(4), 255-268.

Taylor, R. J. (1988). Aging and supportive relationships among black Americans. In J. S. Jackson (Ed.), *The black American* (pp. 259-281). New York: Springer.

Taylor, R. J. (1993). Religion and religious observances. In J. S. Jackson, L. M. Chatters, & R. J. Taylor (Eds.), *Aging in black America* (pp. 101-123). Newbury Park, CA: Sage.

Taylor, R. J., & Chatters, L. M. (1991). Extended family networks of older black adults. *Journal of Gerontology, 46*(4) S210-S217.

Taylor, R., & Nobbs, M. J. (1962). *Hunza: The Himalayan Shangri-la.* El Monte, CA: Whitehorn.

Taylor, S. C. (1993, October-November). The end of retirement. *Modern Maturity,* pp. 32-39.

TIAA Cref. (1974, October). New TIAA-Cref study profiles retired educators. *The Participant,* pp. 1-4.

Tobin, J. J. (1987). The American idealization of old age in Japan. *The Gerontologist, 27,* 53-58.

Tracy, M. B. (1991). *Social policies for the elderly in the Third World.* New York: Greenwood.

Trostchansky, V. F. (1908). Yakuty v ikh domashney obstanovke: Etnograficheskiy ocherk [The Yakuts in their domestic surroundings: An ethnographic sketch]. *ZhS,* Nos. 3-4.

Turner, G. (1884). *Samoa: A hundred years ago and long before.* London: Macmillan.

Turner, L. M. (1894). *Ethnology of the Ungava District, Hudson Bay Territory* (Annual Reports of the Bureau of American Ethnology, Vol. 2). Washington, DC: Bureau of American Ethnology.

United Nations. (1990). *United Nations world population chart 1990* (rev.) (prepared by the Population Division of the Department of International Economic and Social Affairs of the United Nations Secretariat). New York: United Nations.

U.S. Bureau of the Census. (1992a). *1990 census of population: General population characteristics, Kansas.* Washington, DC: Government Printing Office.

U.S. Bureau of the Census. (1992b). *1990 census of population: General population characteristics, United States.* Washington, DC: Government Printing Office.

U.S. Bureau of the Census. (1992c). *1990 census of population and housing: Summary population and housing characteristics, United States.* Washington, DC: Government Printing Office.

U.S. Bureau of the Census. (1992d). *Statistical abstract of the United States, 1992* (112th ed.). Washington, DC: Government Printing Office.

U.S. Bureau of the Census. (1993a). *1990 census of population: Asians and Pacific Islanders in the United States.* Washington, DC: Government Printing Office.

U.S. Bureau of the Census. (1993b). *1990 census of population: Persons of Hispanic origin in the United States.* Washington, DC: Government Printing Office.

U.S. Bureau of the Census. (1993c). *1990 census of population: Social and economic characteristics, California.* Washington, DC: Government Printing Office.

U.S. Bureau of the Census. (1993d). *1990 census of population and housing: Social, economic and housing characteristics, American Samoa.* Washington, DC: Government Printing Office.

U.S. Bureau of the Census & National Institute on Aging. (1991). *Profiles of America's elderly: Growth of America's elderly in the 1980s.* Washington, DC: Author.

U.S. Senate Special Committee on Aging, American Association of Retired Persons, Federal Council on Aging, & Administration on Aging. (1991). *Aging America: Trends and projections.* Washington, DC: Government Printing Office.

Utter, J. (1993). *American Indians: Answers to today's questions.* Lake Ann, MI: National Woodlands Publishing.

Valle, R., & Mendoza, L. (1978). *The elder Latino.* San Diego, CA: Campanile.

van den Berghe, P. (1983). Age differentiation in human societies. In J. Sokolovsky (Ed.), *Growing old in different societies: Cross-cultural perspectives* (pp. 72-81). Belmont, CA: Wadsworth.

Van Steenberg, C., Ansak, M.-L., & Chin-Hansen, J. (1993). On Lok's model: Managed long-term care. In C. M. Barresi & D. E. Stull (Eds.), *Ethnic elderly and long-term care* (pp. 178-190). New York: Springer.

VanStone, J. W. (1962). *Point Hope: An Eskimo village in transition.* Seattle: University of Washington Press.

Van Willigen, J. (1989). *Gettin' some age on me.* Lexington: University Press of Kentucky.

Vatuk, S. (1980). Withdrawal and disengagement as a cultural response to aging in India. In C. L. Fry (Ed.), *Aging in culture and society: Comparative viewpoints and strategies* (pp. 126-148). Brooklyn: J. F. Bergin.

Vatuk, S. (1990). "To be a burden on others": Dependency anxiety among the elderly in India. In O. M. Lynch (Ed.), *Divine passions: The social construction of emotion in India* (pp. 64-88). Berkeley: University of California Press.

Vesperi, M. (1983). The reluctant consumer: Nursing home residents in the post-Bergman era. In J. Sokolovsky (Ed.), *Growing old in different societies: Cross-cultural perspectives* (pp. 225-237). Belmont, CA: Wadsworth.

Voegelin, C. F. (1941). North American Indian languages still spoken and their genetic relationships. In L. Spier, A. I. Hallowell, & S. Newman (Eds.), *Language, culture, and personality* (pp. 15-40). Menasha, WI: Sapir Memorial Fund.

Washburn, S. L. (1981). Longevity in primates. In J. L. McGaugh & S. B. Kiesler (Eds.), *Aging: Biology and behavior* (pp. 11-29). New York: Academic Press.

Watson, W., & Maxwell, R. J. (1977). *Human aging and dying: A study in sociocultural gerontology.* New York: St. Martin.

Wechsler, D. (1958). *The measurement and appraisal of adult intelligence.* Baltimore: Williams and Wilkins.

Weibel-Orlando, J. (1989). Elders and elderlies: Well-being in Indian old age. *American Indian Culture and Research Journal, 13*(3-4), 149-170.

Weyl, N. (1977). Survival past the century mark. *Mankind Quarterly, 17,* 163-175.

Whiting, J. W. M., & Child, I. L. (1953). *Child training and personality.* New Haven, CT: Yale University Press.

Willard, T. (1989, July-August). Old can be beautiful. *The Futurist,* pp. 39-40.

Williams, G. C. (1980). Warriors no more: A study of the American Indian elderly. In C. L. Fry (Ed.), *Aging in culture and society: Comparative viewpoints and strategies* (pp. 101-111). Brooklyn: J. F. Bergin.

Williams, T. R. (1965). *The Dusun: A North Borneo society.* New York: Holt, Rinehart & Winston.

Wirth, L. (1945). The problem of minority groups. In R. Linton (Ed.), *The science of man in the world crisis* (pp. 347-372). New York: Columbia University Press.

Wu, F. Y. T. (1975). Mandarin-speaking age Chinese in the Los Angeles area. *The Gerontologist, 15,* 271-275.

Wylie, F. M. (1971). Attitudes toward aging and the aged among black Americans: Some historical perceptions. *International Journal of Aging and Human Development, 2,* 66-69.

▣ Index

Abkhazia, 34-36, 39-43, 46-47, 49
Acculturation, 183, 252
    of Italian Americans, 212
    of Japanese Americans, 219-220
Aegyptopithecus, 19
African American elderly, 187-196, 223
    friendship networks of, 195
    kin patterns of, 189-191
    political participation of, 195
    religious activities of, 195
    respect for, 190-191, 192
    retirement among, 196
African American ethnicity, 184, 223
    emancipation and reconstruction
        period, influence on, 193
    origins of, 188, 189
    respect patterns in Africa for elders and,
        190, 192
    slave experience and, 189, 191, 192, 193
Age as symbol of defeat by nature, 180-181
Age exaggeration, 44
"Age game," 55, 57
Age grades:

defined, 52
    of Nandi of East Africa, 52-53, 92
    See also Life cycle stages
Age heaping, 41
Age sets, 52
Age-homogeneous communities, 70,
        128-129, 133-134, 143
Age-specific genetic effect on aging, 25
Aged in the United States:
    communities of, 125-128, 130-133
    cultural values and, 172-182
    historical trends, 171-173
    population statistics of, 170
    residence patterns of, 170-171
    See also African Americans; American
        Indians; Asian Americans; Italian
        Americans; Mexican Americans
Aging and Modernization theory, ix, 98-99
    criticism of, 276-277
    generalizations of, 257-270
    salient aspects of, 270-275
Aging as a career, 59-61, 93
    continuity and, 60

sexual dichotomy and, 60
Aging population:
  characteristics of, 30
  United States as, 30-32
Alzheimer's disease, 235
  ethnic/minority support groups for
    caregivers, 236-237
America as melting pot, 168, 183-184
American cultural values, 174-182
  and mental illness in late life, 227-228
  self reliance as core value, 175
American Indian aged:
  morbidity and life expectancy of, 200
  poverty among, 199-200
  reservation conditions, 200
  urban problems, 205-207, 224
American Indian ethnicity, 196-207, 224
  culture areas, 196-197
  government policies (extermination,
    expulsion, exclusion, assimilation)
    and, 198-199
  kinship variations, 197-198
  pan Indian values, 198-198
American retirement in a foreign country,
  130
Anamnestic method of determining
  human age, 41
Antagonistic pleiotropy, 25
Anthropological perspective, 6-15
Anthropology as a discipline, 2-16
Applied anthropology, x, 14, 226, 248-249
Archaeology, 2
Ascribed roles and statuses, 99
Asian Americans, 213-220, 224-225
Asian Pacific ethnicity, 185, 224-225
Assimilation, 183, 186, 199
Australian aborigines, 24
Australopithecines, 2, 19, 21, 22, 23

Babushka role, 263
Baganda of East Africa, 100-101
Benedict, Ruth, 1, 278
Black Caribs of Belize, 101
Boas, Franz, 1
"Brother-sister avoidance" in Samoa, 84, 164

Caloric intake and life span, 24

Caregiving attitudes in modern Japan,
  280-281
Case study approach, 6, 12-13
Childlessness:
  its effect on the elderly, 120-123
  in China, 120
  in Hong Kong, 121
  in Sikaiana, Solomon Islands, 121-122
  in the United States, 122
Chinese-American elderly, 214-216, 224-225
Chinese family, 118-120
Clark, Margaret, 50, 66, 68, 71, 227, 228,
  231, 233, 235, 249
Clinician-ethnic patient belief conflicts
  concerning etiology of disease,
  230-233
  according to degree of acculturation,
    230-231
  African American concepts of illness,
    232-233
  Jamaican causal categories of illness,
    231-232
  magic as cause of illness, 233
Communities, age homogeneous, 124
  Americans in Mexico, 130
  as age-graded phenomena, 133-135, 143
  in France (Les Floralies), 129-130
  in the United States, 125-128
  RVers, 130-132
Community:
  characteristics of, 125-130
  community as process, 125
  Keith's characteristics of, 128
  Redfield's definition of, 125
  "we feeling" and, 129, 130
Comparative analysis, 6, 7-8, 9
  cross-cultural (synchronic), 7
  longitudinal (diachronic), 7, 255
"Compression of morbidity," 29
Context, importance of, for cross-cultural
  understanding, 10, 11, 96, 100-101,
  108-109
Cowgill, Donald O., ix, 53, 98, 109, 270,
  276, 277, 281, 284
Creativity and age, 61-66
  Brahmin folk painters in India, 65-66, 93
  creativity defined, 63
  cultural influences in Bali, 62-63
  jazz musicians, 63-65

productivity and, 62
Cross-cultural communication, difficulties
    in health settings, 228-229
Cross-cultural comparison, 8
Cross-cultural research, 18
Cultural barriers to health care delivery,
    228-236, 249
Cultural change, x, 155-157, 166-168,
    212-213
    diffusion, 252
    externally generated, 252-254
    internally generated, 251-252
    See also Modernization
Cultural factors in longevity, 45-46
Cultural gerontology, x
Cultural pluralism, 183-184, 223
Cultural relativism, 6, 10-12
Culture, 4, 6-7, 9, 11, 13, 15-16, 22, 48
    defined, 6-7, 19
"Culture broker," 228
Culture, personality and aging, 66-68
    contrasted with traditional psychology,
        66
    Guttman's study of ego states in
        mid-to-late life, 67-68

Death and dying, 90-92, 94
    and ceremonies based on age, 92
    in Pacific island societies, 91-92
    reversibility of death, 91
    soul travel and, 91
    Western attitudes toward, 90-91
Death hastening behavior, 107-109
Decrepit elderly, status and treatment of,
    107-109
    abandonment of decrepit elderly, 17, 217
    in harsh climates, 108
    in Niue, western Polynesia, 108-109
    in nomadic societies, 108
    See also Gerontocide
Deculturation, 71-73, 94, 284
Dementia:
    and ethnic caregivers, 236-238, 249
    as stigma, 234-235
Demographic transition, 14, 18, 30, 48-49
    potential social implications of, 32-34
Determinism, racial, economic, biological,
    etc., 9

Disengagement, 8, 73-77, 94 125, 222
    in Fun City, 77
    role of values in, 74
    theory of, 73, 227
Domestication (human), 22
"Dwelling as a forest hermit" in India, 76

East African research, ix
Emic and etic perspectives, 6, 54
Enculturation, 22, 71, 72
"Epidemiologic transition," 28-29
Eskimos, 11, 14
Eskimo elders:
    effect of cultural change on, 155-157
    roles of, 149-151
    spiritual power of, 151-152
    status of, 11, 148
Ethnicity:
    as source of prestige for elders, 187
    defined, 184-185
    Euro-American, 186
    persistence of ethnic identity, 187
Ethnocentrism, 12, 17
Ethnography, 4, 6
Ethnology, 6
Ethnoscience, 9-10, 54
Eviction of elderly parents in Wichita,
    Kansas, 103-104

Fa'aSamoa (the Samoan way), 182, 257
Familism, 100, 113, 209-210
Family and kinship, 111-123
Family:
    American Indian, 205, 224
    Chinese, 118-120
    Eskimo, 148
    extended, defined, 112
    extended and status of the aged, 97,
        261-163
    in colonial America, 172
    Italian American, 221-223
    Japanese, 217
    kinship and, 111-123
    Mexican American, 209-213
    "modified extended family" of Mexican
        Americans, 209
    nuclear, defined, 112

role of the *matai* in Samoan, 161
Samoan, 167, 182
structure and status, 113-115
Filial piety or responsibility, 57, 88, 89, 101,
    118-120, 138, 174, 216, 222, 278
Food preferences, cultural differences in,
    233-234, 249
Food sharing and taboos favoring elders,
    152, 153
Fun City, 70, 125, 126-127
Future emphasis in leisure and recreation
    needs of elderly, 289-290, 294
Future orientation in American culture, 178

Gender roles:
    among Chipewyan Indians, 87
    Eskimo, 147
    in Fiji, 85
    in Hopi culture, 85
    reversal of, 85-86
    in Samoa, 161
Gerontocide:
    Eskimo, 152-155
    Samoan, 165-166
Gerontocracy, 52, 83
Gerontology:
    growth of, 194
    government support of, 293
"Graying of America," 252, 286, 293, 294

Health care for elderly in modern Japan,
    281-282
Henry, Jules, 238, 239, 240, 246, 249
Herskovits, Melville J., 1, 188
Hispanic ethnicity, 185, 224
Holistic approach, 2, 12, 145
Holistic perspective, 6, 8-9
Holocultural analysis, 107-108
Homes for the aged, non-Western, 135-141,
    144
    correlation with industrialization,
        135-136
    in Africa (Zimbabwe), 137-138
    in Hong Kong, 136-137
    in Japan (Fuji-no-Sato), 138-141
Hominids, 2
    evolution of, 19

Homo erectus, 3
Homo sapiens sapiens, 19
lifespan of, 14, 21, 23
Hunza, 34, 36-37, 43-44, 49

Inclusive fitness, 25
Institutionalization rates in aging
    populations, 33
Italian American ethnic population,
    220-223, 225
    attitude toward nursing homes in,
        222-223
    family and family values in, 220-223
    generational conflict in, 222
    respect for elderly in, 221

Japan, x, 251, 277-283, 284-285
    as an aging population, 30
    expansion of elderly population in, 279,
        281
    modernization in, 277-283
    traditional culture values regarding
        elderly, 216-217
Japanese-Americans, 216-220, 224-225
    discrimination and relocation
        experience during World War II, 218,
        225
    Issei, Nisei, and Sansei generations,
        217-220, 225

Kinship systems:
    and residence patterns, 113
    bilateral or bilineal descent, 111
    fictive kinship, 195
    kindred, defined, 112
    marriage and blood ties, 112
    unilineal descent, 111-112
Knowledge, control of, and status of
        elders, 79, 80, 81, 82, 97-98, 100, 157,
        201-202, 261, 273, 274
Kroeber, Alfred, 1

Life cycle stages, 51-52
    behavior and, 53-59, 92
        in Bojaca, Columbia, 57-58

in the United States, 54
in Western Samoa, 57-59
Shakespeare's 51,92
Life expectancy, 18, 19, 21, 27-29, 48
country of residence and, 28
environmental hazards and, 28
variability with occupation,
socioeconomic status, or race, 27
Life history, 55, 60
Lifespan, 18, 22, 48
Lifetable, 20
Linguistics, 3
Longevity, 17-49
individual formulas for, 46-48

Male menopause in the United States, 178
Maximum life-span potential (MLP), 18,
19, 21, 23-25
age of seual maturation and, 24
body weight/brain size ratio and, 23
caloric intake and metabolic rate and, 24
role of culture in evolution of, 19, 21-22
Mead, Margaret, 1, 62, 71, 72, 82, 161, 169, 270
Median age in population aging, 30, 170,
252, 259
Mexican American ethnicity, 207-213
age hierarchy, 210
attitude toward institutionalization of
elderly, 212
change in Mexican American culture,
212-213, 224
familism, 209-210
male leadership, 210
mutual aid and support, 210-211
respect for elderly, 211-212
servidor system, 211
Micronesia, 12
Minority, defined, 184-185
Modernization, 251, 252-254, 257-270
case study of modernization in Japan,
277-283, 284
concept of retirement and, 268-270
definition of old age and, 257, 284
emphasis on youth, 260-261, 284
generation gap and "youth culture,"
274
in Samoan culture, 255
longevity and, 258, 284

loss of leadership roles among elderly,
265-266, 284
Navajo Indians and, 204
proportion of elderly in population, 258,
284
Samoan migrants to California and,
255-257
state responsibility for welfare of aged,
263-265, 284
religious leadership and, 266-268
See also Status of the aged

National Office of Samoan Affairs, 257
Native American ethnicity, 185, 223-224
See also American Indian
Native American urban aged, 205-207, 224
Navajo culture and the aged, 201-205, 224
Network analysis, 141, 143
Nurturing role:
Chipewyan, 87
continuity of, for women, 87, 88
Taiwanese, 88
Nursing homes, 238-248, 249-250
and ethnicity, 242-245
as reflector of American values, 239-240
housekeeper role in, 241
in Navajo country, 204
in other cultures, 245-248
in Samoa (Mapuifagalele), 246-248
in Scotland, 245-246
in United States, 170-171
Italian Americans and, 222-223

Old age, definition of, 53, 93
chronological vs. functional, 53
Eskimo, 148-149, 155
modernization and, 53, 257-258
in Samoa, 158
in United States, 169
Old-old, 221
needs of, in the future, 291-292
Oldest-old, 31-32

Paleodemography, 2-3
Paros, Greece, 35, 37-39, 49
Parent support ratio (PSR), 33

Participant observation, 4, 6, 54
Pensions, 172-173, 282
Performance, 19
Physical anthropology, 2, 14
Population aging, x, 30-34, 48-49
    rates of institutionalization associated
      with, 33
Practitioner-patient conflicts over medical
    roles and responsibilities, 229-230
Precise time orientation in the United
    States, 179-180
Prestige generating components (advisory,
    contributory, controlling, and
    residual), 99-100
Process analysis, 6, 13-15
Project A.G.E., 54-57
Property and/or resource control as source
    of elderly status, 97, 99, 102-107
    Etalese of the Caroline Islands, 104
    Fulani of West Africa, 103
    Heartland farmers in the United States,
      105-106
    Ireland, 104-105
    King Lear, 103
    Kirghiz of Afghanistan, 105
    !Kung Bushmen of the Kalahari, 106-107
    Samoa, 105
Property control and gender differences, 84
"Property game," 103-104

Real and ideal in regard to respect for
    elderly in modern Japan, 282-283, 285
Reciprocal relationships, 97, 132
    African American, 194
    generational and patterns of care,
      116-120
    in Belize, 101
    in Merrill Court, 127
    in RV communities, 132
    in Yugoslavia, 74
    !Kung Bushmen, 106-107
    Mexican American 210-211
    Navajo, 202-203, 224
    Samoan migrants, 256
    with kin, 61
Relativistic perspective of anthropology, 6,
    10-12
Religion in the United States, 173-174

among African Americans, 195
Religious beliefs, Eskimo, 148
Residence patterns of elderly in future, 292
Retirement, 68-73, 93-94, 271, 284
    age-based work categories, 68-69
    as deculturation, 71-73, 94
    continuity of work roles, 69
    gender differences in, 69
    in the United States, 69-73, 93, 172
    new ideas about appropriate age of,
      287-288, 294
    and second careers, 68-69
"Retiring to the porch" in Appalachia, 70
Roles of the aged, 77-90
    based on traditional knowledge, 80-82
    ceremonial and ritual, 77-80
    political, 80-83, 161-162
    See also Gender roles

Samoa, ix, 5, 11-12, 14, 255-256-257, 258
    brother-sister avoidance in, 84, 101
    migrants in California, 5, 166-167,
      256-257
    modernization in, 255-256, 274
    nursing home in, 246-248
Santo Tomás Mazaltepec cultural patterns,
    208-209
Segregation of generations in the United
    States, 126, 175-176
Self-reliance (America's core value), 146,
    175-176, 182, 254
Senescence, 14, 25, 26-27, 48
    as a by-product of natural selection, 26
    evolution of, 24-27
Senior citizen organizations, 287, 294
Services for the aged:
    in aging populations, 32
    in Samoa, 167
    needs in the future, 287, 294
Servidor system, 211
Shamans, 151-152, 266
"Silver seats," 278, 280, 284
Simmons, Leo, x, 14, 17, 50, 78, 83, 84, 85,
    90, 95-97, 107, 111, 116, 165, 181, 197
Shangri-las (areas of alleged extreme
    longevity), 34-45, 277
    validity of longevity claims in
      Abkhazia, 39-43

Hunza, 43-44
Vilcabamba, 44-45
Social and cultural anthropology,
emphases of, 4
Social networks among the aged, 141-143
African American, 195
age-homogeneous housing and, 142-143
Corsican migrants, 142
Mexican American, 209, 211
SRO hotels and, 141-142
Social security system, 32
financing of, 286-287
Societal carrying power, 259
Societal complexity and elderly status,
101-102
Sociolinguistics, 3
analysis of status and ageism through,
3-4
Status of the elderly, 95-111, 123
and control of knowledge, 95-97
and institutional change and, 97-98
and modernization, 98-99, 101, 102, 115,
270-274
and personal achievement, 100-101
and property control, 97, 102-107
cross-cultural analysis of, 95-98
increase with modernization, 293

Simmons's contributions to study of,
95-97
See also Modernization

Thailand, ix, 269

Vilcabamba, 34, 37, 44-45, 49

Women as care givers of the aged, 33, 222-
223, 280
"World's oldest living human being," 18-19

Yagodina, Bulgaria, longevity in, 35, 39, 49
Young-old age grade, future of, 290-291
Young population, characteristics of, 30
Youth-aged potential for conflict in future,
288, 294
Youth emphasis, decline of in America's
future, 289
Youth orientation, 177-179
contrasting attitudes about aging of
men and women, 177-178
fear of aging and, 178

◉ About the Authors

Ellen Rhoads Holmes is Associate Professor and Director of the Department of Gerontology at Wichita State University. After attending Mississippi State College for Women for two years, where her goal was to receive a degree in accounting and become a CPA, her education was interrupted for 10 years by marriage and child raising. Following the death of her husband, she returned to college to pursue an interest in cultural anthropology. She completed the baccalaureate degree in sociology and anthropology (1968) and the master's degree in anthropology (1971) at Wichita State University, and the doctorate in anthropology at the University of Kansas (1981). Her doctoral field research in American and Western Samoa tested the validity of the aging and modernization theory and combined long-standing interests in Polynesian culture and the cross-cultural aspects of aging. Other field research involving Samoan islanders was undertaken in 1988 and 1992-1993. She has been on the faculty of the gerontology program at Wichita State since its inception in 1975, teaching the anthropology of aging, qualitative research methods, and other gerontology courses. Her publications include articles on

Samoan culture, the impact of modernization on the aged, and cross-cultural aspects of aging. In 1992 she coauthored the book *Samoan Village: Then and Now* with Lowell D. Holmes.

Lowell D. Holmes is Distinguished Professor Emeritus of Anthropology at Wichita State University, where he established the anthropology program and taught for 32 years. He received his baccalaureate degree (1950) in English and the doctorate in anthropology (1957) from Northwestern University. He has maintained a lifelong interest in Samoan island culture, having carried out five field investigations in the islands and two among Samoan migrants in California. A pioneer in cross-cultural gerontological research, he has investigated aging in Samoa, has been a lecturer on cultural gerontology at the Midwest Institute for the Study of Aging at the University of Wisconsin and the University of Missouri, Kansas City, and the Scripps Foundation Gerontology Center at Miami University, Oxford, Ohio. In addition to five books on Samoan culture and an introductory anthropology textbook, he coauthored *Aging and Modernization* (with Donald Cowgill) and *Jazz Greats: Getting Better with Age* (with J. W. Thomson).

Ellen and Lowell Holmes have collaborated on numerous research projects over the years including the study of aging and modernization in the Samoan islands and with Samoans in San Francisco, the study of Mapuifagalele, Western Polynesia's first home for the aged, and research on ethnic differences in family caregiving patterns for victims of Alzheimer's disease. In 1992-1993 they investigated adjustment patterns and familial support of elderly Samoan migrants in the San Francisco Bay Area to add a longitudinal perspective on this community they had previously studied in 1977.